NORTHAMPTONSHIRE
IN THE EARLY EIGHTEENTH CENTURY

THE

PUBLICATIONS

OF THE

NORTHAMPTONSHIRE RECORD SOCIETY

Founded in December, 1920

VOLUME XXXIX

FOR THE TWO YEARS ENDED 31 DECEMBER 1994

General Editor: R. L. Greenall

NORTHAMPTONSHIRE
IN THE EARLY EIGHTEENTH CENTURY

The Drawings of Peter Tillemans and others

Edited by Bruce A. Bailey

NORTHAMPTON
1996

Acknowledgements

THIS volume owes its aegis to the inspiration of Sir Gyles Isham, who, in discussion with John Steane, had the idea of reproducing a selection of the drawings from the collection in the British Library (Add MSS 32467). Due to various vicissitudes it failed to reach a state of publication prior to his death in 1976. I undertook to carry on the idea, and it was decided to publish not just a selection but the complete collection. At a crucial moment members of the staff of the Royal Commission on Historical Monuments descended on the county and undertook a survey of both the country houses and churches. I had the good fortune to be associated with the country house survey and I am most grateful to Robert Taylor and John Heward, of the Commission, for allowing me to participate in their work. John Heward has, in addition, read through the text and made many useful comments. Peter Mackay has provided enormous help, not least in checking the typescript and finding all sorts of inconsistencies, and also suggesting many improvements. Michael Vickers of the Ashmolean Museum, Oxford, has provided notes for the section on the Arundel Marbles as they existed at Easton Neston. To all these I am most grateful for their labours and interest.

Ron Greenall, editor for the publications of the *Northamptonshire Record Society*, has constantly encouraged the project and taken endless pains with its publication, and if it is at all successful it owes much to his care and attention. John Munro also gave generously of his time and his expertise in the publication of illustrated books on Northamptonshire.

Very many people have over the years contributed information on individual buildings and, rather than try and list them all, I hope they will allow a general acknowledgement for their assistance. The one person I must single out is the late Victor Hatley, whose early demise robbed Northamptonshire of one of its outstanding local historians. He made many perceptive comments, especially about the Northampton drawings, and it is a great personal sadness to me that he is not alive to see the publication of this volume.

Lastly, on behalf of the Northamptonshire Record Society, I express thanks to the British Library for permission to reproduce the drawings in Add MSS 32467, and to the Marc Fitch Fund for a grant towards publication.

Bruce A. Bailey

Contents

Frontispiece: *A view of Northampton from Queen's Cross on the London Road* (Plate 169)

ISBN 0 901275 60 3

Published by the Northamptonshire Record Society, Wootton Hall Park, Northampton NN4 9BQ
Typeset and printed in Great Britain by Stanley L. Hunt (Printers) Ltd, Rushden, Northamptonshire
and casebound by Woolnough Bookbinding, Express Works, Irthlingborough, Northamptonshire.

Sir Gyles Isham, 12th Baronet, F.S.A., D.L.: a Tribute

WHEN Sir Gyles Isham died suddenly on 28th January 1976, in his 73rd year, the Northamptonshire Record Society announced its intention to publish a Memorial volume "at some future date".

At long last the Society is now able to publish this fine book of Tillemans' drawings of Northamptonshire in the 18th Century. We believe this to be a worthy tribute to one who was President of our Society for eleven years and who, during the thirty years in which he resided at Lamport, took the keenest interest in the N.R.S. and had an unrivalled knowledge of the history and architecture of our county. In fact, before he died he had planned to produce an edition of Tillemans' drawings himself.

The Isham family had lived at Pytchley since the 14th century. In 1560 John Isham, a successful wool merchant, purchased Lamport from Sir William Cecil and built a new house and stables. In 1655 his descendant, Sir Justinian Isham, 2nd Baronet, employed the architect John Webb, a pupil, assistant and son-in-law of Inigo Jones, to add a new West front to the house. This was built in the then innovatory Italian style using Inigo Jones' favourite Northamptonshire Weldon stone. In the following 250 years successive Ishams made additions and alterations, gradually demolishing or enveloping the original Elizabethan house. In particular, in 1732 and 1741, North and South classical wings were added to each end of Webb's central front which we all enjoy to this day.

In 1903 the baronetcy passed to Sir Vere, the 11th Baronet. He was Gyles' father and of necessity lived at St Leonards in Sussex and let Lamport during the long agricultural depression. Gyles (born 1903) and his sister Virginia spent the first half of their lives at St Leonards. Though he was brought up in Sussex he frequently visited Lamport with his father and mother between the Wars. He became acutely aware of his family's history and his future inheritance and responsibility. From an early age his heart was in Northamptonshire, being truly proud of his forebears.

Gyles was a scholar at Rugby (1917-1922) where he took part in school plays and from thence went to Magdalen College, Oxford, obtaining a good degree in history. He greatly distinguished himself, being President of the Oxford University Dramatic Society, President of the Union and the Reform Club and editor of *Isis*. He was a fluent speaker and won acclaim for his Shakespearean acting, particularly for his Hamlet. The theatre then became his profession, acting in the West End with the Old Vic, the newly opened Shakespeare Memorial Theatre at Stratford-upon-Avon, and on overseas tours. On the outbreak of the Second World War he was commissioned into the 60th Rifles.

He served on General Gott's staff in the Eighth Army and subsequently was appointed Intelligence Officer at H.Q. Palestine. He was demobilised in 1946, attaining the rank of Lieutenant Colonel. He then came home to Lamport, aged 43.

The estate had been badly managed and the house neglected, and he decided to give up acting and set about restoring Lamport. He took the keenest interest in the farms, the tenants, the cottages and the woodland. In 1946, with his remarkable knowledge of local history, he arranged with Miss Joan Wake that the Northamptonshire Record Society house their County Records at Lamport. In 1959 they were removed to Delapre Abbey, and again in 1991 to Wootton Hall Park, their present home. In 1952 he was made a Deputy Lieutenant of the County and from 1955-1964 he served on the Northamptonshire County Council. For seventeen years he was Chairman of St. Andrew's Hospital, Northampton. In 1958 he was appointed High Sheriff, and also served as President of the Northamptonshire Agricultural Society. From 1966 to 1973 he edited the N.R.S. Journal *Northamptonshire Past and Present*, and for three years before his death was President of the Northamptonshire Country Landowners Association.

At Lamport disaster struck in 1969 when dry rot was found to be rampant in the house. For five years he waged a bitter but successful battle to renovate the house, disturbing the dust of centuries. Works of art reflecting the interests and tastes of his forebears all had to be restored. Rooms were redecorated to the highest standard including the fine plaster work and marble fireplaces. This was all the more remarkable, bearing in mind that the house was half derelict and there was no endowment, no grants and only a limited income from the estate. In 1972 Gyles, aged 68, opened his house and gardens to the public for the first time. Just before he died, rather than hand the estate over to the National Trust, which required an endowment, he created the Lamport Preservation Trust.

Gyles had a strong sense of public duty and a great interest in the Arts. He was a Trustee of the National Portrait Gallery and of the Royal Shakespeare Company. He was an authority on local history, contributing to Sir Nicholas Pevsner's volume on the *Buildings of Northamptonshire*. He researched the history of the family, the house and its contents, and published various articles on Lamport, and the history of our county.

When young he was physically strong and fine looking. As an undergraduate he was surrounded by adulation, yet remained thoughtful, kind, good natured and good mannered. His enjoyment of life was infectious. He accepted responsibility with zest, and was never swamped by public work. Gyles had a lively sense of humour, and bore no malice. As Robert Speaight said of him, "his kindness, erudition, intelligence and sensibility combined in a peculiarly English way".

The restoration of Lamport Hall, its estate and church are a testimony to the imagination, scholarship and determination of Sir Gyles Isham, 12th Baronet. When enjoying Tillemans' drawings bear him in mind. I am sure you will find this Memorial Volume a worthy tribute to a remarkable man.

Hereward Wake, *President, The Northamptonshire Record Society.*

Introduction

WE, in the last decade of the 20th century, with our heavily built-up areas, motorways and dual-carriageways, and landscape divided into neat fields, have little conception what England looked like at the beginning of the 18th century. It is very rare for an early 18th century series of drawings of any particular county to survive, and Northamptonshire is therefore singularly fortunate that over 200 drawings exist illustrating its countryside, towns and important buildings.[1]

The drawings were commissioned during the second decade of the 18th century as illustrations for a projected History of the county, which was being prepared by a Northamptonshire gentleman, John Bridges. In the event Bridges was to die before his *History* reached publication and when the manuscripts were finally edited for printing in the early 1790s, only a handful of the illustrations, those which had already been engraved, were used. The survival of the drawings and their publication in this volume is a great bonus for historians, and not only for those who specialise in Northamptonshire. The drawings illustrate houses, churches and monuments which form the central source of much of the genealogical information in the *History*. But they do more than this. Views of many of the houses show garden layouts, giving garden historians useful evidence of the current taste *c.*1720. Other views of houses are important for architectural historians since they show the appearance of either long since demolished structures, or views of those which were subsequently rebuilt or altered. Several portrayals of churches have a similar relevance. Views of the towns often show the landscapes around them, with no obvious metalled roads and evidence of open-field cultivation.

The background to the drawings and their commissioning patron is also fascinating.[2] John Bridges was born in 1665 into the world of the gentry. His birthplace was not in Northamptonshire[3] but at Binfield in Berkshire, at the home of his maternal uncle, Sir William Trumbull, Secretary of State under William III. His grandfather had been a staunch Parliamentarian and Governor of Warwick Castle, and his father had made a number of agricultural improvements to the estate at Barton Seagrave, near Kettering in Northamptonshire, which he had purchased in 1665, the year before John's birth.

John was educated at Trinity College, Oxford under the tutelage of Dr. Ralph Bathurst, a leading intellectual of the University. Bathurst was one of the originators of the Royal Society and it is a mark of Bridges' standing that he became a member of that Society in 1708, and in 1712 was voted on to the Council alongside Wren and Newton. Following his time at Oxford, Bridges studied law, being entered at Middle Temple in 1684, and was called to the Bar in 1691. He moved to Lincoln's Inn in 1717 and lived at No. 6 New Square. The law was not to be his main career, however, since he joined the Office of Customs and became Agent and Solicitor in 1695. He left the Customs in 1714 and became Cashier of Excise the following year, holding the post for about twelve months. His antiquarian interests were long founded, and in 1718 he was elected Fellow of the Society of Antiquaries, becoming Vice President in 1723, a post to which he was re-elected in 1724, the year of his death. He had a large library of some 4,000 volumes, including most of the available county histories, English topography, Classics and early printing. He was also associated with Thomas Hearne of Oxford, who was collecting books and materials of a similar nature to Bridges. Hearne, one of the most respected antiquarians of his day, describes Bridges, "his excellent friend" as a "learned generous man".

On inheriting his father's estate in Northamptonshire in 1712, John Bridges was ideally situated to investigate the history of the county. He was extremely well connected, and socially acceptable within the highest circles. It seems likely that he had been collecting material for many years, but the project did not become fully organised till 1718. In 1719 a series of questionnaires were sent out to likely informants and members of the clergy, and a number of replies to this standard format survive amongst Bridges' manuscript collections in the Bodleian Library, Oxford. He also had a number of regular correspondents, with a great deal of information gathered by William Slyford, a professional antiquary, the Rev. Joseph Sparke, archivist at Peterborough Cathedral, Francis Peck of Kingscliffe, who was to produce his own history of Stamford, and others. Another important contributor was Thomas Eayre, a Kettering surveyor, who had a special interest in archaeological sites, and who is responsible for several drawings in the collection here reproduced.[4]

By 1719 things were sufficiently well advanced to think about illustrations, and Bridges

---

1. The drawings are in the British Library, Add.MSS 32467. They have been affectionately known in the county for many years as "The Eayre-Tillemans Drawings", but the great majority are in fact by Tillemans. Eayre's contribution is small, and to some degree is concerned with preparing drawings for engraving, together with another artist, Andrew Motte.

2. Much of the information about Bridges' life and the various contributors to the *History* derives from research undertaken by Tony Brown and Glenn Foard and is published in their *The Making of a County History: John Bridges' Northamptonshire*, University of Leicester, 1994, and I am grateful to them both for their help.

3. *The Dictionary of National Biography* states that he was born at Barton Seagrave, but this is wrong. The entry in the Binfield Parish Register is quite clear.

4. More information on the Eayre family appears in Patrick King, "Thomas Eayre of Kettering and other members of his family" *Northamptonshire Past and Present*, Vol.1 No.5, 1952 (pp.11-23) and on his architectural work in *Colvin*.

Portrait of John Bridges engraved by
George Vertue after the painting by
Sir Godfrey Kneller, the location of
which is unknown.
(By courtesy of A. E. Brown, Esq.)

which he said was full of copperplates from these drawings . . . Some few he had impressions of, which he gave me; unluckily he had given his last copy of Peterborough Cathedral to the present Bishop; the drawing of it is remarkably fine, and more highly finished than Tillemans' drawings usually are; but if it was not better engraven than the specimens I have, I am not much concerned at having missed it. They were done by one Mott, a friend of Mr. Bridges, who, I perceived, had copied some of Tillemans' drawings (who never used a ruler) in a more accurate style.[6]

Few drawings by Tillemans, however, seem to survive. The Northamptonshire series, and another of Wrest Park, Bedfordshire,[7] are the major portions of his oeuvre in this technique so far identified. As the quotation above says, they are executed in a free pen and ink wash. However, examination of existing buildings shows a great accuracy in observation, which adds greatly to their importance for historians.

Two other artists were employed by Bridges, Thomas Eayre and Andrew Motte. Eayre, as we have seen, was also a correspondent and provided information for the proposed text. He was a neighbour of Bridges, Barton Seagrave being the next village south east of Kettering, where the Eayres had established a business as clockmakers and bellfounders some time about 1700. The Thomas of the drawings was born in 1691, and, as well as being engaged in the family business, was also a proficient surveyor and amateur architect. His talents within the latter field were sufficiently well thought of for a new church at Stoke Doyle near Oundle to be built to his designs between 1722 and 1725. It is a sensible if not especially prepossessing building in the Palladian style. It is, however, as a surveyor that his contribution towards the *History* is outstanding. His greatest achievement is a splendid map of Northamptonshire, to the scale of one inch to one mile, conceived in the 1730s, but not issued till 1779. It was reissued in 1791 when the *History* was eventually published.[8] Within the collection of drawings there are smaller maps of Kettering and Peterborough, which were also published, and some less ornate plans of archaeological sites. Eayre clearly had some interest in archaeology, since there survives correspondence between him and Sir Edmund Isham of Lamport in 1738 about the preservation of a newly discovered Roman villa at Weldon. Eayre was not only concerned about recording the remains but also was anxious to secure its preservation, urging Sir Edmund to "think of any way of prevailing with Ld. Hatton to have a Building made over it Directly".[9] Comparing Eayre's archaeological surveys with those of more recent times, one cannot but admire their careful observation. The draughtsmanship may not have the freedom of Tillemans, and his little trees may be rather feathery, but the accuracy of the drawings is admirable.

The other named illustrator in the drawings, Andrew Motte, is rather a shadowy figure. In the

approached Peter Tillemans.[5] Tillemans, born in Antwerp in 1684, had come to England in 1718 with his brother-in-law, Peter Casteels, a painter who specialised in pictures of birds and fowl. Tillemans himself aspired to be a sporting artist, and he worked for a short time with the more famous John Wootton. Unfortunately, he rarely signs his paintings and relatively few have been identified. It does seem, however, that he only had a small success as a painter of larger subjects, relying on smaller topographical works for his main employment. He must have had some standing at the time, for he joined the Academy of Painting founded by Kneller in 1721, and held the post of Steward to the Society of St. Luke, the leading artistic circle of the day, in 1725. His health was not good, and George Vertue, who was collecting material for a history of English art in the early 18th century recorded that Tillemans' death occurred in November 1734 "after many years indisposition that to all who knew him it was wonderful he lived so long, having a continual Ashma".

While he may have been disappointed in his main aim, he worked up a considerable practice as a topographical artist, and many examples of his views of houses exist, with notable examples at Chirk Castle, Floors Castle and Uppark, amongst others. Indeed, his reputation was good enough to be recorded by John Nichols in his *Literary Anecdotes*, where he includes a letter which states that Sir John Cullum visited Bridges' nephew and was shown:

> . . . all the drawings that were done . . . They are chiefly executed in Indian ink, in a slight, but masterly manner, by Peter Tillemans, who was retained by Mr. Bridges, at a guinea a day, with the run of his house. There cannot, I think, be much fewer than 500; those that were dated were all, or chiefly, done in 1719. Mr. Bridges pointed out to me a great box,

---

5.   The fullest account of the work of Tillemans is contained in Robert Raines, "Peter Tillemans, Life and Work, with a list of representative paintings" *Walpole Society*, Vol.47 pp.21-59. To this can be added John Harris, *The Artist & the Country House*, London 1979 (pp.224-238) where there is both text and a number of reproductions of his paintings.

6.   John Nichols, *Literary Anecdotes of the Eighteenth Century*, 1812-1815, Vol.8, p.682. The letter was written by Sir John Cullum of Hardwick House to the antiquary Richard Gough on 1 January 1782. Cullum's estimate of the number of drawings may be the result of an inspired guess. There clearly were more as some views were engraved, but no drawings exist in the collection. A list of possible drawings has been compiled by Brown and Foard and this takes into account drawings indicated in Bridges' MSS, the printed text, etc. Their list needs to be adjusted in the light of some identifications in the present volume.

7.   Bedfordshire Record Office, Lucas MSS 33/127-137.

8.   Eayre's map of Northamptonshire, in its 4 sheets, has been reprinted by Northamptonshire Libraries.

9.   Quoted in Patrick King (*op. cit.*).

published volume there is an engraving of Peterborough Cathedral which bears his signature, and amongst the drawings there is a simple one of Raunds church and another, dated 1719, of an ancient seal connected with Northampton. A portrait of Motte was engraved by Moses Vanderbank in 1718, so he clearly had some reputation. Thomas Eayre was also involved in the preparation of drawings for engraving, and there are careful sections and elevations of Peterborough Cathedral by him, as well as a page of notes concerning All Saints church in Northampton, with an instruction to Motte hoping that a satisfactory plate might result (Plate 189).

In connection with the drawings it remains to note that the distinctive written titles on nearly all the drawings are in the hand not of Tillemans, but in that of another of Bridges' contributors, William Slyford. This perhaps accounts for occasional mis-titling, such as the mistaken identification of monuments at Weekley as being at Geddington. The titles could well have been added some time after the execution of the drawings and perhaps from the itinerary notes.[10]

A good proportion of the drawings bear dates. These vary from an exact date to just a month and year. All the dated drawings, save one or two, fall within the years 1719 and 1721, and then within the later summer months, from July to September. The itineraries of Bridges and the other contributors can be reconstructed from the manuscript notes, and dates within these are also helpful in confirming or suggesting exact dates of drawings where only a month is mentioned in the title.[11] There are two other clues to the dating of the drawings in that the majority bear some numerical notation. This appears either as a number written at the top right-hand corner of the drawing, or is written on the reverse, where a number is preceded by the abbreviation "Num" or "Numb". When these notations are collated with dated examples all the drawings with "Num" or "Numb" fall within the year 1719, and all those with numbers written in the top right-hand corner within the year 1721. While it may be rash to state, categorically, that undated drawings with these number notations do date from those years, a tentative dating by this means does seem reasonable, and has been applied in the catalogue of the drawings. Occasionally, when there are both dated and undated drawings of the same location, a date has been suggested for an undated drawing on the assumption that it is likely to have been done at the same time as a dated drawing. This is, if anything, less satisfactory than the previous method, since it is clear from the itineraries that there were visits to the same location at different times.

It remains to summarise the story of the *History*.[12] Bridges died at his Lincoln's Inn chambers in 1724 at the age of 58. His health had not been good since 1716 when he suffered from gout, and he had a series of severe colds in the 1720s. His manuscripts and collections were inherited by his brother William, a series of 48 notebooks of various sizes. Nothing happened for over ten years, but in 1735 Dr. Samuel Jebb and a colleague Samuel Gibbons, advertised in the *Northampton Mercury* a subscription in order to publish the *History* in parts. In July 1736, in the same newspaper, Eayre's map is advertised, and it is noted that Jebb was hard at work editing the text, and the printer William Taylor was to be employed. Unfortunately, subscriptions did not

Peter Tillemans (1684-1734), from Horace Walpole, *Anecdotes of Painting*, 1862 edition.
(By courtesy of A. E. Brown, Esq.)

come in as expected, and following the issue of two instalments in 1739, the project foundered when Gibbons was declared bankrupt.[13]

Nothing much then happened till 1749 when Brooke Bridges, John's nephew, sold a number of the engraved plates. This perhaps prompted a group of Northamptonshire gentlemen, William Cartwright of Aynho, Thomas Cave of Stanford, Charles Compton of Grendon, Sir Edmund Isham of Lamport and Ambrose Isted of Ecton and others to form a committee and once again try and establish means of publication. The Rev. Benjamin Buckler, fellow of All Souls College, Oxford, was appointed editor in 1755, but, once again, insufficient subscriptions were received and Buckler resigned. In 1757 the Rev. Peter Whalley, vicar of Courteenhall and later of Ecton, took on the task, and by the 1760s portions of the work were approaching completion. In 1778 Sir Thomas Cave, the main inspirer of the project, died, and there was a further lapse in progress. However, largely by the interests of another Northamptonshire squire, Sir William Dolben of Finedon, Whalley was persuaded to continue his task. A London printer Thomas Payne agreed to publish and finally, in 1791, the two volumes of John Bridges' *History and Antiquities of the County of Northampton* were issued. Eayre's map was reprinted to coincide with the publication.[14]

A review of the *History* appeared in the *Gentleman's Magazine* in December 1791, together with a list of the original drawings, a list which corresponds almost exactly with the collection today. Just what happened to the drawings subsequent to 1791 is unclear. The manuscripts were acquired by Dr. Thomas Rawlinson who eventually bequeathed them to the Bodleian Library in Oxford, but the drawings clearly descended via a different route, perhaps connected with the

---

10. Examples of Slyford's hand are reproduced in Brown and Foard *(op. cit.)*.
11. The itineraries have successfully been reconstructed by Tony Brown and Glenn Foard *(op. cit.)*.
12. A useful discussion of the progress towards publication of Bridges' work is contained in Rosemary Eady "John Bridges, Peter Whalley and the History of the County", *Northamptonshire Past & Present*, Vol.IV No.5, pp.287-291 (1970).

13. Copies of Jebb's instalments of the *History* occasionally appear on the market, but they are very scarce.
14. Eayre's map is quite often found bound into copies of the *History*, but strictly it is an extra and not an integral part of the publication, which is complete without it.

publisher Taylor. They were to emerge again when Mrs. E. Codgbrook sold them to the British Museum in 1885.

★   ★   ★   ★   ★

While most of the drawings in the collection are architectural, they portray more than just the buildings. Representation of the Northamptonshire countryside is to be found frequently. Indeed, the very first drawing in the album in which they are mounted, is one of the largest and most detailed views and shows the valley of the Nene near Oundle, with the villages of Lilford and Achurch: a truly superb record, and Tillemans at his best. Here we have the well wooded undulating countryside which anyone familiar with Northamptonshire will instantly recognise. There were, as there are still, plenty of trees and hedgerows. Likewise in the view of Thrapston, the town is almost hidden behind trees, and a prospect of the park at Boughton, Kettering, seems to be almost totally planted with trees.

Also, in Northamptonshire, one is frequently aware of the former open fields, with furlongs and narrow cultivation strips. In the Boughton view just mentioned, the strips run across the park to within a few yards of the great house and its gardens. In the prospects of towns the fields which surround them are also evident: in those of Northampton, especially the view from near Kingsthorpe and that looking towards St. Giles' church, and the views of Brackley and Oundle field systems are evident.

Another feature which will intrigue today's viewer is the number of windmills which scatter the countryside. These are especially obvious in some of the town prospects. In most cases they are of the post-mill type, as compared with those with solid stone or brick towers. Good representations can be found on the South Prospect of Northampton (Plate 169), that of the west Prospect of the town (Plate 172) and of Brackley (Plate 25). The most surprising example is that which appears sitting on its mound in the midst of the planting of the Boughton House garden (Plate 23) – it was not to remain there long!

Roads are not always easy to interpret. To us, used to regular tarmac surfaces, the rutty tracks which, in the winter made Northamptonshire notorious, are barely visible. The prospect of Northampton from Queen Eleanor's Cross (Plate 169) gives really no clear representation of a road, although the coach which descends the hill towards the town must be on one. Roads are most obvious where bridges and causeways cross rivers: notable views are those of Oundle (Plate 193) and Peterborough (Plate 197). The view of Brackley from the south (Plate 25) does show a clear road track, running from the bridge through the town to beyond the market place.

The most impressive town views are, inevitably, those of Northampton, with an especially splendid drawing of the piazza surrounding All Saints church. All the churches in Northampton are recorded and most of the important buildings. At Peterborough, similarly, careful attention is given to the Cathedral, with elevations from almost every direction. The interior is superbly captured and most of the claustral buildings are recorded.

So to other buildings of the county. Looking at the drawings of the churches, it comes as rather a surprise to find that most of them look today pretty much as they did when Tillemans sketched them about 1720. Castor church, near Peterborough, for example, is almost exactly the church of today. The town churches of Northampton are easily recognisable, even the churches of Holy Sepulchre and St. Giles, shown in the state they existed before 19th century alteration and addition. The main differences elsewhere are in roof levels. There are few pitched and tiled roofs; nearly all churches have low angled lead roofs, generally hidden behind parapets. As regards windows, there is much evidence of 17th or 18th century alterations, which were in turn removed in the 19th century. The drawings confirm the notion that a number of churches received far worse treatment in the later 18th or 19th century, than in Cromwell's time! Perhaps the most obvious missing features are tombstones in the church yards. While they did not become widely popular till the middle of the 18th century there were plenty of examples prior to that time. One can only conclude that Tillemans used artistic licence in ignoring them, preferring to concentrate on the architecture.

Tillemans made several drawings of Northamptonshire church monuments. These were clearly felt to be important for their relevance for genealogical study. They vary from medieval figures to high Baroque compositions. One of the most splendid later tombs recorded is that for the 1st Earl Fitzwilliam at Marholm, near Peterborough. He died in 1719 and the drawing which Tillemans has included is not his own, but which, although unsigned, is almost certainly that drawn by the sculptor, James Fisher of Camberwell, and which has variations from the finished memorial. If it *is* Fisher's it is the only recorded drawing by this important sculptor. Another useful drawing is that of the Levinz monument at Evenley, which was savaged by the Victorians, with only the figure allowed to remain, high up under the tower. The best series illustrate some collections of family monuments: examples are the tombs of the Spencers at Brington, the Fermors at Easton Neston, the Chaunceys at Edgecote and the Montagus at Weekley.

The drawings of Northamptonshire country houses are impressive, even if the selection drawn is curiously erratic. Why are some great houses there and others not? Fortunately almost every house of importance which has since disappeared has a drawing. Of special interest are those of Easton Maudit, Fineshade, Greatworth, Horton, and Steane. In some cases we have a drawing of a house which was to be replaced in the 18th century. The most obvious example is Edgecote: Georgian Edgecote is splendid, but one does regret the loss of old Edgecote. And if Edgecote is one's first regret, Steane and Horton must come close behind.

Among houses where there have been major alterations, additions and demolitions since, the most interesting records are those of Astwell, Little Billing, Brockhall, and Deene. Relatively "new" houses in 1720, like Cottesbrooke and Easton Neston, sit wonderfully pristine in their landscapes. In some cases Tillemans has provided an excellent record of garden layouts. These, almost without exception, illustrate the Dutch influence of the reign of William and Mary, with parterres, terraces, small conical trees, urns and statuary. The best examples are those of Aynho, Castle Ashby, Drayton, Horton and Easton Neston. At Easton Neston, in addition, an important record was compiled of the statuary which adorned both house and garden.

As an evocation of early 18th century Northamptonshire these drawings are a superb and unique record. Tillemans did his patron John Bridges proud.

The Tillemans Drawings

(The British Library, Add MSS 32467)

This volume reproduces all the drawings contained in the British Library collection (Add MSS 32467). The collection is basically alphabetical, so the drawings have been left in that order *except* that mis-titled or mis-placed drawings have been placed under their correct location.

Entries are arranged under the following:

The **location** in modern spelling.

Title: as and when it appears on the drawing (in the spelling etc. of the original).

Artist: whether signed, followed by identification when this can be ascertained.

Date: either from the drawing, or based on the evidence of Bridges' MS Notes, or some other source.

Bridges' text: a quotation from the printed text of 1791.

A commentary on the drawing which attempts to point out interesting features and give some background to the subject. The commentaries are, inevitably, of limited extent, and much more could have been said about a number of illustrations. It is hoped that future historians, having this publication at hand, will be encouraged to do further research.

Notes: The British Library reference number. Size of original in centimetres. References to any numbers or letters which appear on the drawing. Bibliographical or other references and notes.

Within the Catalogue of Plates a number of works are cited on frequent occasions. In order not to duplicate endless references these are indicated as below:

Colvin: COLVIN, Howard: *A Biographical Dictionary of British architects 1600-1840* (2nd edition, London, 1978; 3rd edition 1995).

Gunnis: GUNNIS, Rupert: *Dictionary of British sculptors 1660-1851* (Revised edition, London, 1967).

Whinney: WHINNEY, Margaret: *Sculpture in Britain 1530-1830.* Revised by Johy Physick (Pelican history of art, London, 1988).

R.C.H.M.: ROYAL COMMISSION ON HISTORICAL MONUMENTS *An Inventory of the Historical Monuments in the County of Northampton.* Vols. I-IV cover the archaeological sites of the county; Vol.V covers the churches of Northampton; Vol.VI is a detailed inventory of the architectural monuments of North Northamptonshire. (The latter is the only volume intended in this format, unfortunately. Two further volumes are projected: one to cover the major country houses and one to cover the churches of the county as a whole.)

Huxloe

A

1. NORTHAMPTONSHIRE. Nene Valley

Title on reverse of drawing: *A prospect Down the River Nen of Achurch & Lilford*

Artist: Unsigned, Peter Tillemans

Date: Probably 1721. Bridges' MSS notes a visit on 4 Aug 1721.

Bridges' text:

> *LILFORD*, a village of twelve houses is bounded on the north west by the Nyne . . . Here is a very handsome mansion house, built by the family of *Elmes* in 1635, but since much improved by Sir *Thomas Powys*, late lord of the manor . . . The church, dedicated to S. *Peter*, consists of a body, north ile, part of a south ile, the other part appearing from the arches to have been taken down, and

chancel covered with lead. At the west end is a coped tower on which is raised a spire . . .

ACHURCH, usually called *Thorp-Achurch* . . . The church, dedicated to St. *John* the *Baptist*, consists of a body, chancel, and cross ile, tiled. At the west end is a spire steeple, in which are four bells.

This lovely drawing gives an excellent impression of the Nene valley countryside: its gently rolling fields, rich woodland and scattering of villages, church spires and country houses – an 18th century evocation indeed of the "County of Spires and Squires".

On the left is Lilford and on the right Achurch. At Lilford, the triple gables of the facade of the Hall are indicated, although the form is not quite correct, there being a space between each gable; nor is there any suggestion of the round bays which end each wing. Behind the gables is a wide block of chimneys which

are one of the house's distinctive features. The church has a most elaborate cresting to its tower. To the right is the village, with, prominent, a large four-bay house. The village was only to survive till 1755 when the surroundings of the Hall were landscaped. The church lingered on till 1788 when it too was demolished: its monuments were removed to Achurch and three arches from its nave arcades were re-erected as a garden ornament near the river, where they still stand.

Below the village of Lilford can be seen the long causeway with its arched openings running across the valley. Further to the right a tree bisects the view and around are the cultivated fields. Somewhat shadowy figures appear, with a rider and hounds, and a loaded harvest wagon drawn by two horses.

On the far right is Achurch, with its church spire and close by a substantial house. The rest of the village, a row of cottages, is at a slight distance, on the skyline. Below in the valley is seen the winding path of the river, disappearing amongst the trees towards Lilford.

Notes: BL. No.1. 79x14 cm. Other nos: On reverse is Numb. 38 and at the bottom hand corner of the drawing itself a letter 'A'.

View of the Earl of Sunderlands Seat at Althorp with the Old Gate house & Distant View of Brington Church 11 Augᵗ 1721

2. ALTHORP

Title on drawing: *View of the Earl of Sunderlands Seat at Althorp with the Old Gate House & Distant View of Brington Church 11 Augt 1721*

Artist: Unsigned, Peter Tillemans

Bridges' text:

> Here is now only the noble seat of the Earl of *Sunderland.* standing in the midst of a park, very elegantly laid out, well wooded and stocked with deer

A useful view of the house and its surroundings as they existed prior to the alterations of the 1730s. In the centre is the main house, as reconstructed by 2nd Earl of Sunderland during the second half of the 17th century. It was basically a half-H plan, built of red brick with stone dressings, and the view shows the eastern arm of the H. It clearly shows the two main floors with attics in the roof. A wide open forecourt fronts the house, and above the trees rises the upper portions of the towered Tudor gatehouse. This stood just inside the boundary of the earlier moat, already filled in by this date.

In front again, an avenue leads away from the house, and just above the avenue, on the hillside, is the walled kitchen garden, still, in essence, surviving.

Behind the house are indications of formal tree planting, but rather less sign of formality than one might expect.

On the skyline is the village of Great Brington with its square church tower. Further right a line of trees indicates the East Haddon ridge. Also right, but in the foreground, a line of small trees probably follows the route of the drive from the Northampton road, running very much where it does today.

The Spencer family acquired the title Earls of Sunderland in 1644. Robert 2nd Earl, builder of the house as shown here, died in 1702, and the owner, when the drawing was made, was Charles 3rd Earl. The Sunderland title continued till the time of another Charles, 5th Earl, who in 1733 succeeded to the Marlborough peerage and Blenheim upon the death of his aunt, Henrietta, Duchess of Marlborough. The Spencer earldom was created in 1765.

Notes: BL. No.4. 44x28 cm. Other no: Front – 45. This drawing served as original for an engraving in the printed text (Vol. 1 p.480), where it appears with its title, as on the drawing. At the base of the engraving is printed: *Tillemans del.* and *Skelton sculp.*

View of the Earl of Westmerlands house and of the Church & Steeple at Apethorp taken 3. Aug. 1721

3. APETHORPE

Title on drawing: *View of the Earl of Westmorlands House and of the Church & Steeple at Apethorp taken 3. Augt 1721*

Artist: Unsigned, Peter Tillemans

Bridges' text:

Here is the seat of the Earl of *Westmoreland*, neatly built of free-stone, and consisting of a quadrangle, on the east side, with open cloisters.

The house is viewed from the east. A wide avenue encloses the vista, with, in front of the house, screen walls, gazebos and gatepiers. Despite some rebuilding of the facade by Sir Reginald Blomfield *c.*1904, the eastward aspect of the house is much the same today, save that the enclosing forecourt and gazebos shown have gone. Bridges' "open cloisters" are a loggia whose entrance arches are in the centre of the front. A second opened into the inner court and was glazed by Blomfield.

To the right of the house is the village, with, just beyond the outbuildings, the roof and cupola of a circular dovecote just visible, and on the extreme right the spire of the church. The bridge, close by, carried the public road, but this was re-routed in the late 18th century to make way for landscaping and a lake.

The house dates from the 16th century. The Mildmay family acquired the estate in 1550. Sir Walter Mildmay was Chancellor of the Exchequer to Elizabeth I and both he and his son, Anthony, added to the house. The Fanes inherited the property following the death of Sir Anthony in 1617 (see Plate 4), his daughter having married Sir Francis Fane. Fane was raised to the peerage as Earl of Westmorland in 1624 and rebuilt much of the house. In 1904 Apethorpe was purchased by the Brassey family, and in more recent times it was used as a school. It is now in private hands, but not, alas, inhabited.

Notes: BL. No.6. 45.5x30 cm. Other nos: Front – 38; and on reverse Num: 76.

4. APETHORPE

Title on drawing: *The Monument of Sʳ Anth Mildmay in the S. Chancel of Apethorpe Church Lord Westmorlands Church*

Artist: Unsigned, Peter Tillemans

Date: Undated, but probably 1721 although Bridges' MSS record a visit to record the tomb and its inscriptions on 12 August 1719.

Bridges' text:

> In the north ile is an altar tomb of black and white marble, on which are the statues of Sir *Anthony Mildmay*, and his lady; he in armour, in the posture of prayer, with his head on a pillow; she at his left side, in the same posture, and in the habit of the times. Over them is a lofty canopy, and on the north side of it close to the curtains which fall from the canopy, on two pedestals, are figures of Justice, with a sword in her right hand, and a balance in her left, of Wisdom, holding in her right hand a mirrour, with a snake twining round her arm. And on two like pedestals, on the north side, are Charity, pouring out of one flagon into another; and Devotion, holding in her right arm a pillar. Above their heads, IVST, WISE, DEVOVTE, CHARITABLE. At the top of the east end, is a Virgin in a loose robe, as the others, with a tablet in her left hand, and in her right a cross. At the west end is Hope, her eyes raised towards heaven, reposing her left arm on an anchor, and her right hand on

her breast. In the centre, at the top, is a female figure sitting, in her left arm an infant, with an apple in one hand, and holding out the other to take a like apple from another infant standing at the feet of the figure, the right hand of which lies on its back.

This very comprehensive account well describes the tomb, even if the text has too many norths in it! The tomb is in the South chapel and the first pair of standing figures are on the south side of the tomb. It is, in fact, these standing figures which make the tomb so exceptional. Their drapery shows some knowledge of classical sources and the whole is clearly by one of the outstanding sculptors of the day. There are very similar standing figures on the tomb of George Home, 1st Earl of Dunbar, *c.*1611 at Dunbar, and not dissimilar kneeling figures on the tomb of Robert Cecil, 1st Earl of Salisbury d.1612 at Hatfield, and both of these are known to be by Maximilian Colt, the sculptor of the tomb of Queen Elizabeth I in Westminster Abbey. The Apethorpe tomb can, therefore, be confidently attributed to Colt also.

The form of the tomb is extraordinary, rather like a vast marble four-poster, with the figures of Faith, Hope and Charity perched on the canopy, described but not identified in the text. In Bridges' MSS an account dated 12 August 1719 records the tomb with the epithet "beautiful to the Eye" – and many would agree.

Sir Anthony had been Ambassador to the Court of France in 1596.

Notes: BL. No.5. 32.5x20.5 cm. Other nos: Front – 5. There is also a letter A at the bottom left-hand corner. At the end of the title is added 'Extra Good'. For a summary of the work of Colt see *Whinney*. The Dunbar monument is illustrated and described in National Galleries of Scotland, *Virtue and Vision: Sculpture in Scotland 1540-1990* (Edinburgh 1991).

5. ASTON LE WALLS

Title on drawing: *An old Figure of Stone under an Arch in the North Wall of the Chancel 15 July 1721.*

Artist: Unsigned, Peter Tillemans

Bridges' text:

> Not mentioned. This is strange since in Bridges' MSS is a note dated 15 July 1721, the same as the drawing, is the statement: Under the N wall of the Chancel an antique figure under an Arch, drawn by Mr Tillemans.

The drawing shows a low arched recess containing a recumbent effigy, with the architecture elaborated with a wide cusped arch and on each side pinnacles, with that on the left hand broken. The figure is that of a priest in vestments, somewhat worn, of 14th century date and usually identified as that of John de Ardele who held the living at the end of that century.

Notes: BL. No.7 (part of a composite sheet with Edgecote, Plate 104). 32x22.5 cm. Other no: Front – 7.

View of the Front of the Lord Ferrers' house at Astwell in Wappenham Parish

6. ASTWELL CASTLE

Title on drawing: *View of the Front of the Lord Ferrers' House at Astwell in Wappenham Parish*

Artist: Unsigned, Peter Tillemans

Date: Undated, but probably 1721. Bridges' MSS record a visit on 17th July 1721.

Bridges' text:

> At about a mile's distance from *Wapenham*, to the south west lies *ASTWELL*, an old seat belonging to Earl *Ferrers*. Behind the gate-house is a little court and an entry into the hall. The hall windows project *en ronde*, and have battlements over them. The wainscot, and chimney-pieces in several rooms, are adorned with the arms of the family, and with other carved work: and the windows, which are of chrystal, are stained with flowers, birds, horses and other ornaments.

Unfortunately most of this house has gone, save for the tower and a portion of the wing to the left. As this and the following drawing show, it was a house of considerable extent and age.

The tower dates from the end of the 15th century and is part of the rebuilding programme put in hand by the Lovett family shortly after they had acquired the estate in 1471. It is entered through a heavily panelled door, with a wicket gate, and its upper storeys are reached by a stair turret, whose battlements appear at its rear right-hand corner. To the left of the tower, above the lower battlemented wall, other battlements are seen, presumably the top of one of the hall windows described in Bridges' text. Beyond again, on the left, the two main gables of the west range, each of three floors having arched mullioned windows. There is a further projection behind, and within the range a large chimneystack.

To the right of the tower there is another gabled wing, also of three floors with mullioned windows. Both of these gabled ranges accord with a date shortly after 1600, and in Bridges' MS Notes he records a carved shield with the date 1607. The Shirley family had just acquired the property and it remained in their possession through the 18th century. However after being created Earls Ferrers in 1711 they resided mainly at another of their properties, Staunton Harold in Leicestershire, and Astwell gradually fell into disrepair and was reduced to the status of a farmhouse.

One wishes that its hall and painted windows had survived.

Notes: BL. No.2. 44x28 cm. Other no: Front – 12.

Another View of the Lord Ferrers' House to the North

7. ASTWELL CASTLE

Title on drawing: *Another View of the Lord Ferrerss House to the North*

Artist: Unsigned, Peter Tillemans

Date: Undated, but probably also 1721.

Bridges' text:

See previous drawing.

This view is taken looking across the valley from the north side, and shows the back of the courtyard block. Another tall three storey range of early 17th century date is evident, and above it, just detectable, the battlemented top of the stair turret of the gatehouse. The wing on the right is an irregular affair, with a number of gabled projections. To the right of the house is a walled garden, and to the left a thatched barn.

Notes: BL. No.3. 45x28 cm. Other nos: Front – 13. Above the frame of the view is pencilled: ?Astwell. This was probably added *c.*1885.

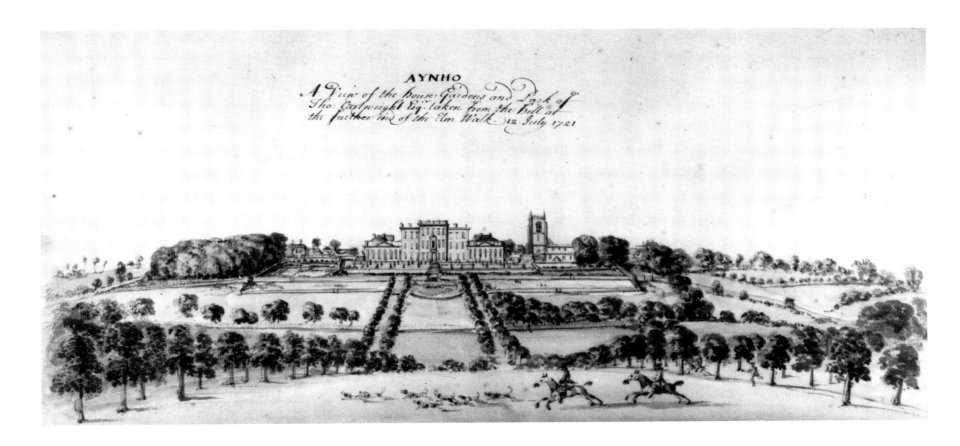

A View of the house Gardens and Park of
Tho: Cartwright Esq. taken from the hill at
the further end of the Elm Walk. 12 July 1721

8. AYNHO

Title on drawing: *A View of the House Gardens and Park of Tho Cartwright Esqr taken from the Hill at the further end of the Elm Walk 12. July 1721*

Artist: Unsigned, Peter Tillemans

Bridges' text:

> *Aynho* is a village of one hundred houses seated on the west end of an hill, of gentle ascent from the east, but falling abruptly to all the other expositions.
>
> *(There is no actual mention of the house in the text.)*

This is one of the most attractive and more typical of Tillemans' drawings in the collection, with the garden terraces showing especially well. The view is looking northwards, along the wide double avenue of the 'Elm Walk', across which speeds the hunt, perhaps led by Mr Cartwright. The farmland is divided from the park by a fence, and then higher up the slope the gardens begin. A series of walled terraces can be identified, with a curved projection in the centre. Closer to the house a formal parterre spreads either side a pathway with steps, and on either side of the parterre are lower levels with other forms of planting; perhaps a kitchen garden with fruit trees on its walls, to the left.

The house appears in its early Georgian form, without the extensions and alterations made by the architect John Soane *c.*1800. In its centre is the tall three storey block designed by Edward Marshall, the King's Master Mason, *c.*1660, with the entrance and arched window above. To either side are low wings with pediments and tall windows, all added 1707-1714 by the architect Thomas Archer, that on the left being an orangery. Just visible over these are the roofs of the wings which form the entrance forecourt on the north side of the house.

The church tower stands proudly alongside the garden to the right (see Plate 10).

The Cartwrights became owners of Aynho in 1615, and the Thomas of the title succeeded in 1676.

Notes: BL. No.10. 46x28 cm. Other no: Front – 7. For the work of Marshall, Archer and Soane, see *Colvin.*

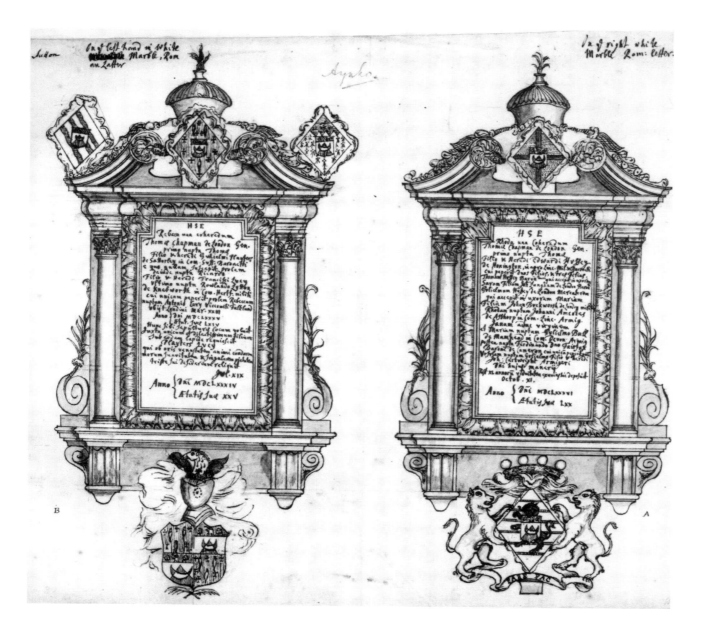

9. AYNHO

Title: No title as such on drawing

Artist: Unsigned, unknown hand

Date: Probably 1734, since on the back of the drawing is written "W.S. 5. Augt. 1734".

An impressive, if somewhat heavy handed, drawing of two monuments which were either side the chancel of the old church, and were placed in a similar position when the church was rebuilt in the 1720s (see Plate 10). The monuments commemorate the coheiresses of Thomas Chapman of London, Rebecca and Rhoda. Rebecca married into the Lucy family of Charlecote and died in 1685; Rhoda was the wife of Ferdinando, Baron Fairfax, who died in 1686, and her daughter became the wife of Thomas Cartwright of Aynho (d.1676), hence why they were buried at Aynho.

Both memorials are typical of the workshop of William Stanton of Holborn, London, one of the most fashionable carvers of his day.

Notes: BL. No.9. 34x30 cm. For the Stantons of Holborn see *Gunnis.*

10. AYNHO

Title on drawing: *AYNHO South Prospect of the Church taken 12. July. 1721*

Artist: Unsigned, Peter Tillemans

Bridges' text:

> The church, dedicated to St. Michael, consists of a body with two iles, a burial place joining to the south ile, a chancel all leaded, and a vestiary which is covered with slate. At the west end is a handsome embattled tower, with a small pinnacle at each corner.

This small sketch records the church in its medieval form, only to survive till 1723, when 'by the Pious Care, Generous encouragement and prudent management' of Thomas Cartwright, it was rebuilt in a Vanbrughian classical style – all, that is, save for its medieval tower. The drawing suggests that during the 17th century there had been much patching up and rebuilding, with hardly a window that is anything other than of post-1600 form. The tower is a fine example of 14th century work and of a type typical of the south Northamptonshire/north Oxfordshire region, and survived the 18th century rebuilding.

Notes: BL. No.8. 25x16 cm.

AYNHO

South Prospect of the church taken. 12. July. 1721.

View of Bernack Church to the South July 1721

11. BARNACK

Title on drawing: *View of Bernack Church to the South July 1721*

Artist: Unsigned, Peter Tillemans

Date: July 1721. Bridges' MSS record visits on both 27th and 28th of that month.

Bridges' text:

> The church, dedicated to St. *John* the *Baptist*, consists of a spacious body, two iles, and chancel, covered with lead. At the upper end of the south ile is a leaded embattled chapel, and a like chapel at the upper end of the north ile. The pillars and arches which support the iles are neat and adorned with fretwork. At the west end is a pyramidal steeple, in which are four bells. On the south side is a handsome porch, with four seats under old arches on each side, with stonework running up pyramidally, with narrow embowed arches crossing one another at the roof. On the ridge of the middle division, on the north and south side of the tower, is stonework, and on it the figure of a cock.

A splendid drawing showing the south side of this remarkable church with its striking Saxon tower. Almost equally remarkable is the late Norman bell stage and spire. The late 12th century porch described by Bridges drew equal admiration from Sir Nikolaus Pevsner, who describes it as "a superb piece". The tracery of the windows is accurately drawn: the fine Decorated style south aisle, with, to its east, the richly decorated Perpendicular Walcot Chapel, with its unusual double window. The roofs, as Bridges states, are of lead, the nave rising above the aisle as a plain wall topped by a low parapet: today that plain wall is pierced by small trefoil clerestory windows.

To the left and behind the church are the chimneys and gables of the Manor House, also described in Bridges' text, and to the east of the church there is a fine circular dovecote.

Notes: BL. No.12. 43x28 cm. Other no: Front – 29.

12. BARNACK

Titles on drawing: *A Monᵗ at the upper end of the S Ile in Bernack Church July 1721. The Fragments of Stone Work on each side of the East Window of the S Ile July 1721. Painting upon wood at the upper end of the N Ile July 1721. NB On the back of this a Monᵗ in Peterborough Cathedral*

Artist: Unsigned, Peter Tillemans

Bridges' text:

No specific reference to these items

The drawings gathered on this sheet relate mainly to the Walcot chapel on the south side of the church. The monument is one of two at Barnack carved from grey Alwalton stone, both of Tudor date and both having tomb chests within an arched recess. This one is the most elaborate with its panelled base and large heraldic achievement of the Walcot family.

The window and two niches are part of the east wall of the chapel. The left-hand niche contains a sculpture of the Annunciation, and both, with their crocketed gables fit in period with the chapel itself, late Perpendicular.

The wooden panel with its painting of the martyrdom of a saint no longer exists.

Notes: BL. No.14. 43x28 cm. On the back of the bottom drawing is another of two tombs in Rockingham Church (Plate 233).

Two Figures Cut in Wood in a Seat in Barnack Church. July 1721.

Two other Figures of Stone lying under 2 Arches at the upper end of the N Ile in the S Church July 1721

13. BARNACK

Title on drawing: *Two Figures Cut in Wood on a Seat in Barnack Church July 1721. Two of the Figures of Stone lying under yᵉ Arches at the upper end of the N Ile in this Church July 1721*

Artist: Unsigned, Peter Tillemans. Bridges' MS Notes record under 27 July 1721: "On the Pew at the upper end of the N side of the Church are handsome Carvings drawn by Mr Tillemans".

Bridges' text:

> In the wall, on the north side of the chapel, is the monument of a man cross legged, lying on his back, and under an arch at his feet, the monument of a woman.

The two drawings on the left are of stall ends. They are exceedingly fine examples of early Renaissance design and probably early 16th century in date. Unfortunately they are no longer in the church.

On the right are the two monuments mentioned in Bridges' text. That at the top is the figure of a knight wearing a surcoat over his mail suit. His right arm crosses his body to hold his sword and his legs are crossed. Today the figure is so worn that it is difficult to interpret. The lower effigy is that of a lady, her hair in plaits under a wide netted headdress, and wearing a long gown. Both memorials are 14th century in date.

Notes: BL. No.15. 44x28 cm.

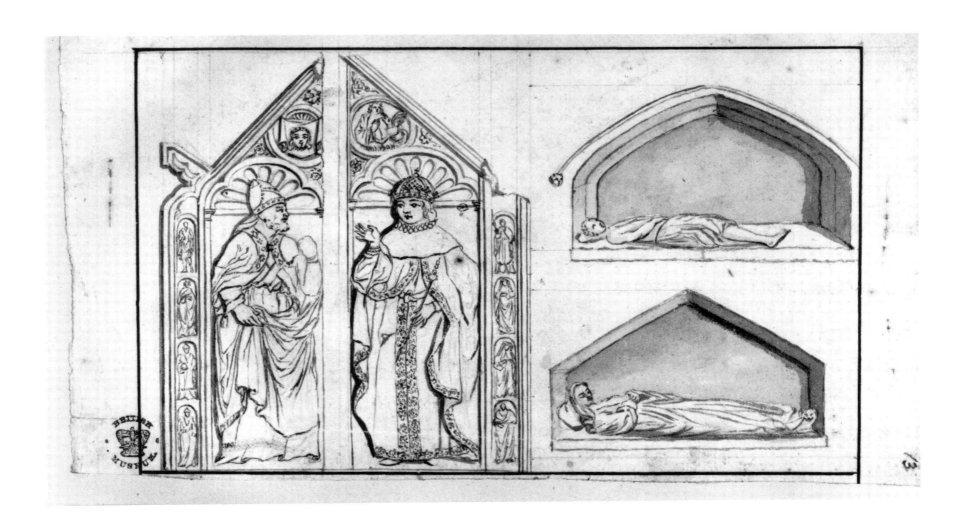

14. BARNACK

Title on drawing: *Bernack Church*

Artist: Unsigned, perhaps A. Motte

Date: After 1721.

This is a smaller version of the drawings on Plate 13.

It is presumably a reduced version made as a preliminary to engraving, hence its attribution to Motte.

Notes: BL. No.13. 23x14 cm.

The Ruins of Barnwell Castle taken Southward

15. BARNWELL

Title on drawing: *The Ruins of Barnwell Castle taken Southward*

Artist: Unsigned, Peter Tillemans

Date: Probably 1721. There is an entry in Bridges' MS Notes dated August 1721, although another dated 7 Aug 1718 says "View of the ye ruins of ye Castle taken".

Bridges' text:

In the reign of *Hen.* I. a castle was built here by *Reginald le Moine*, the remains of which now standing are four round bastions, a great gateway to the south-east, a small door on the west, with doors into the bastions, and doorcases still intire. The walls, which are about three feet thick, are yet subsisting, except on the western side, the middle part of which is open. Lord Chief Baron *Montague* resided here about thirty-five years ago: since that time it hath been in a great measure demolished.

There is not much to add to Bridges' description. It all looks very much as it does today. The date usually given for the building of the castle is *c.*1266. Le Moyne bestowed the property on Peterborough Abbey and it was after the Dissolution that the Montagus acquired it. It is the house built close by, by Sir Edward Montagu, in the late 16th century, which forms the core of the present house at Barnwell. The ruins of the castle stand in the grounds and must rank as one of the most thrilling garden buildings on any property.

Notes: BL. No.11. 31x20 cm. Other nos: At the base of the drawing is a letter A, and on the reverse is written, Numb. 37. The drawing has been squared over, suggesting preparation for redrawing for engraving.

16. BARTON SEAGRAVE

Artist: Unsigned, Peter Tillemans

Date: Probably 1719. A visit is recorded on 5 October 1719, but, of course, Tillemans lodged with Bridges when he came to Northamptonshire.

Bridges' text:

> The manor, which is within the *Gloucester* fee, with considerable estate, is now in *John Bridges*, Esq; as successor to his father, who about the year 1665. purchased of Mr. *Humfrey*, Lord *Cullen*, and others.

This is a view of Barton Seagrave manor house, the home of John Bridges. It comes as no surprise to find that this particular house receives great attention from Tillemans, and the drawings of it are some of the most delightful and highly finished in the series.

This, the first of three, shows the south front, set above a sunk garden, with a gazebo on the left. The oldest part of the house is to the left of the porch and is partly Elizabethan with mullioned windows, while the right-hand wing appears to be mid-17th century, with cross-mullion and transom windows, perhaps a rebuilding by Bridges' father shortly after 1665.

In John Morton's *Natural History of Northamptonshire* (1712) occurs the statement: "The Worshipful J. Bridges, Esq; has in his own Grounds in and about Barton Seagrave, planted at least 40000 Trees of several Kinds: The Advantage whereof in part he himself has liv'd to enjoy, and his Posterity will enjoy it, in still greater Measure". Evidence of the planting can be seen in the garden beyond the wall on the left and is further amplified by the view in another drawing (Plate 18).

It would be nice to identify the figures. John Bridges himself was a bachelor and perhaps it is him we see looking out of the window above the porch. But who is the lady exercising the dogs? Perhaps his aunt, Lady Trumball.

Notes: BL. No. 266. 45x20 cm. Morton's *Natural History*, 1712, contains several references to Bridges' planting as well as that quoted (p.486 para 28).

17. BARTON SEAGRAVE

Title on reverse of drawing: (Not easy to read) *Wignell or Wiguel Guys*
Artist: Unsigned, Peter Tillemans
Date: Probably 1719.

Another view of Bridges' house, this time taken from the south-west, with the west front and its large early Georgian sash-windows prominent. The pretty gazebo looks into a walled topiary garden where a variety of trees are growing. Behind the wall are four large pine trees and even though we cannot see the full detail of the garden it is clear that Morton's description (Plate 16) is borne out by the drawing.

The title on the back of the drawing is puzzling and has, so far, not been explained.

Notes: BL. No.262. 24.5x12 cm. Other no: On reverse is written Numb. 16.

18. BARTON SEAGRAVE

Title: None on drawing

Artist: Unsigned, Peter Tillemans

Date: The absence of any numbers on the drawing make dating difficult, but it may also be 1719.

This is a more distant view of the house, taken from the east, along a wide double avenue. The central part of the avenue has trees which have been trimmed of their lower branches and some of their central branches to improve their shape. In the foreground is the Ise Brook with its banks lined with pollarded willows. Right in the centre Tillemans has placed himself, sketching, and beyond, in the avenue, two more people are strolling, doubtless John Bridges and one of his colleagues – Thomas Eayre of Kettering, perhaps?

Notes: BL. No.267. 29.5x12 cm.

19. BARTON SEAGRAVE

Title: None on drawing

Artist: Unsigned, but probably Tillemans

Date: Uncertain.

This rather rough sketch records the tympanum of the north entrance doorway of Barton Seagrave church. The building is a good example of a Norman church, with a large squat tower standing between the nave and chancel, and despite later alterations remains almost as built in the 12th century. The chancel was partially rebuilt in the 13th century, when an aisle was added on the south side of the nave. In 1878 the aisle was rebuilt.

The church is the burial place of John Bridges and there is a memorial tablet to him, carved by the Northampton sculptor, John Hunt.

Notes: BL. No.268. 24 x 15 cm. For John Hunt see *Gunnis*, Hunt is also mentioned in connection with All Saints church, Northampton (see Plate 173).

20. BILLING, LITTLE

Title on drawing: *The Ruines of the Longvilles House at Billing Sepr 1721*

Artist: Unsigned, Peter Tillemans

Date: Bridges' MS Notes record a visit on 4th September 1721.

Bridges' text:

> Part of the Mansion-house, which was formerly inhabited by the *Longevilles*, is still left standing, and hath great marks of antiquity remaining. The first storey is supported with broad arches, where is the appearance of a chapel. The doorcases, of *Harleston* free-stone, are thick and large. And at the south end is a turret with a stair-case leading up to the leads. A part of it is embattled. In the yard is a farm-house, made out of the ruins, adjoining to the ruinous part.

It is worth quoting the description from Bridges' MS Notes, since there is further detail:

> ye Ruins of a house belonged olim to Sr Edw Longeville ye last yt inabited in't – Marks of great Antiquity still remaining in ye Shell of good part still standing – Bowd Windows like Chappels, wth Narrow Arches & hollow Stone dores & Stairs with Broad Arches, Supporting ye 1st Story, where was appearance of a Chappell – narrow Stone staircase lead up ye 2d Story. Thick Door Cases of large freestone of Harlestone. Ruins in ye yard of Chimneys of ye Hall & Kitchen a Turret to ye S end with a Staircase to ye Leads.

> A Farmers house of Mr Thursby, made out of ye ruins, now joining to ye ruinous part

What we have here is a most interesting survival of the medieval house of the Longuevilles and it is sad that it no longer exists. This is clearly the chamber range of the house with the chamber and possibly a chapel on the first floor above a vaulted undercroft. The tracery depicted in the windows suggests an early 14th century date, with remains of geometrical designs and transoms dividing the window horizontally. Similar windows can be seen at Stokesay Castle in Shropshire. The right-hand section of wall has the remains of a southern extension with a broken wall and arched opening. To the left of the broken wall is a small trefoil shaped opening, very like the one in the courtyard at Canons Ashby. The staircase tower is presumably that on the left, partly embattled as Bridges states, while that on the right, a broader affair with cross slit may well have been a garderobe, and is comparable to a similar one at Broughton Castle, near Banbury.

The north side of the house was similar, and was engraved by Samuel and Nathaniel Buck in 1729.

The left hand wing, the farmhouse, is late 17th century in appearance and may well be a conversion or re-utilisation of earlier portions. This is probably due to William Thursby of Abington, who owned the manor, and who did much rebuilding on the Abington estate in the late 1670s. This is the only portion of this house now remaining, and even that was rebuilt in 1880.

Notes: BL. No.16. 44x28 cm. Other no: Front – 57.

A

21. BLISWORTH

Title on drawing: *Draught of Rog^r Wakes Mon^t at the upper end of the South Isle of Blisworth Church taken 9 July 1719*

Artist: Unsigned, Peter Tillemans

Bridges' text:

> At the upper end of the south ile is an altar monument of freestone covered with grey marble, and round the marble is this inscription in brass. Here lyeth Roger Wake Esquyer lord of Blysworth in the Counte of Northampton and Elizabeth his . . . which Roger decessyd the xvi day of Marche the yere of our Lord God MCCCCCIII. on whose soule Jeshu have mercy. At the right corner at the top, and left corner at the bottom are the arms of *Wake*; and at the left corner at the top, and the right corner at the bottom are the arms of *Wake* impaling *Catesby, two lions passant crowned*. On the north side of the monument are the arms of *Wake, viz. Argent, two gules, in chief three torteauxes,* impaling *two lions*; and of *Wake,* impaling *three cheverons.* Behind the monument is an arch in the wall, wherein it appears to have formerly stood.

This simple sketch well records the appearance of this brass. It commemorates Roger Wake, d.1504, and his wife, their seven sons and three daughters. The heraldry is indicated with the arms of Wake being obvious, but slightly mis-emblazoned in Bridges' text: the true emblazon is – Argent, two bars gules, in chief three torteaux.

Notes: BL. No.17. 20x15.5 cm. Other nos: Front – 57; on reverse Num. 83.

View of Buckton church now in Ruines with a View of the Town   Sep.ʳ 1721

22. BOUGHTON. Boughton Green

Title on drawing: *View of Buckton Church now in Ruines with a View of the Town Sepʳ 1721*

Artist: Unsigned, Peter Tillemans

Date: The date can be made more exact from Bridges' MSS Notes as 5 September 1721.

Bridges text:

> The church, dedicated to S. *John* the *Baptist*, stands upon the green about half a mile distant from the town. It now lyes in ruins, no part of the roof remaining, and the walls in several places levelled with the ground. It consists of a body, chancel, and north chancel or chauntry-chapel. At the west end is a spire of eight sides, raised upon a plain coped tower: both these are still left standing.

The title on the drawing uses the old name of the village, Buckton, which differentiated it from Boughton near Kettering. The view looks north-west across the expanse of the Green towards the village. It shows in the church such medieval features as then survived: the east wall with its wide single gable enclosing a small oval rose window in its head. The spire stood till 1780, when it collapsed. The site of the building, built into the hillside, is comparable with Wadenhoe near Oundle (Plate 256).

On the horizon, to the left of the spire, is a windmill, which stood near the Northampton-Harborough road.

Notes: BL. No.79. 43x26 cm.

*View of the Duke of Mountagues house at Boughton taken on ye
Rising Ground in Geddington Feild . July .1721*

23. BOUGHTON HOUSE

Title on drawing: *View of the Duke of Montagues House at Boughton taken on yᵉ Rising Ground in Geddington Feild July 1721*

Artist: Unsigned, Peter Tillemans

Bridges' text:

> In *Weekley* parish is *Boughton*, a distinct manor, and the seat of his Grace the Duke of *Montagu.*

One might have expected Bridges' text to say just a little more about this important house. The view is taken from a north easterly point and looks across the field cultivation, down to the house, set within its formal layout, as it was created in the early 18th century.

On the left an avenue runs down from the Geddington road to the stables, a fine block with a domed entrance archway. Then comes the forecourt, with its park wall and archway entrance in shadow. In front again is a large square pool, with, on the house side, a row of conical trees. Above the pool, and forming the central feature of the view, the tall elegant block of the house itself. The drawing does not make quite clear the form of this front – a half H plan, the view being taken across the wings of the H. Behind the tall front, built at the end of the 17th century, runs a lower range also of two floors, somewhat more irregular in effect, which forms the west side of the larger of the two courtyards at Boughton. To the right of the house a sloping bank is visible, leading to further formal planting fronting another pool, still remaining today. Below, and running to the right of the house, is the rest of the layout, an intricately planned series of walks, water canals and pools. The regular boundaries and more open area indicate the canals and pool, and some of the avenue planting which bounded the layout is clear to the far right. Also at this point is a windmill on a tall mound, a relic of the earlier open farmland. The mill was to disappear during alterations to the layout under the landscape gardener Charles Bridgman, shortly after this drawing was made, but its mound survived, converted into a mount allowing views over the layout.

Notes: BL. No.65. 45 x 28 cm. Other no: Front – 24. The whole layout is carefully and amply described with plans in R.C.H.M. Vol. II, pp.156-162. There is also some discussion of it in Tessa Murdoch, *Boughton House, the English Versailles*, London, Faber/Christies 1992.

24. BOUGHTON HOUSE

Title on drawing: No title on drawing. Sheet 47 of a series of consecutive drawings of statuary.

Artist: Unsigned, Peter Tillemans

Date: Uncertain, but possibly July 1721, when the house was drawn.

This page from the series of drawings of statuary is the only one which relates to Boughton, despite that the title-page of the series says: *Boughton near Kettering D. of Montagu's Draught of the Busto's.* For further comments on this series see Easton Neston (Page 54). The sheet shows the ten plaster busts which decorate the arcade on the north front of Boughton House. They rest on splendidly carved wooden brackets with acanthus decoration, one of which is sketched in under the first head. Precise identification of the heads is difficult: they fall within that category which is usually described simply as "antique".

Notes: BL. No.64. 32x20 cm.

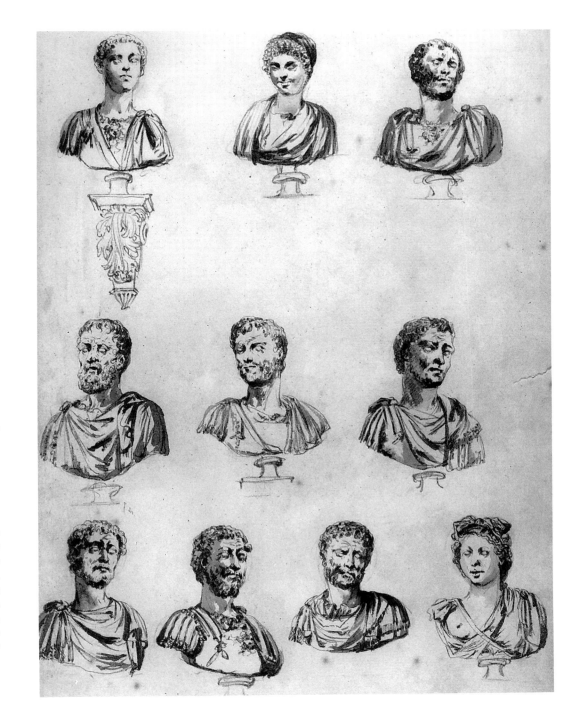

25. BRACKLEY

Title on drawing: *A View of BRACKLEY to the South taken 12 July 1721*

Artist: Unsigned, Peter Tillemans

Bridges' text:

> The town is situate on a gentle descent to the south, and consists chiefly of one long street from south to north . . . On the south border the river *Ouse* hath a small current, which at the entrance into *Brackley* passeth under a stone bridge of two arches, where it divides the parish from *Evenley*. From the bridge the great street of the town runs up to the top of the hill, and then turns eastward to *St. Peter's* which is the parish church . . . In the southwest end of the town, on the left hand side of the river, was a fair castle. The site, and hill where it stood, is yet to be seen, and hath the name of *Castle-hill*, though the walls have been long since demolished.

The drawing effectively captures the hillside location of the town and the path of its main street.

In the foreground are the strip formations of the fields, running down to the river, which is crossed by a two-arched bridge. Just over the bridge is the church of St. James, which as described further in Bridges' text, was in a decayed condition. It has a west tower and nave and south aisle, both lead covered, and survived till about the middle of the 19th century. At the top of the hill stands the fine Market House with its striking cupola, built at the expense of the Earl of Bridgewater in 1706. The properties to the left of the main street have long gardens running back to an access lane. Above and beyond them is a conspicuous post-mill, standing on Castle Hill. In the centre of the view is the tower of the chapel of SS. James and John, whose main facade is recorded by another drawing (Plate 28). On the far right, in the lower portion of the town, is the parish church of St. Peter, with its fine tower, again the subject of a further drawing (Plate 27). In the distance, in the valley, is a large house, presumably Turweston Manor.

As interesting as the buildings is the representation of the rural setting of the town, with gardens, orchards and much planting. Indeed, it is the quantity of trees which makes the drawing so attractive.

Notes: BL. No.67/ 44x28.5 cm. Other no: Front – 6. This is the larger of two views drawn from the south-west (see also Plate 26), and is the more detailed. It served as the original for an engraving in Bridges' printed text (Vol. 1, p.150) where it is given a key listing the principal buildings. There are two wash drawings in the Overstone Collection, Reading University (Vol. A-B, fol. 71) of the Chapel of St James, which presumably show the remains of that church. Although not dated or signed, they are probably the work of Thomas Athow and date from about 1800, but there is no tower.

26. BRACKLEY

Title on drawing: *Prospect of Brackley to the South taken to yᵉ right hand of the Road from Oxford July 1719*

Artist: Unsigned, Peter Tillemans

Date: The drawing of St Peter's church, Brackley (Plate 27) is dated 1st July 1719.

This is almost identical to the previous drawing, save that it is taken from a position a little further to the west, and the 1721 drawing presumably supplants it.

Notes: BL. No.66. 30.5x20.5 cm.

28. BRACKLEY

Title on reverse of drawing: *Draught of Sᵗ Johns Hospital at Brackley at the West Taken 1 July 1719*

Artist: Unsigned, Peter Tillemans

Bridges' text:

> The hospital dedicated to St. *James* and St. *John* . . . now in lease from *Magdalene* college to Mr. *John Welchman* of *Brackley*, lies in a ruinous condition. The old hall was taken down about fifty years since. In the modern hall are one hundred and five shields, which were removed thither out of a garret, and contain the arms of many of the nobility and gentry, and of eleven bishops sees. The chapel is still subsisting, but stript of all its former decorations, the glass taken out of the windows, the seating gone, and the tomb-stones removed out of their places. It is about one hundred and twenty foot in length, and two and twenty in breadth, and hath only one ile, with a low broad tower on the north west side, coped at the top . . .

The sad state of the building, as recorded in Bridges' text, is obvious in the drawing. The doorway shows its late Norman decoration surviving from the time of the founding of the Hospital *c*.1150, while above is a wide triple lancet window of Early English design, with columns dividing the lights and dog-tooth ornament around its arches. Either side the niches have medieval statues, still surviving. Having long ceased to be used for religious purposes, other buildings have encroached across the facade and the lancets have been partially blocked.

The building was restored by Buckeridge in 1869 for use as a chapel for Magdalen College School.

Notes: BL. No.69. 19.5x15.2 cm. Also incorporated in the composite plate in the printed text (Vol.I, p.150).

27. BRACKLEY

Title on reverse of drawing: *Draught of Sᵗ Peters Church, at Brackley taken 1ˢ July 1719*

Artist: Unsigned, Peter Tillemans

Bridges' text:

> The church dedicated to St. *Peter*, is seated near the river on the east side of the town, and about a quarter of a mile distant from it. It consists of a body, north and south ile leaded, and chancel tiled, except on the south side, which is also leaded. At the west end is a low embattled tower, in which are five bells.

This drawing shows the fine 13th century tower with its arcaded facade and statuary in niches above the doorway. The statuary, which is original, is still there, and when the drawing was used for an engraving in Bridges' printed text they were shown in larger detail.

Notes: BL. No.68. 18.5x15.3 cm. Engraved as part of a composite plate in Bridges' text (Vol. I, p.150).

29. BRINGTON, GREAT

Title on reverse of drawing: *Draught of Sr Rob. Spencers Mon^t standing at the East End of the N. Chancel ag^t the N Wall at Brington taken 6 July 1719*

Artist: Unsigned, Peter Tillemans

Bridges' text:

No mention.

The title is incorrect, since the tomb is that of Sir William Spencer d.1532 and his wife Suzanna. Today only the tomb chest survives, the canopy and back panel with its heraldry having been destroyed at a date prior to the 1820s, when it was drawn for inclusion in George Baker's *History of Northamptonshire*, published in 1822. The destruction probably took place shortly after 1785 when the chapel was rearranged to accommodate the memorial by Nollekens for the 1st Earl Spencer (d.1783).

Notes: BL. No.70. 18.2x15 cm. The title ends with "ii". At the bottom left is written "F".

F

30. BRINGTON, GREAT

Title on reverse of drawing: *Draught of Sr John Spencers Mon^t Standing between the North & South Chancell near the East End taken 6 July 1719*

Artist: Unsigned, Peter Tillemans

Bridges' text:

> Under an arch of freestone, in the north chancel or burying-place, curiously embellished, are the figures of a Knight in armour with his Lady . . . (Bridges' text quotes the complete inscription).

This splendid tomb, whose canopy is carved from Totternhoe stone, remains one of the finest pieces of Tudor decoration in any parish church. The figures are of alabaster with their original colouring largely intact.

Notes: BL. No.71. 26x18 cm. The title ends with "ii".

31. BRINGTON, GREAT

Title on reverse of drawing: *Draught of Sʳ John Spencers Monument agᵗ the North Wall of the N. Chancel Taken 7. July 1719*

Artist: Unsigned, Peter Tillemans

Bridges' text:

> Again the inscription is recorded only.

This is a further fine example of the series of tombs erected at Brington *c.*1599 to designs of Hollemans (see Plate 32). It commemorates Sir John Spencer (d.1599) and his wife Mary. This example is notable for its pillared side piers, its fine cresting and the magnificent display of heraldry.

Notes: BL. No.72. 30.5x18 cm. The title ends with "ii". At the bottom left is written "D".

32. BRINGTON, GREAT

Title on reverse of drawing: *Draught of Robt Lord Spencers Mon^t between N & South Chancel (at the lower end) at Brington Taken 7. July 1719*

Artist: Unsigned, Peter Tillemans

Bridges' text:

> The inscriptions are recorded but there is no description of the tomb.

This is the tomb in the arch furthest west from the altar. It commemorates Robert, 1st Baron Spencer (d.1627) and his wife Margaret (d.1597) and was erected by Lord Spencer two years after his wife's death. It forms one of a series of tombs erected in 1599 or thereabouts to designs of Jasper Hollemans, a carver who worked from the alabaster workshops near Burton-on-Trent. All have somewhat heavy handed detailing, but as essays in late Elizabethan Renaissance design, with their colouring and heraldry, are almost unrivalled. Typical of its time is the canopy with its wide arch obelisk finials. The heraldry in this instance is used in a most unusual way on the coverlet which lies across Lady Spencer's figure, rather like an embroidered counterpane.

Notes: BL. No.73. 30 x 18 cm. The title ends with "ii". For Jasper Hollemans see *Whinney.*

33. BRINGTON, GREAT

Title on reverse of drawing: *Draught of Willm Lord Spencers Mon^t at ye lower end of the North Chancel in the Area at Brington Taken 7. July 1719*

Artist: Unsigned, Peter Tillemans

Bridges' text:

> Upon a black marble tombe are the figures of a Baron and Baroness in their robes of state, with their hands lift up, over them is an arch of black and white marble, supported by eight pillars of black marble of the Corinthian order, with white Capitals . . .

Bridges was clearly impressed by this tomb, allowing a description as well as recording the inscription. It is, indeed, a superb affair and was the work of Nicholas Stone and his assistants and cost £600. It comes as a welcome relief with its black and white marble as against all the colour and heraldry of the earlier tombs. The details are splendid, most notably the central figures of Lord and Lady Spencer, where much attention has been paid to detailing of the costumes. William Baron Spencer died in 1636 and the tomb was finished two years later.

Notes: BL. No.74. 29x18.5 cm. The title ends with "ii". The entry in *The Notebook of Nicholas Stone* (Walpole Society, Oxford, 1919) reads: 'In 1638 I mad a tombe for the Lord Spencer and his Lady and sett up at Althrop in North hantshear for the which I had very well payed me 600£.' The work of Nicholas Stone is also discussed in *Whinney*.

c

35. BRINGTON, GREAT

Title on reverse of drawing: *Draught of Sr Edward Spencers Mont standing at the East end of the North Chancel agt the North Wall at Brington taken 6. July 1719*

Artist: Unsigned, Peter Tillemans

Bridges' text:

> Again only the inscription is given.

This extraordinary memorial commemorates Sir Edward Spencer (d.1655) and is the work of Nicholas Stone's son, John. The singular design prompted the late Sir Gyles Isham to refer to this tomb, somewhat irreverently but appropriately, as "The potted Earl" – one can forgive the erroneous peerage!

Notes: BL. No.77. 29x19 cm. The entry in the *Stone Notebooks* (Walpole Society, Oxford, 1919) reads: 'In Ano. 1656, I sett up a Tombe for Sir Edward Spencer att Brainton neare Althrop in Northamptonshire for wch I had 64£'.

34. BRINGTON, GREAT

Title on reverse of drawing: *Draught of Sr John Spencer & his Lady Katherines Mont standing in the middle between the North & South Chancel at Brington taken 6. July 1719*

Artist: Unsigned, Peter Tillemans

Bridges' text:

> Inscription only recorded.

This fills the central arch of the three between the chancel and the Spencer Chapel and commemorates Sir John Spencer (d.1586) and his wife and was, as previously noted with the other monuments, erected in 1599 by Hollemans (see above, Plate 32). It is the least satisfactory of the three monuments relying for its effect on its painted colour and heraldry.

Notes: BL. No.75. 30 x 18.5 cm. The title ends with "ii". At the bottom left is written "C".

Front of Mr Thorntons house at Brockhole 21 July 1621

36. BROCKHALL

Title on drawing: *Front of Mr Thorntons House at Brockhole 21 July 1721*

Artist: Unsigned, Peter Tillemans

Bridges' text:

> Here is one neat seat, the residence of Mr. Thornton Lord of the Manor, supposed to be built by the family of *Eyton*.

This is a most interesting record of the appearance of this house as originally built by Edward Eyton *c.*1610-20. The facade has the usual gables, arched mullioned windows and projecting wings, not dissimilar to the wings on the north front of Canons Ashby. The forecourt gateway has a typical gable and its archway leads through to the entrance to the Hall of the house. To the right is a range with a clock tower and the forecourt is bounded by outbuildings with similar Jacobean details.

The Thornton family acquired Brockhall in 1625 and when George Baker saw the house about 1820 he recorded in his *History* (1822) that it had been "considerably altered and improved by the present possessor", that is Thomas Reeve Thornton who inherited in 1790. What was done, quite skilfully, was to reduce the height of the gables and then incorporate them into a flat parapet, so that the house now looks rather severe and square. In addition a second projecting wing was built on the right making a symmetrical facade. Finally, in order to balance the design, the entrance doorway was moved to the centre of the facade. The outbuildings were removed and new stables built in 1799, which is probably the date when most of the alterations were accomplished.

Whilst one might bemoan the loss of the gables and irregularity, the house today is a most interesting mixture of genuine and fake Jacobean. Internally little remains of its original decoration but there is a pretty staircase and some charming "Gothick" plasterwork.

Notes: BL. No.78. 44x26 cm. Other no: Front – 21.

37. CASTLE ASHBY

Title on drawing: *Prospect of the Earl of Northamptons House & Gallery at Castle Ashby, Taken 1. Aug. 1719*

Title on reverse of drawing:

> *Prospect of the Earl of Northamptons House & Gallery at Castle Ashby, Taken 1. Aug. 1719*

Artist: Unsigned, Peter Tillemans

Bridges' text:

> The Earl of *Northampton*'s seat, which is built into a square, and forms a quadrangle within, was finished in 1624. The sides to the east and south were designed by *Inigo Jones*.

The view is looking at the south front of the house with the Elizabethan wings linked by the range attributed to Inigo Jones. Although the basic appearance of the facade is the same today, there are one or two significant differences. These mainly concern fenestration. The link building, for example, in this view retains its original cross-mullion and transom windows, which were later replaced by Georgian sashes. Then to the left, the first ground floor window past the link range, which in the drawing is shown as a four-light mullioned window, was later made to match its counterpart in the opposite wing, by being lengthened and given a transom. Note also the sundials on the projecting oriels of each wing.

Above the roofline appear various chimneystacks, with to the left those of the kitchen range and to the right those of the Hall range. In the centre, through the archway the entrance into the Hall is indicated.

The tradition of work at Castle Ashby being by Inigo Jones is of long foundation. While no documentary proof has been found, reference has been discovered in the accounts to a surveyor named Carter, and in Jones' office one of his principal assistants was an Edward Carter (d.1663), an elusive designer about whom little is so far known. Perhaps, therefore, the attribution should not be totally dismissed.

Notes: BL. No.80. 41x26 cm. Other no: On the reverse is written Num: 103. The discovery of Carter's name was made by Gervase Jackson-Stops and was published in an article in *Country Life* (1986, 30 January).

38. CASTLE ASHBY

Title on drawing: *Prospect of the Earl of Northamptons House at Castle Ashby taken in yᵉ Gardens*

Title on reverse of drawing: *Prospect of the Earl of Northamptons House at Castle Ashby taken in the Gardens 1. Augᵗ 1719*

Artist: Unsigned, Peter Tillemans

Bridges' text:

> That [facade] on the east was originally open with cloisters to the garden, but they are now filled up.

This is an important record of the appearance of this facade prior to alterations made later in the 18th and 19th centuries. The most obvious change is the disappearance of the high gabled roof on the right. This is the attic storey above the Great Chamber (King William Room), which was removed when this range was altered following the collapse of the Hall roof in 1771. Elsewhere the main differences are, as on the previous drawing, in the windows. At ground level can be seen the arches of the Jacobean loggia – Bridges' cloister – filled with large rectangular sash windows. These were later lengthened and their heads made to fit the curve of the arches *c.*1805. The open doorway is today a French window.

On the first floor there is a mixture of windows, some cross-mullion and transom openings and some plain mullioned type. At the left-hand end of the facade two three-light mullioned windows appear on both first and second floors. These discrepancies are to some measure the result of remodelling following a fire in the middle of the 17th century, the scorch marks of which are still apparent above many of the windows on the upper floors today.

In Bridges' MS Notes this facade is also credited to Inigo Jones: " "ye side towd ye S E Chace by Inigo Jones taken by Tillemans ye E as also towds ye Gardens wch Ld N sd was built by the same Architect. Sevll Chiney peices in ye Gallery supposed to be of that Architects".

As for the garden, the chief difference is that it seems to have been walled on its southern side. From the house a terrace falls with a sloping bank to the parterre, where there are urns, conical trees and other small flowering shrubs. The central path no longer exists, but the sloping banks remain, as do the steps on the left hand side, and even today the stone curbing of the top path has a break opposite the French window, so recording the position of the steps shown in the drawing. It is clear, therefore, that the present Victorian terraced garden retains a good deal of the layout as created in the 1680s and '90s.

Notes: BL. No.81. 41x26 cm. Other no: On reverse is written Num.102. What are these small flowering shrubs? August is not a month when there would have been roses. Might they be hibiscus or hydrangeas? I am grateful to Peter Mackay, who has intimate knowledge of the house, for checking these entries.

Nassaburgh

The Church & Steeple of yͤ ancient Town of Castre near Peterborow to yͤ S.

39. CASTOR

Title on drawing: *The Church & Steeple of yͤ ancient Town of Castre near Peterborow to yͤ S*

Artist: Unsigned, Peter Tillemans

Date: Probably 1719, and in Bridges' MS Notes a visit is recorded on 8th August 1719.

Bridges' text:

> The church, dedicated to St. *Kyneburga*, consists of a body, north and south ile, chancel, and cross ile from north to south, all covered with lead. In the middle is a broad tower, on which is raised a pyramidal steeple. The embattlements of the tower are curiously wrought, and underneath are two rows, the upper of small pillars, and the lower of the same, mixed with arches running round the square of the tower.

This simple drawing shows the church almost exactly as it appears today. The only difference is that the transept window clearly has foliated tracery in its head, a typical Geometrical Decorated design, and this was later removed to leave just plain circles. Bridges was much taken with the decoration of the rich Norman tower and has noted the pierced battlements.

Notes: BL. No.82. 31.5x20 cm. Other no: On the reverse Num.90.

40. CHESTER

Title on drawing: *THE ROMAN CASTRUM of CHESTER*

Artist: Thomas Eayre (signed)

Date: The caption is dated 1723.

Bridges' text:

> *CHESTER*, antiently an hamlet of four or five houses, is so named from the adjoining *Roman* encampment or *Castra* . . . Here is at present only one house, the residence of captain *Thomas Ekins*. This fortification or burrow as they now call it, was an oblong square, near twice as long as broad, and containing in the area about eighteen acres . . . Among the ruins on the south side, have been found two plain oblong quadrangular stone pillars, about four foot long and almost two in breadth. They seem by their form to have been sepulchral altars, but having no inscription, nor any other marks, it is not easy to determine for what end they were made.

This is a good example of Eayre's careful archaeological survey work. It can be compared with a modern plan (RCHM Vol.II p.91) and this shows that he has caught the general shape of the site with the two portions at different angles. Various hedge-lines are detectable today, and the walling at the top of the plan, described in the caption, is also confirmed by other records. At the bottom of the plan is a sketch of one of the "stone pillars".

The caption above the plan reads:

> The upper half of ye bank of ye W: side is ye most Remarkable, its about 9 Foot high and is ye same within as without –. the other parte of this bank is ye same height without, But is even with ye Surface of ye ground within. The N. Side is at ye E: corner about 20 Foot high and Very steep but diminishes off gradually so that its not about 10 Foot at ye other end - – All the E: side is about 12 Foot high without but the ground is even with it within – – The S: side is much ye same with ye upper parte of ye W: but is but about 4 Foot high within & without A great quantity of earth was brought into it to make it as high as the banks on these sides; And the whole Camp is of a different sort of earth; lighter and blacker than ye feilds adjoyning – 1723

Notes: BL. No.83. 33.5x21 cm.

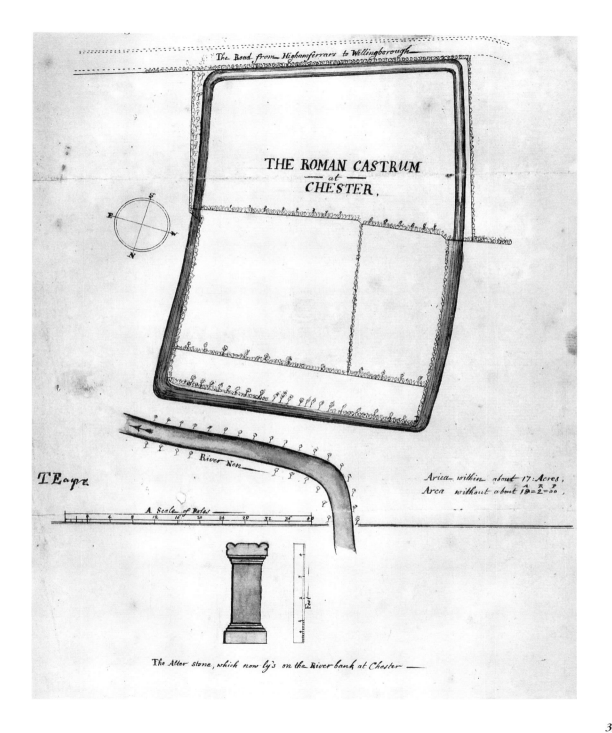

The Road from Highamferrars to Wellingborough

THE ROMAN CASTRUM at CHESTER.

T Eayre

River Nen

Aric̄a within about 17: Acres,
Area without about 18=2=00

A Scale of Poles

The Alter stone, which now ly's on the River bank at Chester —

View of Cliffords hill & Country adjacent taken in houghton par[ish] Feild 8. Aug. 1721
a. Cliffords hill b. great Billing. c. little Billing. d. Weston

41. CLIFFORD HILL

Title on drawing: *View of Cliffords Hill & Country adjacent taken in Houghton par Feild 8 Aug.t 1721*
a. Cliffords Hill b. great Billing c. little Billing d. Weston

Artist: Unsigned, Peter Tillemans

Bridges' text

> In this parish on the bank of the river stands *Clifford-hill*. It is of a circular form encompassed with a wide and deep ditch, and resembles the muniment at *Towcester*, named *Berryhill*, but is much larger. Around the top of it was formerly, as is reported, a mound of earth, which was pared off by *William Ward*, Esq: the father of the present possessor, with a design to use it as a bowling green.

The view is taken from near the Houghton-Cogenhoe road, looking across the strip cultivation of the slope of a field. The track running down to the river, lined with trees, is on the left, as it is today. The mound is an important but slightly mysterious monument. It is thought to be 11th or 12th century in date and built as a defence of the river ford. The name existed by the 13th century and it is one of the largest mottes in the country. *(See also next drawing entry.)*

Several villages appear in the view. On the far right is Great Billing, whose church appears with a spire, which it had till 1758 when it was demolished by lightning. In the valley, to the right of the mound, is Little Billing, where the church is shown with a substantial tower. Then on the skyline to the left is Weston Favell, also shown with a spire. This survived until May 1725 when, as the *Northampton Mercury* records it was "split assunder by the violence of a clap of thunder". Such damage to church spires was common and few in Northamptonshire survive as original medieval structures.

Notes: BL. No.84. 45x28.5 cm. Other no: Front – 41. For a full assessment of the archaeology of Clifford Hill see RCHM Vol.II pp.87-8.

View of Cliffords hill Sepr 1721 Taken from ye Mill with a distant View of Houghton Steeple

42. CLIFFORD HILL

Title on drawing: *View of Cliffords Hill Sepr 1721 Taken from yᵉ Mill with a distant View of Houghton Steeple*

Artist: Unsigned, Peter Tillemans

Date: The exact date is probably 18 September when visits to Brafield and Cogenhoe are recorded in Bridges' MS Notes.

A further view of this monument, made highly picturesque by the romantic mill buildings in the foreground. The combination of stone banks, thatched roofs and a somewhat tumbledown quality would make this an ideal subject for an artist today!

The tower of Little Houghton church is on the skyline.

It is worth quoting the description in Bridges' MS Notes:

> Cliffords hill is round emcompassed with a Ditch hill much in form like but larger than Berry hill at Toster. Elders, Thorns grow & Rabbets Burrow – stands within a Close of Mr Wards & ye Close near a Watermill upon ye River Nen yt runs to Northton wch Mill is at ye bottom to ye W of ye Hill & belongs to Mr Ward. The Top seems to have been pared away or even'd, like ye end of a Sugar loaf, taken away by Mr Wards Father to make a Bowling Green. It Overlooks at ye Top ye Country at a great distance on all sides except S wards where other high grounds interpose.

Notes: BL. No.85. 45x28 cm. Other no: Front – 56.

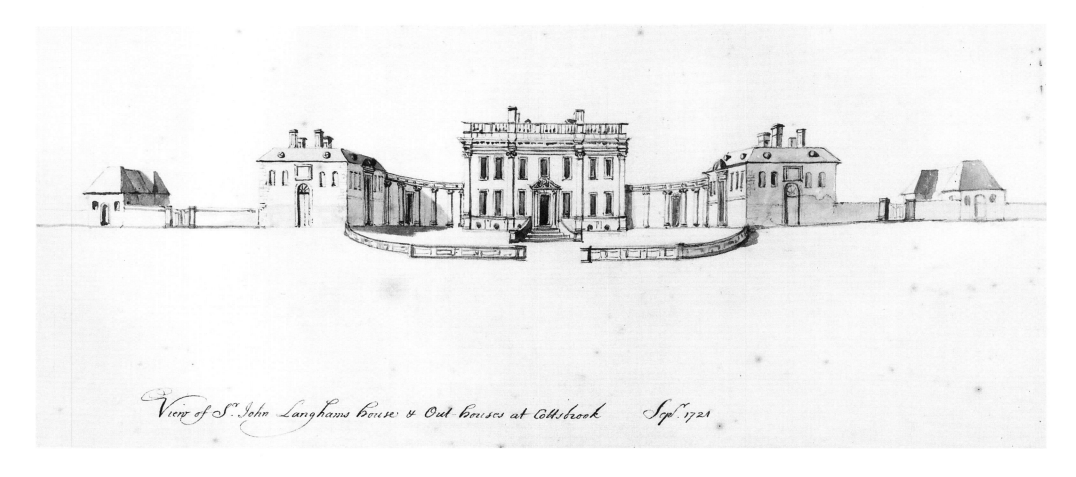

View of Sr john Langhams house & Out houses at Cottsbrook   Sepr 1721

43. COTTESBROOKE

Title on drawing: *View of Sr john Langhams House & Out Houses at Cottsbrook Sepr 1721*

Artist: Unsigned, Peter Tillemans

Date: No precise date appears in Bridges' MS Notes, although visitations in the area are recorded about the 20th of that month.

Bridges' text:

Here is one seat, the residence of Sir *John Langham*, an elegant modern-built brick house, standing at the entrance of the town.

This is another useful record of the original effect of this house, with the full symmetry of its architecture and its entrance forecourt and matching outbuildings. Much of what is shown here survives today although the effect is masked by 20th century planting.

Cottesbrooke was built between 1702 and 1713 probably by Francis Smith of Warwick, basing his ideas on Buckingham House in London, a favourite model for early 18th century architects. It is basically a Palladian plan with central block linked by curved quadrants to pavilions, and like Buckingham House, Cottesbrooke is also built of red brick and stone. The drawing shows that the pavilions had doorways in the end walls, no longer existing, and also suggests that the archways into the quandrants were also open, while they are now blocked.

The house remained in the possession of the Langhams till 1910, and after a number of changes of owner, it was acquired by Sir Reginald and Lady Macdonald Buchanan in 1937, with whose family it still remains. Tillemans shows the original entrance front, now the garden front. The sloping forecourt has been replaced by a planted parterre with statuary, much enhancing the handsome facade.

Notes: BL. No.86. 45x28.5 cm. Other no: Front – 54.

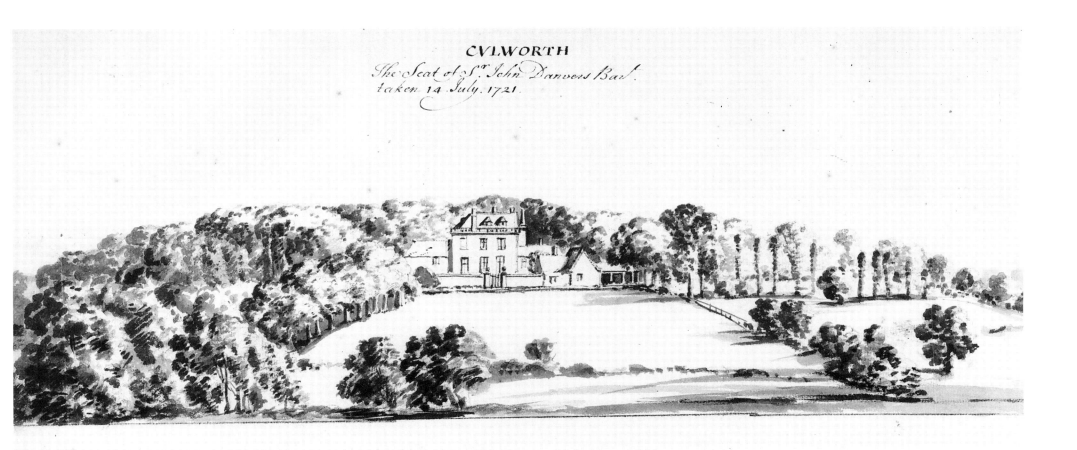

44. CULWORTH

Title on drawing: *CULWORTH The Seat of Sr John Danvers Bart taken 14. July 1721*

Artist: Unsigned, Peter Tillemans

Bridges' text:

> There are two mineral springs in this Lordship, whereof one is in Sir *John Danvers*'s grounds, and the other in Mill-piece.

This house is still known as Danvers House today. It was probably built by Sir Pope Danvers, who died in 1712 – the name Pope deriving from his mother, Anne, daughter of Sir William Pope of Wroxton, Oxfordshire. The Sir John of the title succeeded in 1712 and may well have made further additions to the building.

We see the south facade of the house and its garden, from across the valley. The front ends rather abruptly on the right, possible because it was intended to create a larger facade. There are the usual cross-mullion and transom windows, a balustrade and roof dormers. To right and left of the main block are lower wings and at the corner of the garden an outbuilding with a pillared shelter beyond. There is some sign of formality in the planting with a line of tall slender trees to the right of the house, and the vista we look across is bounded on the right by a regular line of trees.

Today the house looks less impressive. The tall range in the drawing is now partnered by others almost the same height, and the balustraded roof has been replaced by a series of more simple roof levels. The garden wall and gatepiers are no more.

Notes: BL. No.87. 45x28 cm. Other no: Front – 9.

South Front of the Earl of Cardigans house at Deen
5 Aug. 1719

45. DEENE

Title on drawing: *South Front of the Earl of Cardigans House at Deen 5 Aug 1719*

Artist: Unsigned, Peter Tillemans

Bridges' text:

> The earl of *Cardigan*'s house here is built of stone, embattled, with a turret at each corner, covered with lead, and with a rising roof. Before the east front, now used as the principal one, are erected some offices which hinder that part of the view. The hall and other apartments are spatious, and the house and library windows are illuminated with arms and matches of the *Brudenell* family . . .

This is another important record of a house where, while the basic structure survives, alterations have taken place so that it is barely recognisable. Within a year or two of this drawing being done, the house was "modernised" and nearly all the mullioned windows in the drawing were replaced by Georgian sashes. Furthermore the tall turrets were removed and the corner towers finished with battlements in line with the general roof level, and several windows in the towers were blocked. It is interesting to compare Tillemans' view with that on an estate map at Deene by Thomas Brasier, drawn in 1746.

Tillemans shows us the south facade, with the two octagonal towers marking the extent of the Tudor south range probably built by Sir Thomas Brudenell *c.*1530. Above to the left arises the roof of the Hall and immediately over the range is the apex of the gable of the east range containing the Great Chamber. The

chimneys of the range also appear as does, just visible, the battlements of the north tower which ends the east side. Windows appear in a rather informal arrangement and these were replaced by a regular row of sashes in the mid 1720s, although it is still possible to trace the blocked surrounds of many of them.

The tall block of tower-like form on the left has now gone. Its windows with a tall one just visible to the side of the smaller octagonal tower, suggests that it housed a staircase which rose immediately south of the end of the Hall, and there is some evidence in the structure today which supports this concept. The wide arched doorway connects with the Hall.

On the far left a lower range of offices and kitchens is indicated, and the 1746 plan shows these were retained. They were removed some time after the middle of the 18th century and the present south facade was doubled in length with a slightly taller battlemented and towered facade about 1800.

Bridges' reference to the East front as being the "principal" one is odd, since there does not seem to have been anything like a grand entrance on that side, simply access from a large parterre garden. The MS Notes however emphasise the fact with an entry dated July 1721 stating: "This Front [the North] was intended for ye Principal Front tho yt of ye East is now used." And a little later: "The East side of this House now ye Entrance side is Embat".

The Brudenells acquired Deene in 1514 and were raised to the peerage as Earls of Cardigan in 1661. The owner when Tillemans drew the house was George, 3rd Earl, who was to give Bridges access to the library at Deene.

Notes: BL. No.88. 32x20 cm. Other no: On reverse – Num:73.

46. DEENE

Title on drawing: *The Monument of Sr Robert Brudenell under an arch wth his 2 wives at the upper end of the S Ile at Dene 4 Augt 1719*

Artist: Unsigned, Peter Tillemans

Bridges' text:

> Under an arch in the south ile is an altar monument of marble, on which is the figure of a Judge in his robes, between his two wives in the habit of the age, with their hands in the gesture of prayer.

This fine alabaster monument is for Sir Robert Brudenell (d.1531) and his two wives, Margaret (d.1501) and Philippa (d.1532). The tomb chest displays typical early Renaissance detailing with a mixture of Gothic traceried panels and classical balusters and twisted columns. The effigies are of fine quality, with Sir Robert in his robes as Chief Justice of the Court of Common Pleas, a post he held from 1521 until his death. His first wife wears a pedimented headdress, while his second, a widow's habit, suggesting it was erected before her death. The workmanship is comparable to another fine tomb in Northamptonshire, that of Sir Richard Knightley (d.1534) at Fawsley.

Sir Robert had acquired the Deene estate in 1514.

Notes: BL. No.90. 32x20 cm. Other no: On reverse Num:74.

47. DEENE *(right)*

Title on drawing: *The Portico of the Inner Front of the Earl of Cardigans House at Dene 5 Aug 1719*

Artist: Unsigned, Peter Tillemans

Bridges' text:

> At the south corner of the east side you enter into a court, where is a free-stone porch, with four pillars of the Ionic and Corinthian order above and below.

This simple drawing is of the porch leading into the Hall on the south side of the courtyard. It faithfully records the rich Renaissance decoration and also suggests within the arch a series of openings, through into the house and beyond, reflecting the screens passage axis. The porch dates from *c.*1571 when Sir Edmund Brudenell added considerably to the earlier house, creating an especially splendid Hall with magnificent open timber roof.

Notes: BL. No.89. 29x20.5 cm. At the bottom left-hand corner of the drawing is written "A".

Huxloe (top left annotation)

Drayton House towards y^e Park (caption within drawing)

48. DRAYTON HOUSE

Title on drawing: *Drayton House towards yᵉ Park*

Artist: Unsigned, Peter Tillemans

Date: Probably 1719. Bridges' MS Notes record a visit on 14 August 1719.

Bridges' text:

> *Drayton*, the capital mansion of *Drayton* and *Lufwick* manors, an antient but very elegant structure, was built by *Henry Green* about the latter end of *Henry* VI's reign, It had been formerly a castle, is now embattled, and hath turrets at each end of it. Here are many good pictures and portraits, particularly of the *Mordaunt* family, and amongst others valuable ones are those of *Hen*. VII and *Hen*. VIII by *Holben*.

Amazingly this house still looks very much today as it does in this drawing. Except for some changes in interior decoration the architecture as it existed in 1719 remains unaltered. The forecourt is entered through elaborate gatepiers with ironwork. On either side are low walls, now topped by further rails. Then on the right are the

formal gardens laid out during the early years of the 18th century. On the extreme right is one of a pair of banqueting houses which form the corners of the parterre. The gabled building in the trees is a brick built orangery. To the left of the house is a square building with a pyramidal roof, designed as a dovecote.

The house dates from *c*.1300 and a good deal of its medieval structure still stands, although transformed in the decades either side of 1700 into a Baroque palace. Appearing above the lower battlemented wall are the upper portions of a splendid decorative facade designed by William Talman and built between 1702 and 1704. Bridges' statement that the house is "now embattled" is interesting since evidence has recently come to light that the left hand tower complex was not created till the second decade of the 18th century. It would have been brand new when Tillemans visited, if this is the case. Another interesting feature is the diamond shape over the main entrance. In reality there is a square panel with a carved coat of arms, and what the diamond may represent is the funeral hatchment of Sir John Germaine, Talman's employer, who died in December 1719. It was customary to hang a hatchment over the door of a house to denote a period of mourning.

The reference to portraits by Holbein refers to copies of Royal portraits set within panelling in the Hall.

Notes: BL, No.91. 41x23.5 cm. Other no: On reverse – Num:98.

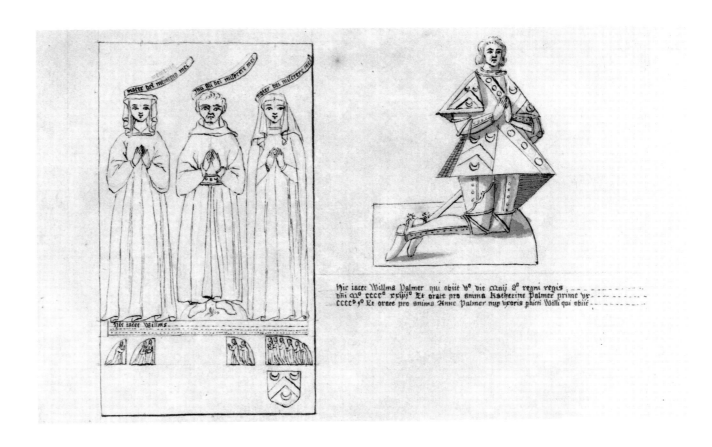

49. EAST CARLTON

Title on reverse of drawing: *Stoke Doyle*

Artist: Unsigned, Peter Tillemans

Date: Uncertain. There are two visits recorded in Bridges' MS Notes, one on17 September 1719 and the other on 27 July 1721. The larger itinerary is 1719 and this seems the more likely date.

Bridges' text:

On the south side of the Palmers place of burial, is in brass the portraiture of a man in a gown, between his two wives in the dress of the times: in a label over the man's head, *Jesu fili Dei misere me*; over the woman on his right hand *Mater Dei memento mei*; above the woman on the left, *Mater dei miserere mei*. At the top were three shields of arms, and at their feet an inscription, which are torn away. Below are the figures of three sons and four daughters, at the bottom three shields of arms, of which that only at the left corner is remaining, *A chevron between three crescents*.

Despite the title written on the reverse of the drawing, the figures at the top of the drawing are clearly those described in Bridges' text at East Carlton, although the figures of children do not exactly correspond, there being three daughters under the first wife and two sons and six daughters under the second. No brass now exists at Carlton and perhaps it was destroyed when the church was rebuilt in 1788.

The other figure is of a kneeling knight wearing an heraldic tabard bearing the arms of Palmer, and the Latin inscription records William Palmer (d.1424) and his wife Anne. It also has the appearance of a brass, but no memorial of this type is described in Bridges' text.

Notes: BL. No.240. 29x20 cm.

50. EASTON MAUDIT

Title on drawing: *View of the East Front of the Earl of Sussex' House at Easton Maudit taken in the Coach Yard 7. Aug 1721*

Artist: Unsigned, Peter Tillemans

Bridges' text:

> The earl of *Sussex* hath an antient Mansion-house, the chief residence of the family, since the purchase of this estate by Sir *Christopher Yelverton* in the reign of queen *Elizabeth*. It is ornamented with many portraits of the nobility and gentry, about the end of the last century, chiefly collected by *Barbara* viscountess *Longueville*. But what is most valuable in this seat, is a large well-furnished library, of printed and manuscript books, in all languages and faculties.

This is another excellent record of a long vanished house. The Yelvertons acquired the estate in 1578, and were raised to the peerage firstly as Viscounts de Longueville in 1690 and then in 1717 as Earls of Sussex. The Sussex peerage continued till 1799, when following the failure of the male line, the properties passed to the Grey de Ruthin family. In 1801 the estate was purchased by the 1st Marquis of Northampton and the house was demolished.

Architecturally it must have been an interesting house, for though at first sight it seems almost entirely Elizabethan, of *c.*1570, the somewhat irregular pattern of both gables and windows suggests that this was a reworking of an older structure. The central porch would appear to have to the left a Great Hall with long windows to the ground. Behind is a suitably large chimneystack. To the left again the large blank gable suggests a cross-wing with rather lower windows on its ground floor, but no openings above, but probably representing the Great Chamber suite. To the right of the porch a more haphazard arrangement of windows and chimneystacks suggests the service rooms. It is interesting to find two porches: an attempt to give the facade some symmetry.

From the left-hand end of the main block there is a connecting range which links through the wing on the edge of the forecourt. This is a tall affair of three storeys, largely still with mullion and transom windows, and even the enlarged sashed opening on the first floor still have their Elizabethan hoodmoulds over them. The introduction of sashes here suggests an apartment of importance – perhaps a Gallery housing the Longueveille portrait collection?

The entertaining series of finials on the gables is typical of this area, with a similar clutch existing at Gayhurst just over the Buckinghamshire border.

Notes: BL. No.97. 45x30 cm. Other no: Front – 40.

51. EASTON MAUDIT

Title on drawing: *Sr Christopher Yelvertons Mon in Easton Maudit Church Aug 1721*

Artist: Unsigned, Peter Tillemans

Bridges' text:

> Upon a tomb upwards of two foot in height, in the north chancel, is the figure of Sir *Christopher Yelverton* in a judge's robe, and of his lady in widows weeds; both resting on cushions, and with uplifted hands. On the north side are two compartments in each of which are four daughters, and two compartments on the south side, and two boys in each. Over their heads are turned two arches, upon three rows of flat pillars.

This monument is freestanding in the centre of the north chapel at Easton Maudit. Sir Christopher Yelverton (d.1612) was Speaker of the House of Commons in 1597 and a Judge of the Queen's Bench from 1602. His wife was Mary Catesby (d.1611), one of the Ecton and Whiston Catesbys. The pillars of the monument are cut from Stanwick ragstone, polished to appear like marble: a memorable example of the use of this stone.

Note: BL. No.98. 24.5x22 cm.

52. EASTON MAUDIT

Title on drawing: *Sr Hen. Yelvertons Mont in Easton Maudit Church Aug 1721*

Artist: Unsigned, Peter Tillemans

Bridges' text:

> Under an arch in the north wall, adorned on each side with small statues of Faith, Hope, Charity, &c. in apartments one above the other are the effigies of Sir *Henry Yelverton* and his lady; he in a judges robes, she in a dress of a widow. Both of them have books in their hands, and rest on cushions. On the sides of the tomb below, are four sons and five daughters kneeling, with a desk between them. The arch on each side is supported by an alms-man clothed in black, as large as the life.

This is one of the more unusual of Northamptonshire tombs, notable for the use of books within its decoration, not only in the hands of the principal figures, as the text describes, but acting as pillars behind the almsmen or bedesmen on each side. Is this an allusion to the library in the house which causes remarks in Bridges' text?

In the drawing the figure of Charity, from the apex of the monument, is drawn alongside the main design; the two other small sculptures of Hope, with the anchor, and Faith, with the Cross, are in their proper positions.

Sir Henry Yelverton (d.1629) was a judge of the Court of Common Pleas and read the warrant for the execution of Mary Queen of Scots, and pronounced the execution order on Sir Walter Raleigh. His wife Margaret had died four years before him.

Notes: BL. No.99. 28x23 cm.

Front of the Lord Lempsters house at Easton to the West

53. EASTON NESTON

Title on drawing: *Front of the Lord Lempsters House at Easton to the West*

Artist: Unsigned, Peter Tillemans

Date: Probably 30 July 1719 (see Plate 56).

Bridges' text:

> The only house now in *Eston* is the magnificent seat of the Earl of *Pomfret* or *Pontefract*. The wings are of brick, and were built by Sir *Christopher Wren*. The body is of a fair, white, and durable stone, brought from the pits at *Helmedon*, and was finished in 1702, about twenty years after the erection of the wings. It was built by *Hawkesmore*, who hath very much departed from the first design. Mr *Morton* tells us, that in the opinion of good judges there is no seat in *Europe*, which exceeds this at *Eston* in the folowing particulars; first, "in the stone of which the structure is built":secondly, "That notwithstanding the appearing smallness it hath so many rooms of state": and thirdly, "That there is no part of the space or room within useless."

Here is the prospect of this house as it had been completed in 1702, showing the large entrance forecourt, the main block of the house in the centre, and either side recessed wings. On the left the wing is backed by a stable court, while on the right the wing looks towards the church, and beyond that is a thatched barn. Only the left-hand of these two wings survives today, and the stable block behind was rebuilt later in the 18th century. Rising above this wing is the top of a column which ornamented the garden (see Plate 58).

Architectural historians are now generally agreed that the design of the house did originate in Wren's office – Sir Christopher being a distant relation of Sir William Fermor, later 1st Lord Lempster, who built the house. The facades as we see them today were the work of Nicholas Hawksmoor, and a wooden model in the house shows indeed that he "hath very much departed from the first design". Bridges' text well summarises the case!

Notes: BL. No.94. 46.5x10 cm. Other no: On reverse – Numb.51.

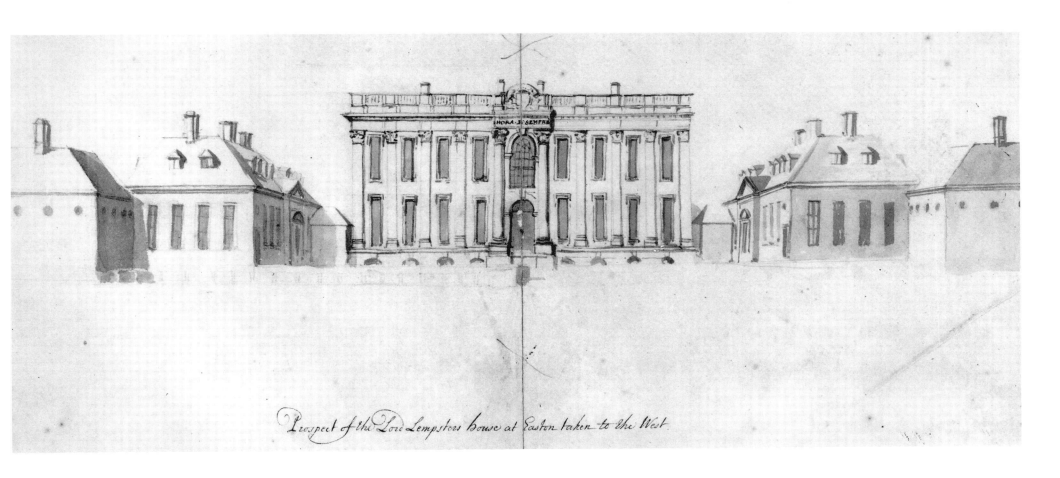

Prospect of the Lord Lempsters house at Easton taken to the West

54. EASTON NESTON

Title on drawing: *Prospect of the Lord Lempsters House at Easton taken to the West*

Artist: Unsigned, Peter Tillemans

Date: Probably 30 July 1719 (see Plate 56).

This magnificent drawing shows the full west prospect of the house with its architecture carefully delineated. It brings out the importance of the recessed wings in creating a symmetrical Palladian effect. It is worth comparing it with a similar spread of some ten years later at Cottesbrooke (Plate 43).

When this drawing was made it would seem that the entrance to the house was at ground level, with what is now the front door, in the centre of the main floor, being treated as a window. However, it is clear on the previous drawing (Plate 53) that there were steps up to that opening, so perhaps a little artistic licence?

Otherwise the drawing compares closely with that of the previous Plate.

Notes: BL. No.93. 41x26.5 cm. Other no: On reverse – Num: 91.

Prospect of the Lord Lempsters house taken in the Garden

55. EASTON NESTON

Title on drawing: *Prospect of the Lord Lempsters house taken in the Garden*

Artist: Unsigned, Peter Tillemans

Date: The drawing of a monument in the church is dated 30 July 1719 and this is the likely date of this drawing although a series of visits are recorded in July 1721 when the statuary in the house was measured.

Bridges' text:

> The garden . . . is richly adorned with antique statues, and with other valuable pieces of ancient sculpture; a collection of vast value, being all the more ornamental part of the *Marmora Arundeliana.*

This delightful drawing shows the east side of the house and its formal gardens. The main house is in the centre with wings on either side. By the steps to the doorway are statues, and there are busts over the ground floor windows. In front of the house is a circular pool, in the midst of a formal parterre with conical trees and smaller shrubs, all interspersed with further statues. To the right in the background is a tall column topped by another statue, and to the right again, a long garden wall, broken by a gateway with ornamental piers.

Today there are no such gatepiers on this side of the house, but a pair identical to these now stands about a quarter of mile to the west of the house in the centre of an avenue. There is also today a circular pool in front of the house, but the present one was created in the 1920s and is closer to the house than the one shown by Tillemans.

The medieval tower of the church appears over the garden wall and enough is visible to show that the chancel had a classical east window, probably part of the alterations put in hand by Sophia Lady Lempster in 1718 when she beautified that part of the church with panelling, altar rails and a wrought iron screen.

The statuary is indeed "antique" and as Bridges' text notes is the major portion of the famous Arundel Marbles, and these are the subject of a series of further drawings (Plates 58-102).

Notes: BL. No.92. 44.5x19.5 cm.

56. EASTON NESTON

Title on drawing: *Mon^t of Sr George Farmer ag^t the N Wall of ye Chancel of Easton Church*

Title on reverse of drawing:

> *Mont of Sr George Farmer agt the N Wall of ye Chancel of Easton Neston Church 30. July. 1719*

Artist: Unsigned, Peter Tillemans

Bridges' text:

> Against the north wall of the chancel is a beautiful monument of white marble . . . which is supported by two pillars of white marble of the Corinthian order, lye upon a tomb the effigies of a man in armour and a woman in the habit of the times in a praying posture . . . Under the arch are pennons cut in stone . . . at the head, side, and foot of this tomb, are the figures of seven sons and eight daughters in a praying posture; the eldest son in armour . . .

As Bridges' text suggests this is an exceptionally fine tomb. It is carved from a very pure form of alabaster and Bridges can be forgiven for thinking it to be white marble. The main effigies are of Sir George Fermor (d.1612) and his wife Mary (d.1628), and behind them is a splendid display of heraldic pennants like a peacock's tail, and above either side of the central achievement two small figures representing Justice and Truth.

Only the heraldry is in full colour, with the figures having a little gilding to highlight details of costume and armour, and it is likely that it was never fully in colour. Together with other monuments in the church it was beautifully restored in the 1950s.

Notes: BL. No.95. 32x20 cm. Other no: On reverse – Num:92.

57. EASTON NESTON

Title on drawing: *Sr Hatton Farmers Mon^t ag^t the S Wall of the Chancel of Easton Church*

Title on reverse of drawing:

> *Sr Hatton Farmers Mon^t ag^t the S Wall of the Chancel of Easton Neston Church 30. July 1719*

Artist: Unsigned, Peter Tillemans

Bridges' text:

> [Following an emblazon of the shield of arms on the monument] Beneath these arms is an arch supported by two black marble pillars of the Corinthian order with white capitals; and under this arch the busto of a man upon a pedestal . . . on the right side of this busto is the statue of an armed man in jack-boots, with a batton in his right hand, a skull on a pedestal by him . . . On the left side of the busto is the statue of a woman, with her left hand upon an hour-glass, and over her head the same arms as over the head of the man.

This fine if eccentric monument fills much of the south wall of the chancel. Sir Hatton Fermor (d.1640) is shown as a swaggering figure with a large cravat and high gambado boots, together with his second wife Ann. Various children are represented as demi-figures within the pediment and by the bust in the centre. The monument is a curious late use of alabaster, and is attributed to Pierre Besnier, a French-born sculptor, whose signature is on the memorial of Sir Hatton's son-in-law at Shuckburgh, Warwickshire – also incidentally, of alabaster.

Notes: BL. No.96. 32x20 cm. Other no: On reverse – Num:93. For Pierre Besnier see *Gunnis* and *Whinney*.

58-102. EASTON NESTON, THE ARUNDEL MARBLES

Title on drawing: No titles on drawings, but notes on the reverse of some. They all form part of a series of consecutive drawings of statuary of which the title-page bears the heading: *Boughton near Kettering D. of Montagu's Draught of the Busto's.* In fact, only one sheet relates to Boughton (see Plate 24).

Date: July 1719 (see Notes below).

The sheets in this series of drawings are numbered 1 to 47, although 35 is missing. The last sheet, no. 47 is that referred to above, showing busts under the arcade at Boughton House. The rest clearly show statuary which decorated the house and garden at Easton Neston. Several drawings show plinths carved with a coronet and linked Ls, denoting the title of the owner of Easton Neston, Lord Lempster.

This collection of statuary has an interesting history. It originated with Thomas Howard, Earl of Arundel, who, in 1613, accompanied by his wife and the architect Inigo Jones, spent some eighteen months touring northern Italy. In Rome and elsewhere he acquired many of the items portrayed in these drawings. Jones was the designer of a covered gallery for Arundel House in the Strand about 1615 to house the collection. Items were added until the middle of the century when it contained several hundred pieces. Lord Arundel's later years were beset by problems and he retired abroad, dying in Italy in 1646.

After the Civil War Arundel's grandson, who had no interest in the sculptures, was prevailed upon by the diarist John Evelyn to present the inscriptions to the University of Oxford in 1667. The items portrayed here remained in the gardens of Arundel House till 1691 when, for the price of £300, Sir William Fermor purchased them. In 1692 they were taken to Easton Neston and there set up as decorations for the house and garden. In 1721 a note in Bridges' MSS records a visit on 18 July where he met "an Italian employed by the present Lord L in making perfect the statues maimed". This is a reference to Giovanni Battista Guelfi, a protégé of the Earl of Burlington, who had brought him from Italy in 1718. The results of Guelfi's restoration of heads, arms and other appendages were not admired and George Dallaway, in his *Anecdotes of the Arts* 1800 describes them as "misconceived" and that he had "ruined the greater number of those he was permitted to touch".

George Vertue, an important antiquary of the arts in 18th century England, compiled in 1734 a *Description of Easton Neston*, which was published in 1758, and records the disposition of the sculptures. Vertue's description gives a good idea of the way in which the sculptures decorated the gardens. For example he describes going from the east front doorway into the garden, going down steps "which go down on each side, and are adorned with antique statues; and all that front richly adorned with fine antique bustos over the windows". These are clearly visible in Tillemans' view of that front (Plate 55). He goes on: "in front of the steps is a piece of basso relievo of the trojan war; several pieces more, two altars with a dog's head at the corner, and a lion's at the other; a horse's head in the middle between festoons, and an antique lion and a Sea monster, besides innumerable altars, pedestals, and basso relievos, which the gardener could give no account of". Further on he tells us: "The East front looks into a parterre, the evergreens of which are taking up, to bring it to a modern taste. On the left hand from the house is a terrace, which hath at the beginning of it next to the house an antique Corinthian fluted pillar, with an antique statue of Apollo at the top". There is an elaborate description of one of the main features of the collection, "The Tomb of Germanicus", an extraordinary pastiche affair, of which Tillemans' drawing provides one of the best contemporary representations.

By the time Vertue visited the gardens, Easton Neston had descended to Lord Lempster's son, Thomas, who was created Earl of Pomfret in 1721. When he died in 1753 his son George, who was encumbered by debts, decided to sell the sculptures. With great foresight, his mother, Henrietta, Countess Pomfret, bought them in at the sale and in 1755 presented them to the University of Oxford, and they were once more reunited with the marbles which had come to the University in 1667.

In the 1880s the whole collection was rehoused in the new galleries of what we know as the Ashmolean Museum. Guelfi's unfortunate restorations were removed, and there they remain to this day, variously known as "The Arundel Marbles" or "The Pomfret Marbles". In 1882 Adolf Michaelis' *Ancient Marbles in Great Britain* appeared and is still cited as the main authority for the Marbles. In the subsequent plates *Michaelis* catalogue numbers and identifications are given.

Notes: BL. Nos. 18-64. The fellow antiquary and bibliophile, Thomas Hearne, records in a letter in July 1719 that Tillemans was drawing the sculptures at Easton Neston (Tony Brown and Glenn Foard, *The Making of a County History: John Bridges' Northamptonshire*, University of Leicester 1994 (p.36)). The information above is largely based on material in D.E.L. Haynes, *The Arundel Marbles*, Oxford, Ashmolean Museum, 1975.

Michael Vickers of the Ashmolean Museum, Oxford, has kindly supplied the *Michaelis* references.

58 (BL 19). *On reverse* 'The Entire Shafte of a Pillar of ye Temple of Apollo at Delphos wth ye Statue of Apollo at ye Top". A tall column which stood to the north of the house and appears in the background of the view of Easton Neston from the east (Plate 55). Conspicuous on the base is the coronet and L for Lord Lempster. (*Michaelis* 130 refers to the column; *Michaelis* 58 to the statue of "Apollo"). 32x20 cm.

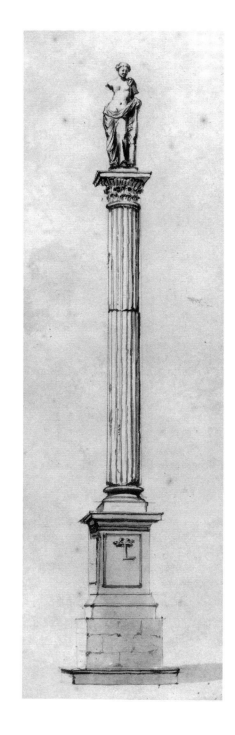

59 (BL 20). [*Michaelis* 40, identified as Dionysis]. 32x19 cm.

60 (BL 23). *On reverse* A Nymph returned from Bathing. [*Michaelis* 10, identified as Venus Genetrix]. 32x19 cm.

61 (BL 47). [*Michaelis* 36, identified as Eros]. 32x19 cm.

Plates 59, 60 and 61 show statues standing within niches within walls in the Hall inside the house. These existed till late 19th century alterations and are recorded on photographs held at the National Monuments Record.

63 (BL 22). *(right)* One of the many "altars, pedestals and *basso relievos*" noted by Vertue. *On reverse* "An Altar Peice". 32x19 cm.

62 (BL 21). *(left)* This composite pastiche structure was south of the house "at the end of the terrace on the left hand of the house, adjoining the garden wall". It was known as the "Tomb of Germanicus", a title which derives from the central sarcophagus, which when it was at Arundel House, had been surmounted by a supposed bust of Germanicus. On the keystone of the central arch can be detected the crossed Ls and coronet for Lord Lempster.

Vertue's description is worth quoting: "it is formed thus, viz. an alcove or arch in the middle, and upon a large oblong pedestal stands the Sarcophagus or tomb of Germanicus, which is long like a coffin, only strait and square; it is of marble, and basso relievo on the outside; upon the tomb is cut a round pedestal and on that a marble Statue of Jupiter, less than the life; on each side of this pedestal are busts of two women, and on each side of this arch or alcove are doric pilasters, which support a pediment, in which there is in basso relievo the figure of a man as big as the life, with his arms extended as if he was crucified, but no lower than about his paps is seen, the cornice cutting him off as it were; and this extension of his arms is called a grecian measure, and over his right arm is a grecian foot; on the top of the pediment stands the god Terminus, and likewise on each side of this alcove are two smaller niches; in that on the left hand, as you look at the tomb, is the trunk of a body, the fore part towards you, the proportiion and the muscles very fine, and both well executed; so as to be worthy a sculptor's study. On the outside of both these niches are dorick pilasters, which go up and support the cornice, and at the top on each side two pedestals with each a statue, very fine and perfect".

For a discussion see M. Vickers, "Germanicus' Tomb", *The Ashmolean* 15 (1988-89) pp. 6-8. Size of drawing, 32x20 cm.

64 (BL 24). *On reverse* Qu. Fabius Masimus. [*Michaelis* 46, Statue of a Roman]. 32x19 cm.

65 (BL 25). *On reverse* A Mathematician or an Architect because he has part of a Square in his hand. [*Michaelis* 41, A man]. 32x19 cm.

66 (BL 26). [*Michaelis* 19, Athena]. 32x19 cm.

Plates 64 to 72 represent some of the major sculptures in the collection and were raised on plinths with the Lempster cypher and set within the garden. Several can be seen in the eastern view of the house (Plate 55).

67 (BL 29). [*Michaelis* 5]. *On reverse* Ab^t ye Fountain A Grecian Lady. 32x19 cm.

68 (BL 30). [*Michaelis* 3]. *On reverse* Ab^t ye Fountain A Grecian Lady. 32x19 cm.

69 (BL 31). [*Michaelis* 6]. *On reverse* A Grecian Lady round the Fountain. 32x19 cm.

70 (BL 32). [*Michaelis* 4]. *On reverse* A Grecian Lady round the Fountain. 32x19 cm.

71 (BL 33). *On reverse* Marcus Tull. Cicero. [*Michaelis* 45, "Cicero"]. 32x19 cm.

72 (BL 34). *On reverse* A Greek Orator. [*Michaelis* 47, Statue of a Roman]. 32x20 cm.

73 (BL 27) *On reverse* A Scipio. (G. 1150). 32x19 cm.

74 (BL 28) *On reverse* A Scipio (G. 1151). 32x19 cm.

73 and 74 represent statues which are not part of the Arundel Marbles but are in the Ashmolean collection.

75 (BL 35). *On reverse* Melapomene. [*Michaelis* 32, A Muse]. 32x19 cm.

76 (BL 36). *On reverse* This supposed to be Clio. [*Michaelis* 31, A Muse]. 32x19 cm.

77 (BL 37). *On reverse* Venus now mended. [*Michaelis* 26, Venus]. 32x19 cm.

78 (BL 38). [*Michaelis* 8, A woman]. 32x19 cm.

Plates 75 to 83 represent various groups within the gardens at Easton Neston.

79 (BL 39). *(Above)* [*Michaelis* 11, Venus Genetrix], *(below)* [*Michaelis* 91, Grave relief of Menelaos]. 32x19 cm.

80 (BL 41). [*Michaelis* 20, A woman]. 32x19 cm.

81 (BL 42). Not identified. 32x19 cm.

82 (BL 43). *(Above)* [*Michaelis* 28, Leda and swan], *(below)* [*Michaelis* 92, votive relief]. 32x19 cm.

83 (BL 44). Judith with the head of Holophernes (G. 1277), *(below)* [*Michaelis* 112, A relief]. 32x19 cm.

84 (BL 40). [*Michaelis* 1, A woman]. 32x19cm.

85 (BL 45). [*Michaelis* 2, A woman]. 32x19 cm.

86 (BL 46). *On reverse* A Dalmatian soldier. [*Michaelis* 48, Barbarian]. 32x19 cm.

87 (BL 48). [*Michaelis* 41, A man]. 32x19 cm.

Plates 84 to 91 show statues in the niches on the staircase of Easton Neston.

88 (BL 50). [*Michaelis* 30, Hygieia]. 32x19 cm.

89 (BL 52). *On reverse* Diana. [*Michaelis* 22, Artemis]. 32x19 cm.

90 (BL 53). *On reverse* Drana Antinous. 32x19 cm.

91 (BL 54). *On reverse* Caius Marius. [*Michaelis* 44, "Marius"]. 32x19 cm.

92 (BL 49). [*Michaelis* 39, a statue of Heracles], with *(below)* [*Michaelis* 115 and 117, part of a sarcophagus relief]. 32x19 cm.

93 (BL 51). This shows the large alcove which was formerly in the centre of the fireplace wall of the Hall at Easton Neston. The scrolls were created, perhaps by Guelfi, to support the back panel. Photographs in the National Monuments Record show this alcove and the other niches in the Hall as they survived till the late 19th century, when alterations were made and the walls rendered flat. [*Michaelis* 38, Heracles (a statue)]. 32x19 cm.

94 (BL 55). *(Top left)* [*Michaelis* 33, Scylla], and *(right)* [*Michaelis* 23, statue base for Artemis]; *(middle left)* [*Michaelis* 107, Putto relief], and *(middle central)* [*Michaelis* 90, a grave relief]; *(middle right)* not identified; *(below)* [*Michaelis* 114, Oval sarcophagus]. 32x19 cm.

95 (BL 56). A drawing which shows, around the lower relief, indications of the rusticated stonework of the exterior of the house. *(Top)* [*Michaelis* 111, A sarcophagus]. *(Below)* [*Michaelis* 84, Attic relief]. 32x19 cm.

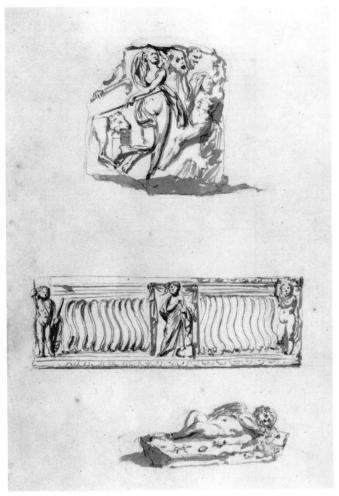

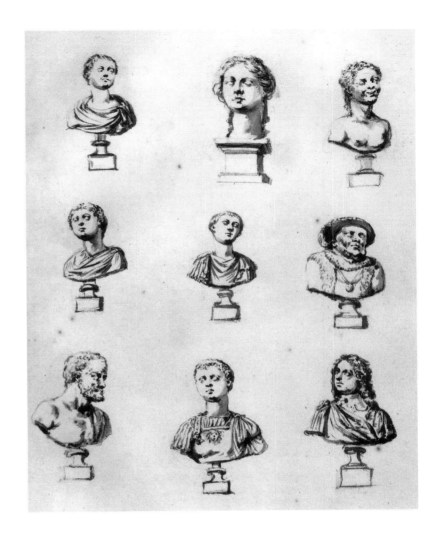

96 (BL 57) *(Top)* [*Michaelis* 109, Sarcophagus fragment]. *(Middle)* [*Michaelis* 115, Sarcophagus relief]. *(Below)* [*Michaelis* 37, Sleeping Eros]. 32x19 cm.

97 (BL 58). Noted in Vertue's description. [*Michaelis* 123-4 lists a 17th century table-end]. 32x20 cm.

98 (BL 59). *On reverse* A Colossus near the old Banquetting House. (This probably refers to the central bust on the top line.) The busts on the smaller pedestals were situated above the windows on the garden front of the house and can be seen in the drawing of the garden (*Plate 55*). Not all these are "antiques" judging from the third bust on the second line, which is of Henry VIII (G. 1228), and the middle bust on the lowest line, which looks early 18th century in manner. The final bust on this line is late 17th century, and is a bust of Prince Rupert of the Rhine in the Ashmolean (G. 1152). 32x19 cm.

99 (BL 60). *(Above left) Michaelis* 62, Niobe; *(above right) Michaelis* 78, Aphrodite; and *(below) Michaelis* 63, Niobid. 32x19 cm.

100 (BL 61). Identified are, *(top centre) Michaelis* 120, Nereid relief, and *(below) Michaelis* 56, A sphinx. 32x19 cm.

101 (BL 62). *(Top) Michaelis* 72, Bust of a man. *(Below)* Not identified in *Michaelis.* 32x19 cm.

102 (BL 63). *(Above left) Michaelis* 184, Bust of a satyr. *(Below right),* Bust of a bearded man. Others unidentified in *Michaelis.* 32x19 cm.

103. EDGECOTE

Title on drawing: *EDGECOTE The Seat of Toby Chauncy Esqr 15 July 1721*

Artist: Unsigned, Peter Tillemans

Bridges' text:

> The Manor-house inhabited by *Tobias Chauncy* Esq; hath in its several marks of antiquity . . .

This view is a fascinating record of a house which was demolished to make way for the present Edgecote Hall, built between 1747 and 1752. One wishes that the porch in the centre of the facade had been saved: it is a splended piece with a mass of decoration with ornamental pilasters, heraldry, statuary and a curved gable with a fan-like top. All this is reminiscent of an equally elaborate confection on the porch at Dingley, near Market Harborough, built in the middle of the 16th century. In Bridges' MS Notes occurs the note: "ye Porch pave del gusto del tempore Elizabeth Tillemans has described it". He also notes a dated chimneypiece of 1598. There is also a delightful quote: "Rooms have Dorecases & some Windows like Chappel Windows – evry where almost footsteps of antiquity". There are, indeed, features such as the tall Hall windows, left of the porch, and upper windows in the gables, which indicate a late 15th or early 16th century date. The octagonal tower with flat parapet and arched windows on the far left is comparable with a similar one at Dingley. So we may have a house here of early origin with mid-16th century work, embellished towards the end of the century.

Notes: BL. No.100. 45x28.5 cm. Other no: Front – 10. The late Victor Hatley drew my attention to a description of a house contained among the poems of Mary Leapor (1722-1746) who spent her early years at Marston St. Lawrence, only a few miles away. The poem is called "Crumble Hall" and the following extract seems very apposite:

> Of this rude palace might a poet sing
> From cold December to returning Spring;
> Tell how the building spreads on either hand,
> And two grim giants o'er the portals stand;
> Whose grisled beards are neither com'd nor shorn,
> But look severe, and horribly adorn.

There indeed on the porch are the "grim giants" and the fact that the house was eventually pulled down supports the "Crumble Hall" allusion. Trevor Hold, who has also studied Mrs Leapor's poems, supports the idea that Edgecote is the house of the title.

104. EDGECOTE

Title on drawing: *The Monument of Sʳ Toby Chauncy & his 2 Wives in the S Ile 15. July. 1721*

Artist: Unsigned, Peter Tillemans

Bridges' text:

> On the altar-tomb of marble between his two wives . . .

This small sketch is of a large tomb still in the south aisle at Edgecote, and one of a number of memorials in that church to the Chauncey family. It commemorates Sir Toby Chauncey (d.1607) and his two wives, Bridget (d.1579) and Elizabeth, and is carved from alabaster. There are a number of tombs of this type and workmanship in the Midland counties: they are somewhat coarsely carved and have Renaissance decorative details, especially on their tomb-chests, the shield shapes being especially distinctive. They are all associated with a family of carvers named Roilley who worked from the Burton-on-Trent quarries. Originally they would have been highly coloured and this would have eased the effect of the clumsy carving. Today there are still considerable traces of colour on the figures of the tomb.

Notes: BL. No.7. (Part of a composite sheet with Ashton le Walls (Plate 5). 32x22.5 cm. Other no: Front – 7. The Roilley family of carvers are referred to in Whinney *(op. cit.)*. The main discussions of their work are contained in two articles in the *Transactions of the Birmingham Archaeological Society* (P. Chatwin: 'Monumental effigies in the County of Warwick" (Vol.XLVIII, 1992, and S. A. Jeavons: 'Monumental effigies of Staffordshire' (Vol. LXX. 1952).

105. EVENLEY

Title on drawing: *Imley Church the Monument of Sʳ Creswell Levinz in the Chancell 11 July. 1721*

Artist: Unsigned, Peter Tillemans

Bridges' text:

> On the south wall near the communion table under a monument of veined marble is this inscription on a square marble tablet . . . [inscription quoted]

> [Also] This parish gave birth to Sir *Creswell Levinz*, Knt. attorney general to King *Charles* II. and afterwards one of the justices of court of common-pleas. He was descended from the antient family of *Levinz*, of *Levinz-hall* in the county of *Westmorland*.

This sketch is a useful record of the original appearance of this monument. Unfortunately when the church was rebuilt in 1864 it was savagely mutilated and only the figure was allowed to survive skied on a bracket under the tower. The monument compares with a similar figure of a judge at Silton in Dorset and has something in common with the memorial to Baroness Rockingham at Rockingham, and both of these can be confidently attributed to the sculptor John Van Nost, more famous for his lead garden ornaments than for his church monuments.

Levinz-hall in Bridges' text is, of course, Levens Hall.

Notes: BL. No.143. 28x23 cm. There is another record of the monument drawn *c.*1800 by Thomas Trotter in the collection of the Northamptonshire Libraries, which confirms the accuracy of Tilleman's representation.

View of the Scite of Finshed Abby now Mr Kirkham's House

106. FINESHADE

Title on drawing: *View of the Scite of Finshed Abby now Mr Kirkham's House*

Artist: Unsigned, Peter Tillemans

Date: Probably 1721 and there are visits in the area in Bridges' MS Notes in August 1721. Fineshade is, however, mentioned specifically only on 6 May 1719 and 7 October 1719.

Bridges' text:

[There is a long account giving the history of Fineshade Abbey of which the following are extracts:]

Here was originally a castle, named *Castle-Hymel* in *Laxton* parish demolished in the reign of King *John* . . . upon the ruins of it was afterwards erected a priory of black canons . . . Mr *Kirkham*'s house, as appears by the arched roofs, and pillars in the lower rooms, which composed the cloisters, is built on the scite and foundations of the priory.

Another useful record of a house no longer in existence. Without Bridges' description one might imagine it to have been largely Jacobean, since there is nothing visible in the drawing to indicate medieval architec-

ture. The embanked site of the castle, then the Priory, is evident, as it is today. Among the outbuildings to the right is a circular dovecote and the woodlands which lie behind the house appear much as they do today.

Lightly sketched in, just beyond the forecourt gates, are two tiny figures sitting on a bench. Perhaps one of them is "the ingenious Mr. Kirkham", that is Charles Kirkham, one of Bridges' correspondents, mentioned several times in the text. The Kirkhams acquired the property from John Lord Russell who had been granted it after the Dissolution.

In Bridges' MS Notes in addition there is mention of the Castle ditch appearing "on all sides except to the House where 'tis levelled for Conveniency" and "one gate of ye Pry lately pulld down to ye NW of his house".

The house survived till 1749 when it became submerged in a Georgian mansion, and this in its turn was submerged in a palatial pile in 1856. Exactly a hundred years later, following a period of neglect, the house was demolished and only a small portion remains, although the Georgian stable block still survives and was skilfully converted into a house in the early 1990s.

Notes: BL, No.103. 45x27 cm. Other no: Front – 28. A full discussion of the site is contained in RCHM Vol.1 p.38.

107. FOTHERINGHAY

Title on drawing: *Fotheringhay Church & Bridge*

Artist: Unsigned, Peter Tillemans

Date: This drawing was engraved for the printed text where it carries the date August 1718 and this accords with a visit recorded in the MS Notes on 7 August. It is one of the few drawings which can be confidently dated during the 1718 preliminary itinerary.

Bridges' text:

The church, part of the old Collegiate church, dedicated to Virgin *Mary*, and *All-Saints*, consists of a body and two iles, high and spacious, covered with lead. At the west end is a square tower, containing four bells, on which is raised an octagonal tower of later erection.

The bridge of wood . . . is of four arches, covered with wood, and stone laid upon it, partly walled, and partly railed in. On the right-hand as you enter the bridge from *Fotheringhay* is a stone tablet with this inscription; *This bridge was made by Queen Elizabeth in the 15 yere of her Reygne*; Ao Dni 1573. Above is, *God save the Queen*; and in a round over it E R. with a knot between. The castle is quite defaced . . .

A well known view and easily recognisable. The bridge as described in the text is clear, with beyond it the splendid church. Behind are thatched roofs of cottages and then on the right is the boundary wall of the castle site, with some blocked arches within it, and behind that the tree-clad mound of the keep. A typical and charming Tillemans touch is the figure on the river bank in the centre of the view.

The drawing is lightly over drawn with squares as a preliminary stage to it being engraved. The diminutive figure was not included in the engraved version.

Notes: BL. No.101. 47x25.5 cm. Other no: On reverse – Num:35 ee. The engraved plate is in Bridges Vol.II, p.453.

Mon.ᵗ of Ric. Plantagenet Duke of York on the N. side the High altar at Fodringhay.

108. FOTHERINGHAY

Title on drawing: *Monᵗ of Ric Plantagenet Duke of York on the N side of the High Altar at Foderinghay*

Artist: Unsigned, Peter Tillemans

Date: See previous drawing (Plate 107).

Bridges' text:

> Bridges quotes William Camden to the effect that ". . . Queen *Elizabeth* commanded two monuments to be set up . . . which nevertheless (such was *their* narrowness who had ye charge of the work) are looked pon as very mean for such great princes . . ."

What Tillemans has drawn is one of a pair of memorials; the other for Edward Duke of York is on the south side of the altar. Both are identical and were erected in 1573. They are carved stone and rely on their architectural design for effect, and while the carving is not of the highest quality, there is much to admire. They are almost certainly by the same carver who carved decoration at Deene, notably that on the porch into the Hall (Plate 47) and the fireplace within, dated 1571. He was also probably working at Kirby Hall during the early 1570s.

Notes: BL. No.102. 31.5x20.5 cm. Other no: On reverse – Num:77.

109. GEDDINGTON

Title on reverse of drawing: *North Prospect of Geddington Church Taken 10 July 1719*

Artist: Unsigned, Peter Tillemans

Bridges' text:

> At *Geddington* was antiently a royal seat, in a close to the north-east of the church, called the castle or hall-close. The surface of the ground is here very uneven, and many foundations still visible.

This delightful drawing is taken from the north-east across the uneven ground described, the foundations of a Royal Palace or Hunting Lodge which fell out of use *c.*1300. The church is carefully drawn, and on the north side of the chancel can be seen a blocked arch, which it is clear from later reference in the text led to "a chapel on the north side of the chancel, taken down some years since by the family of Maidwell, to whom it belonged". To the right of the church are the ruined gables of a substantial 17th century house, and then behind further chimneys, the main village, with the Eleanor Cross rising above the roofs.

Notes: BL. No.104. 31.5x20.5 cm. Other no: On reverse Num:87. The site of the Hunting Lodge is discussed in RCHM Vol.II p.51.

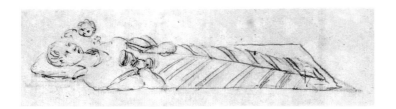

110. GEDDINGTON (above)

Title on reverse of drawing: *Draught of a Mon^t lying flat on the Ground in Geddington Ch. Cut in Basso Relievo nr the N. Isle at y^e upper end under the N. Wall Taken 10 July 1719*

Artist: Unsigned, Peter Tillemans

Bridges' text:

> [Bridges lists various monumental inscriptions and amongst them is:]
>
> . . . the portrait in stone of a person, with a chalice in his right hand; supposed by tradition of the place to have been a priest who died as he administered the sacrament. But the cup is added only to shew that he was in priest's orders, and therefore the power of administering the eucharist.

This memorial is shown exactly as described in the text, and it is amusing to find Bridges squashing a local tradition! Only the upper part of the figure appears revealed, the lower section being covered by a ridged cover. There was a fashion for such memorials, with only the upper parts of figures shown, in the 13th century, the date of this monument.

Notes: BL. No.106. 20.5x12 cm. Other no: On reverse Num:89.

For some reason this monument is not included in Hartshorne's *Recumbent Effigies* (1876) although it is contained in *Pevsner* where the covering of the figure is described as a shield.

111. GEDDINGTON (right)

Title on drawing: *Geddington Cross*

Title on reverse of drawing:

> *Q^u Eleanor's Cross Geddington Co. Northants By T. Eayre July 29 1718* [Written in a different hand to other titles]

Artist: Unsigned, Peter Tillemans

Date: 29 July 1718 would fall within Bridges' preliminary itinerary, and in Bridges' MS Notes occurs references to the Northampton and Waltham Crosses on 21 and 22 July 1718, so the date may well be accurate. The fact that the other Geddington drawings were taken on 10 July 1719 gives weight to that being the date of it.

Bridges' text:

> In the middle of the town, where the three principal streets center, is a neat triangular cross, built by *Edw.* I. in honour of his consort queen *Eleanor*. Of the three crosses yet remaining this is the

most perfect: being neither much injured by time like *Waltham*-cross, nor much altered like that near *Northampton* by modern additions.

This fine drawing was used for an engraved plate in the published text, where it appears in reverse.

The Cross looks very much as it does today, save that the stocks have been moved to another site, and the sundial above the niches, a 17th century addition, has been removed.

The title on the reverse of the drawing is puzzling. There is no reason to think that this drawing is by Eayre, it is totally in Tillemans' vein.

Notes: BL. No.107. 31.5x19.5 cm. Other nos: On reverse Num:23. At the bottom of the drawing is a letter D.

112-124. GLENDON

Title at beginning of series of drawings: *Paintings in the Windows of the Chapel at Glendon and a Draught of Queen Catherine Parr – 1719 12 sent to me by the Revd B. Bridges 15 Apr 1790 W D*

Artist: Signed Peter Tillemans on the first drawing

Bridges' text:

> The church or chapel, dedicated to St. *Helen*, consists of a body and chancel. In the north window are six pieces of painting of scripture incidents, four of which representing the story of *David* and *Abigail* have the following inscriptions under them. Below the portrait of *David*, Then said David unto his men . . . men . . . yrde, His swearde about him, and David . . . his . . . weard. Under the feast. Hi^c dronken churle being come to sence, he told what had betide, Which quailed to his currish heart he shortly dyed. Below *David*, and *Abigail* on her knees: And meets with David in the way and huymbly falls on face, And sayd my Lord this fault be mine, and so obtained grace. Under the asses loading; But Nabal's lad tells Abigail howe gently David passes, Their hurt . . . flocke than she in hast With food doth lade hir asses. Over each of these inscriptions is this date. 1563. In the east window are six more historical pieces without inscriptions.

The church at Glendon no longer exists, it having been, together with the village, obliterated when the park was landscaped around Glendon Hall. Just when this happened is not exactly recorded, but it would seem to have been about the time the Booth family acquired the estate, *c.*1758. The glass was saved and inserted in the first floor bay window of the older part of the Hall, which had formerly formed part of the Gallery. The framed panels are set within the lower lights of the window, the roundels in the upper lights.

The note on the leaf beginning the series of drawings is interesting since it would appear to indicate that these drawings were added to the collection in 1790 by W.D., presumably Sir William Dolben of Finedon, who was highly instrumental in achieving the final publication of Bridges' text.

Notes: Bl. Nos.109-120.

112 Crucifixion (BL 109). Size of drawing 41x31.5 cm.

113 David and Abigail story (BL 110). 41x31.5 cm.

114 David and Abigail (BL 111). 41x31.5 cm.

115 David and Abigail (BL 112). 41x31.5 cm.

116 David and Abigail, the Feast (BL 113). 41x30.5 cm.

117 Not identified (BL 114). 41x31.5 cm.

118 Not identified (BL 115). 40x31.5 cm.

119 Not identified (BL 116). 40x31.5 cm.

120 Not identified (BL 117). 40x31.5 cm.

121 Not identified (BL 118). 41.5x31.5 cm.

122 Not identified (BL 119). 41.5x31.5 cm.

123 Not identified (BL 120). 41x31 cm.

124. GLENDON

Title: *A Draught of Queen Catherine Parr – 1719*

Artist: Unsigned, but Peter Tillemans (see Plate 112)

Bridges' text:

> In the gallery of Mr. *Lane*'s house are various coats of arms and family portraits; and amongst other pictures, a full length of queen *Catherine Par*, in a rich habit of the times, for which the family was offered an hundred pounds.

This splendid portrait now hangs in the National Portrait Gallery in London. It was acquired for the Gallery in 1965, but had been previously sold from Glendon in 1953. While at Glendon it had been much admired and a fine engraving of it is contained in George Baker's *History and Antiquities of the County of Northampton*, Vol.II. It is now accepted that the portrait is, in fact, not Queen Catherine, but Lady Jane Grey. The Lane family of Glendon was related to William Parr of Horton, uncle of Queen Catherine, which probably led to a mis-identification.

Notes: BL. No.121. 32x20 cm. A full discussion of the portrait and its identity is contained in Sir Gyles Isham, "Queen Catherine Parr and Lady Jane Grey", *Northamptonshire Past & Present*, Vol.IV, No.5, pp.293-4, and in Roy Strong, *Tudor and Jacobean Portraits*, National Portrait Gallery, 1969.

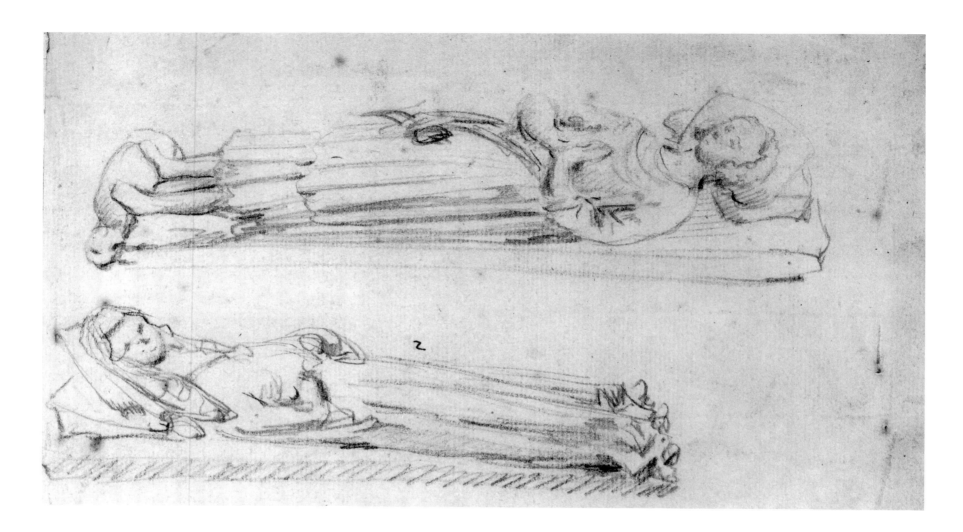

125. GLINTON

Title on drawing: *1.2 Two old battered Figures of Stone lying in the Church Yard 31 July 1721*

Artist: Unsigned, Peter Tillemans

Bridges' text:

In the churchyard are two old stones, with battered figures of Ecclesiastics upon them.

Bridges seems to have taken scant notice of these two effigies since, while they are badly worn, they are reasonably recognisable for what they are. They are no longer in the churchyard but have found shelter within the church.

The figure above is of some interest since it represents a man in the dress of a Forester. The belt across his body supports a horn and sheaf of arrows, and under his left arm is a large bow. The figure of the lady is much simpler and also more worn. She has a draped headdress and long gown. Both are dateable about 1300.

Notes: BL. No.122. 21.5x18.5 cm.

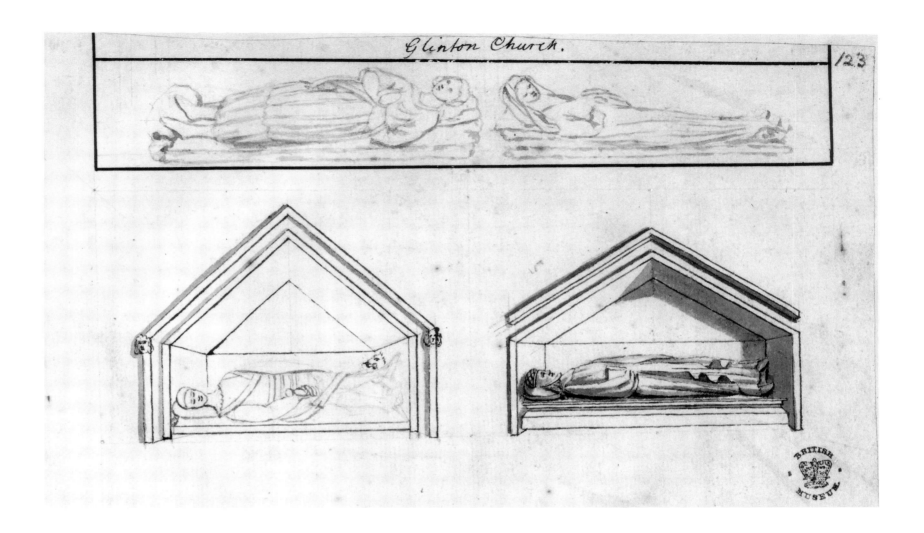

Glinton Church.

126. GLINTON

Title: *Glinton Church*

Artist: Probably A. Motte

Date: Uncertain.

This is a reduced drawing of the two figures at Glinton based on the previous drawing (Plate 125) together with sketches of two arched recesses which appear to be those at Barnack (Plate 14) and is probably a preliminary study for an engraved plate, hence its attribution to Motte.

Notes: BL. No.123. 21x13 cm.

GRETWORTH

The House of Charles Howe Esq.
taken 11 July 1721

127. GREATWORTH

Title on drawing: *GRETWORTH The House of Charles Howe Esqr taken 11 July 1721*

Artist: Unsigned, Peter Tillemans

Bridges' text:

> Mr. *How*, the Lord of the Manor, hath here a very good house built about twenty years ago, and situated with the town upon the hill.

The hill, with village and house, is just as Bridges describes. The slope of the hillside has strips of field cultivation running up to the walls of the enclosed gardens around the house. The strips are interrupted by a fence and ditch, still detectable in that position today.

The main block of the house, shown in dark wash, suggesting it was of dark ironstone (probably that from Eydon), is of two and a half storeys, of five bays, with a balustrade and tall chimneys. The roof is flat suggesting a prospect platform. The house was built by Charles Howe about 1700, and must have been somewhat similar in appearance, if not in colour, to Harrowden Hall, near Wellingborough, built about 1719. On either side of the main block can be seen lower ranges with mullioned windows indicated and these are probably of earlier date to the main block. Just by the house are two gatepiers with finials, and these are almost certainly the pair that survive, with magnificent carved pineapples on top. The house unfortunately was burnt in 1793 and subsequently demolished.

Notes: BL. No.125. 45x28 cm. Other no: Front – 5. The site is discussed in RCHM Vol.IV p.65-6.

The Mon.t of . . . Visct hatton ag. the S.
Wall of the chancel of Gretton 4 Aug. 1719

129. HARROWDEN, GREAT *(right)*

Title on reverse of drawing: *A Brass Plate in the Church of Harroden magna*

Artist: Unsigned, Peter Tillemans

Date: Uncertain, although a visit to Harrowden is recorded in Bridges' MSS Notes on 10 October 1721.

Bridges' text:

> On a large antique marble at the entrance into the chancel, are the portraits of a man in armour, and his wife in a winding-sheet. Over their heads were coats of arms and labels, now torn away, and round the verge the remains of the following inscription . . . [quoted].

It is interesting that this splendid brass was already badly damaged when Bridges saw it, but curious he should describe the lady as being in a shroud, when she is dressed in a simple draped habit. The figures are of William Harrowden (d.1423) and his wife Margaret. Both stand on the inscription plaque which is supported upon two decorative pedestals. Above them was an elaborate canopy with three shields, while the inscription had at its corners the signs of the Evangelists, with two remaining.

Note: BL. No.126. 22.8x18.7 cm.

128. GRETTON

Title on drawing (partly torn): *The Mont of . . . Visct Hatton agt the S Wall of the Chancel of Gretton 4 Aug. 1719*

Artist: Unsigned, Peter Tillemans

Bridges' text:

> Against the south wall of the chancel, on a sort of chest of black marble lie two weeping children, and on the pediment between them, under a viscount's coronet, these arms, *Hatton*, impaling *Haselwood*.

This rather curious mural monument at Gretton is one of the few memorials to the Hattons of Kirby: one might have expected a whole host of splendid tombs. The actual monument is rather more unbalanced as a design than the drawing suggests, with the putti, one with a skull, sprawling somewhat uncomfortably on the edge of the black marble sarcophagus.

The monument commemorates Sir Christopher Hatton who succeeded his father to the Barony and also to the post of Governor of Guernsey. In 1672 he had the misfortune to see both his wife and his mother killed in a gunpowder explosion on Guernsey. He was created Viscount Hatton in 1683 and was the creator of the magnificent parterre garden at Kirby where he is recorded to have had an impressive plant collection.

Notes: BL. No.124. 30x18.5 cm. Other no: On reverse – Num:105. The gardening activities of Viscount Hatton and his brother, Charles, are discussed in Miles Hadfield, *A History of British Gardening*, London, 3rd edition 1979 (pp.134-9), and there are other references in David Jacques and Arend Jan van der Horst, *The Gardens of William and Mary*, London 1988.

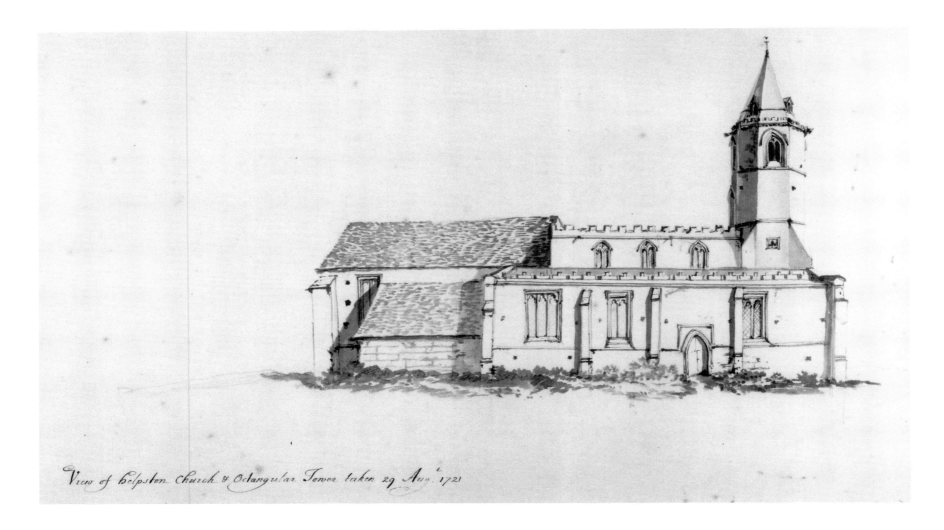

View of Helpston Church & Octangular Tower taken 29 Aug.¹ 1721

130. HELPSTON

Title on drawing: *View of Helpston Church & Octangular Tower taken 29 Aug.ᵗ 1721*

Artist: Unsigned, Peter Tillemans

Bridges' text:

> The church, dedicated to S. *Botulph*, consists of a body, north and south ile covered with lead, and a tiled chancel. At the west end is a tower, consisting of three divisions, the second and third of which are octagonal; and an hexagonal spire, with low battlements.

This excellent drawing well depicts this largely 14th century church. The chancel was rebuilt in 1609, and the window and large flat buttress seen would fit this date, and perhaps also the curious form of battlements on the aisle. The buttresses along the aisle are regular, except those at the ends, which again may be 17th century. The contrast between the flat lead roofs and pitched tiled roofs shows clearly.

Notes: BL. No.127. 42x28 cm. Other no: Front – 50.

131. HEYFORD, NETHER

Title on reverse of drawing: *Draught of the Figures of Sʳ Walter Mauntells Monᵗ at the North side of the Chancel at Heyford Taken 7. July 1719*

Artist: Unsigned, Peter Tillemans

Bridges' text:

> On a tomb under an arch on the north side of the chancel, is the portraiture in brass of a man in armour, and his wife in the habit of the times, joined hand in hand . . .

This is one of the finest brasses in the county, with clearly engraved figures some four feet long. It is however no longer on a tomb, but the lid stone of the tomb, bearing the brasses, is now set into the floor of the chancel. Sir Walter died in 1467 and such clearly engraved figures are unusual at this date.

Notes: BL. No.76. 18x15 cm.

132. HEYFORD, NETHER

Title on reverse of drawing: *Draught of Judge Morgans Monument at yᵉ upper end of the South Isle of Heyford Church Taken 7 July 1719*

Artist: Unsigned, Peter Tillemans

Bridges' text:

> Against the south wall at the upper end of the church is Judge *Morgan*'s monument supported by the statue of *Faith* on one side, and that of *Hope* on the other: In the middle compartment are the effigies of himself, wife, and children. At the top of the monument are arms and crest of *Morgan* . . .

This is the fine monument in the south aisle at Heyford for Judge Francis Morgan (d.1558) one of the Judges of the King's Bench, who, as Bridges' text further records "pronounced sentence of death on Lady Jane Grey: soon after which he is said to have gone mad, crying out in his fits, 'take the Lady Jane from me.' and in this distraction he ended his life."

The monument is one of a series of similar design in the county, the others being at Charwelton (1590), Harrington (1558), Thorpe Mandeville (1597) and Welford (*c.*1570). It is likely that the monument was not erected for some years after the judge's death, probably after the death of his widow. It is carved from stone and after some years of neglect has been superbly restored.

Notes: BL.No.128. 21.2x18.1 cm. The drawing has at its base the letter A.

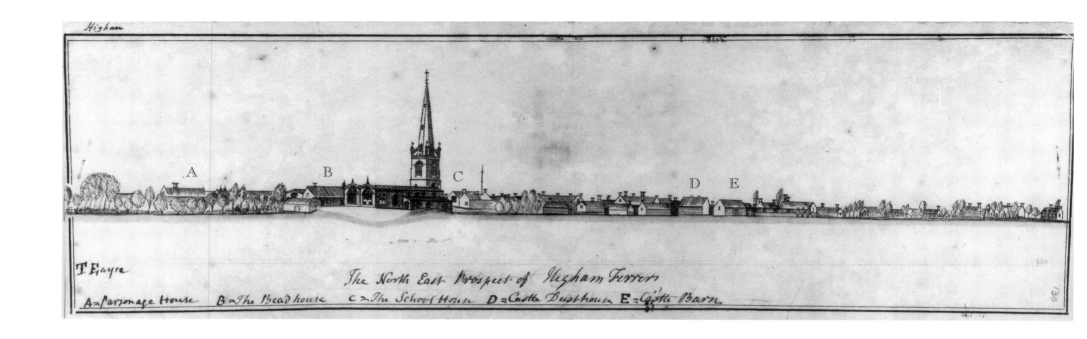

133. HIGHAM FERRERS

Title on drawing: *The North East Prospect of Higham Ferrers   A = Parsonage House   B = The Beadhouse   C = The School House   D = Castle Dusthouse   E = Castle Barn*

Artist: Thomas Eayre (signed)

Date: Uncertain.

Bridges' text:

> HIGHAM-FERRERS, situated on a rocky elevated ground abounding with springs, about the distance of half a mile to the north east from the *Nyne* . . . The lordship from east to west extends about three miles, from north to south two small ones. In Higham are an hundred and twenty houses, chiefly built of stone. Northward of the church is the castle-yard, where was antiently a castle erected probably by one of the *Ferrers* family.

This narrow but charming view is taken from the north-east, and the caption at the base allows identification of the individual buildings, faint though the initials are above the respective shapes. The drawing is more basic than Tillemans would have produced, and Eayre's small trees are a distinctive difference. There is a fair use of the ruler for the smaller buildings, where Tillemans would have relied upon free-hand drawing.

Just to the right of the church is a tall pillar or pole. Bridges' text mentions not only the Market Cross in the square near the church, but also two other crosses, Stump Cross in the north end of the town, and Spittle Cross in the south. What appears must be in the Market Place area and may be connected with one of the many fairs for which the town was well known.

Notes: BL. No.130. 42x13 cm.

134. HIGHAM FERRERS

Title: None on drawing

Artist: Unsigned, Peter Tillemans

Date: Probably 1719. A number of visits are recorded in Bridges' MS Notes: 2 August 1718, 2 September 1719 and 25 September 1721. Most of the other drawings in that area were produced in 1719.

Bridges' text:

> The church, dedicated to the blessed Virgin, consists of a south ile, and ile leading to the chancel, and two north iles, leaded, and embattled. On a handsome embattled tower, at the west end, is a beautiful hexagonal spire with crockets at the angles.

This rather shadowy drawing shows the church from the north-east, with the double gables of chancel and Lady Chapel towards the viewer. In the centre of the drawing is the splendid spire which dominates the town.

The church is one of the finest medieval churches in Northamptonshire, not only displaying a variety of architecture from the 13th to the 17th century, but also retaining inside medieval screens which divide the interior into separate areas – a feature rarely found today, common though it was in medieval times. The medieval effect of the spire is the result of rebuilding after its collapse in 1631, leaving us an intriguing puzzle as to how much is genuine.

Beyond the church on the left is the chapel and gable of the Bedehouse, and on the right the School, with a stump of one of its pinnacles sticking up between the buildings. Rising above the roof tops is the tall standard with a cross finial shown on Eayre's Prospect (Plate 133).

Notes: BL. No.131. 30.5x20.5 cm. Other no: On reverse is written Numb. 41 dd.

135.   HIGHAM FERRERS

Title: None on drawing

Artist: Unsigned, Peter Tillemans

Date: Probably 1719 (see previous drawing).

Bridges' text:

The college stood north-west from the church, at some distance in the town. It appears to have been a quadranglar building, about fifteen yards square within. There were two wings projecting westward, one of which is still standing, the ruins of the other are visible. The east front on the outside is about thirty yards long, the north side, comprehending the wing, about sixty yards. The entrance was on the east-side, through a gate now standing, over which are three niches. The hall was in the western part, and some remains of the doors and window frames are yet to be seen. The

chapel as appears from the windows, was on the south side; the east window is shut up, and the chapel converted to a kitchen. The whole building, now an inn with the sign of the *Saracen*'s head, is in a very ruinous condition.

This rather clumsy drawing shows the sad state of the building. Its gateway, with crude representation of the niches over, is in the centre, and on either side, amongst a mixture of windows can be seen a number of 15th century windows with arched heads under square hood moulds. The large decayed gable on the left contains the outline of the chapel window mentioned by Bridges, and the two large corbel heads are still there today. The window to the left of the entrance archway later became a doorway. Projecting at an angle to the left of the top of the entrance archway is the inn sign of the Saracen's Head. The drawing has been squared over ready for copying prior to engraving.

The college was founded by Archbishop Chichele in 1431 and it is regrettable that so little now remains of this building. Since it was in such decay by 1720, perhaps it is amazing that there is so much!

Notes: BL. No.132. 23.5x14 cm. Other no: On the reverse is written Numb.32 dd.

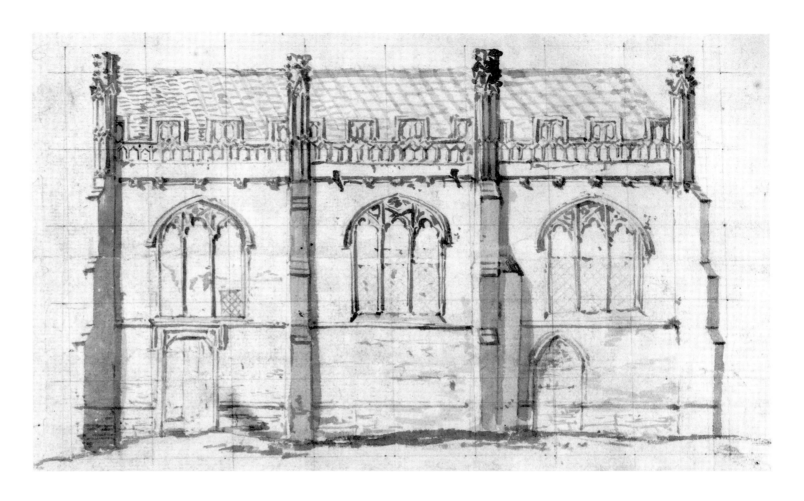

136. HIGHAM FERRERS

Title: None on drawing

Artist: Unsigned, Peter Tillemans

Date: Probably 1719 (see Plate 134).

Bridges' text:

At the north-west end of the church is the school, built of stone, tiled and embattled, in length thirty six foot six inches, and sixteen foot six inches in breadth. It is supported with-out by four buttresses on each side, with a pinnacle at the top of each. On the north side are three windows intirely filled up; at the east end is a window of five divisions, and a like window at the west end. On the south side are three windows, consisting each of three divisions, and between the two upper windows to the east is a stone pulpit fixed in the wall, with stone stairs to ascend it. The roof was formerly wainscotted, and painted with different colours, but is now most of it fallen down. Great part of the windows on all sides is stopt up.

This splendid little building, much finer in its architectural character than the drawing would suggest, was almost certainly built following the refounding of the school at Higham by Archbishop Chichele in 1422. It is an especially fine example of Perpendicular architecture and bearing in mind Chichele's status in the land, could easily be by Royal masons.

Bridges' text decries the sad state of the building, but it is now in excellent condition, having been restored following the First World War.

Notes: BL. No.133. 23.5x17.5 cm. On reverse is written "dd".

137. HIGHAM FERRERS

Title: None on drawing

Artist: Unsigned, Peter Tillemans

Date: Probably 1719 (see Plate 134).

Bridges' text:

> On the south side of the church is the bead-house, or alms-house, founded and endowed by archbishop *Chichele* for twelve men and one woman, with a daily allowance of one penny to each of them. It is divided into two parts, the upper of which, divided from the lower part by a screen of wood, you ascend by six stone stairs. This seemeth to have been formerly used as a chapel. The windows have been with glass finely stained, and several imperfect portaits of saints and kings are yet remaining. On each side of the east window are two niches for statues, and on the south side near the east is an holy water bason . . . . . On the top of the west end without, under a stone arch, is a small bell, to give notice of prayers twice a day.

Another rather rough drawing, also squared over. It does not give any indication of the construction of the west wall, built of alternate dark and light sandstone courses (perhaps the wall was lightly rendered?). The bell in the bellcote was to be remade by Thomas Eayre in 1737. As a Bedehouse it was founded in 1428, and has been restored in recent years for use as a parish hall.

Notes: BL. No.134. 20.6x17.3 cm. Other nos: On reverse Numb.32 dd; and at the base of the drawing a letter C.

138. HIGHAM FERRERS

Title on drawing: *Belfrey door*

Artist: Unsigned, Peter Tillemans

Date: Probably 1719 (see Plate 134).

Bridges' text

> Over the steeple door without, are ten bas reliefs within circles
> of our Saviour's crucifixion, several of which are much defaced.

The drawing, once more squared up for copying, shows the inner face
of the western porch, with the double doorways into the church. Even
considering some adjustment when the spire was rebuilt in 1632, this
doorway is one of the finest pieces of late 13th century carving in the
county and its quality has been compared with work in Westminster
Abbey. The doorways are unusual in having low segmental heads rather
than a pointed archway, and each is surrounded by a deep band of
carving with a mixture of foliage patterns and small figures, which
together with the stem rising between the doors is related to a Tree of
Jesse. The work is usually dated between 1250 and 1280.

Notes: BL. No.135. 19x13.5 cm. Other nos: On reverse is written Numb.30
dd. At the base is a letter A.

On the Breaſt. Fili dei miſerere mei.

140. HIGHAM FERRERS *(right)*

Title on reverse of drawing: *Two Brass Plates in the church of Higham Ferrers of the Chicheley's. Nº.1.William Chicheley and his Wife, as tis Said, the Brass where their names were being taken off. Nº.II. Thomas Chicheley and his Wife Agnes, the Father and Mother of the Said Wm and Henry Archbishop of Cant. and of William.*

Artist: Unsigned, Peter Tillemans

Date: Probably 1719 (see Plate 134).

Bridges' text:

> Upon a stone in the same chancel, are the effigies in brass in a niche supported by pillars, of a man in the habit of a religious, and a woman in that of a vowess or nun, reputed to be of *William Chichele* and *Beatrix* his wife. Beneath their feet were inscriptions on a brass tablet, which are now taken away. On different escutcheons were the arms of *Chichele*, and another coat now lost.

> Upon a marble in the north chancel, laid down, as supposed, at the charge of archbishop *Chichele* . . .

The first of these simple drawings shows the fine brass of Archbishop Chichele's brother William, who died in 1425 and his wife, standing beneath a canopy with two shields above their heads, that on the right missing, as Bridges' text relates. Bridges is incorrect in thinking that William and his wife are dressed in religious habit: he is costumed as a civilian with full length gown and she in a simple draped habit as might befit a widow. Around the edge of the slab is an inscription with at each corner the signs of the Evangelists, with only one remaining today at the bottom left, the winged lion for St Mark.

The second brass is not described in Bridges' text but only recorded by its inscription. It is nevertheless a fine example of a cross brass with symbols of the Evangelists and Christ, drawn separately alongside. They are given numbers 1. for St John (an eagle); 2. for St Mark (a bull); 3. for St Matthew (an angel); 4. is missing, but is for St Luke (an ox); 5. is for Christ. The brass is indeed for Chichele's parents and records the death of his father, Thomas, in 1400.

Notes: BL. No.137. 32.5x19 cm. At the base of the drawings the letters G and H.

139. HIGHAM FERRERS *(above)*

Title on reverse of drawing: *A Brass Plate in the Church of Higham Ferr of Laurencius de Santo Mauro, formerly Rector of this Church, See the Inscription Mr. Bridge's Book Page 7.*

Artist: Unsigned, Peter Tillemans

Date: Probably 1719 (see Plate 134).

Bridges' text:

> Under an arch, on the north side of the altar steps, is a free stone monument covered with marble, on which is a brass portrait with this inscription on the breasts, *Fili Dei miserere mei.* On the top and sides were eighteen brass figures of the apostles and others, of which some are now taken away. On the arch over his head, *Susipiat me Cristus qui vocavit me – In sinu Abrahe Angeli diducant me.*

On the marble is this inscription;

Hic iacet Laurentius de Sto Mauro quondam rector istius Ecce cuius anime propicieture Deus.

This small sketch shows the brass in its damaged state, as it remains today. Only the left hand side of the canopy support, with its niches holding figures of saints, exists entire, with just one niche on the right, at the top. Laurence St. Maur died in 1337 and the brass is one of the finest in Northamptonshire, and indeed in England. The engraving has a superb clarity of draughtsmanship which makes the best brasses of this period so memorable.

Notes: BL. No.136. 25.5x19 cm. At the base is a letter F. There is an engraving of the brass, together with another in the church (William Thorpe, mercer, d.1504) on an engraved plate by Schnebbelie and Basire, both well known late 18th century engravers (Copy in the collection of Northamptonshire Libraries). They both provided plates for the published text, although this one was not included.

141. HOLDENBY

Title on reverse of drawing: *Holdenby Ruins now down*

Artist: Unsigned, Peter Tillemans

Date: Uncertain. The only recorded visit in Bridges' MS Notes has the date 1722, but no other drawing by Tillemans comes from that year. The numbering system would suggest a date in 1719 and there are visits and drawings for places not far distant in July of that year.

Bridges' text:

> *Holdenby* is famous for its antient Manor-house, a very noble and magnificent structure, built in the reign of Queen *Elizabeth* by Sir *Christopher Hatton*, as he himself expressed it, for the last and great monument of his youth . . .

A really superb drawing combining all the delight of architectural detail together with the charm of the figure composition – observers, like us, viewing the prospect of the ruins.

The view takes in the spread of the forecourt or Base Court as it was known, with the archways on either side. To the left is all that remains of the tall three storey range, each floor having its own order of pilasters, with the Ionic clearly denoted at ground level. Variously intact are wide six-light mullion and transom windows, and at roof level remnants of a balustrade. The wing ends in a canted bay. Then across the first court are impressive remains of a double arcaded facade which is part of the range which formed the service to the Hall.

Beyond the ruins of the mansion is the house created after 1651 by Captain Adam Baynes, a Parliamentary officer who purchased the site in that year and demolished most of the rest of the house. It is on the site of Baynes' house that the present Holdenby House was erected between 1873-75 in a style suggested by what was known of the first house together with some inspiration from Kirby Hall.

Notes: BL. No.138. 46x24 cm. Other no: On reverse is written Numb.43 bb.

There are supposed survey drawings of Holdenby among the Thorpe collection in Sir John Soane's Museum, London. (John Summerson ed. "The book of architecture of John Thorpe in Sir John Soane's Museum", *Walpole Society* 1966.) A plan dated *c.*1607 shows the facade looking into the Base Court with canted bays projecting into the court, rather than the flat facades shown in the drawing.

142. HOLDENBY

Title on reverse of drawing: *Holmby House in Northamptonshire*

Artist: Unsigned, Peter Tillemans

Date: Uncertain (see previous drawing Plate 141).

Bridges' text:

> Of this structure, which we apprehend was demolished by order of the Parliament after the death
> of the King, only some gateways, and fragments of the pyramids with arms are now remaining . . .
> In the garden walls which are standing are several arched niches.

Here is shown one of the gateways, that is one of the arches which gave entrance into the Base Court, both

of which bear the date, clear in the drawing, 1583. The archways have a crested top and niches in their side
piers. Also noteworthy are the circles carved in the spandrels of the arches and above the niches. Very similar
archways occur at Kirby Hall, which had also become a Hatton property by the 1580s. Above the wall to
the left can be seen the chimneys of Captain Baynes' house, and to the far left a rough mound incorporat-
ing what Bridges' text describes as "several arched niches".

There is no evidence of the tall facades of the previous drawing, and the note on the reverse of the previous
drawing "Holdenby Ruins, now down" perhaps suggests they had been demolished. They do appear,
however, on the canvases painted by John Wootton in the Entrance Hall at Althorp, part of the work done
in the early 1730s.

Notes: BL. No.139. 38x20 cm. The garden layout of Holdenby is extensively described in RCHM Vol.III pp.106-9.

143. HOLDENBY

Title on reverse of drawing: *Holdenby ruins now down*

Artist: Unsigned, Peter Tillemans

Date: Uncertain (see Plate 141).

Bridges' text:

[Bridges' text quotes John Norden's description:]

> . . . in the hall there are raised three peramides very high standing instead of a shryne, the midst whereof ascendeth unto the roofe of the Hall, the other two equal with the syde walls of same hall, and on them are depainted the armes of all the gentlemen of the same shire, and of all the noblemen of this land.

[In Bridges' MS Notes an entry with the date 1722 says:]

> . . . ye top of ye Mid. Pyramid wanting, ye pedestall of ye left hand only standing, yt on ye right quite gone: pieces of the Pyramids I saw made support for Hovels in ye Ministers yard, some with ye Arms upon em.

These then are the remains of elaborate obelisks which formed part of the interior decoration of the Hall. They are reminiscent of similar decorations on a number of church monuments, such as those of Sir Christopher Yelverton at Easton Maudit (Plate 51) and the Spencer tombs at Brington (Plates 31 and 32).

Notes: BL. No.140. 28.5x14.5 cm. Other no: On reverse of drawing is written Num,b 46 bb.
There is a slight pencil sketch on the reverse of this drawing of a house of farmhouse character, but it is too indefinite to allow identification.

144. HORTON

Title on reverse of drawing: *Lord Parr of Hortons Mon[t] in Horton Chancel Aug 1721*

Artist: Unsigned, Peter Tillemans

Bridges' text:

> Upon a square tomb of white marble, raised two foot six inches from the ground, are the figures of a man and a woman: the man in his hair, with a large beard, reposing his head upon his helmet and gauntlets, and his feet upon a dog: the woman in a resembling habit with those of the preceding monument, having a mantle clasped with a buckle, hanging down behind to her feet, and a bracelet round her neck; her head lying on a pillow, and supported by two angels lying under it on another pillow.

This is the splendid tomb of Queen Catherine Parr's uncle, William Lord Parr (d.1546) and his wife (d.1555). Both had been at the Field of the Cloth of Gold in 1520, he serving the King, she the Queen. The effigies are excellently detailed and around the tomb is much heraldry, together with small figures representing their five sons and five daughters. Both in design and workmanship the tomb can be compared with that at Fawsley for Sir Richard Knightley (d.1534).

Notes: BL. No.141. 21.5x14 cm.

The Earl of Halifax' House and Gardens taken 9 Aug 1721 at Horton

145. HORTON

Title: *The Earl of Halifax' House and Gardens taken 9 Aug¹ 1721 at Horton*

Artist: Unsigned, Peter Tillemans

Bridges' text:

> The parish is inclosed, and contains eight or nine families, beside the Earl of *Halifax*'s, who hath here a very good seat and gardens. Part of Lord *Halifax*'s house is new-built, the old part is embattled.

This is a most important record of a house which was to be almost totally rebuilt within twenty years or so of the date of the drawing. To the left is an octagonal tower attached to a wing with panelled parapet and large windows, all having been built by the Parrs probably *c.*1550-60, and similar to work at Dingley Hall.

Bridges' "new-built" portion is the wing on the right, which with its detailed cornice, decorative doorway and long casement windows, is likely to have been built *c.*1700. The way the doorway is drawn suggests that the wing is only one room thick, and the awkward way the wing joins the rest of the house suggests that this is the beginning of a new facade to overlook the garden.

The garden is a charming example of the early 18th century parterre fashion, with a mixture of conical trees, small shrubs, grass plots with small circular beds, and further planting against the walls.

To the extreme right is the church, with its elegant wrought iron weather vane, and in front stands the Rectory (now the French Partridge restaurant). Bridges' MS Notes record: "The Church new Casd & handsomely Pewd with Oak & well pavd with free Stone. Here is an handsome Oak Screen supported by flooted Pilasters of the Ionick Order. The Church repaired by the Earl of Halifax about three years since. At ye Top of this Tower is a Weathercock sett upon Iron Work." The ironwork, alas, is no longer there.

Notes: BL. No.142. 45x28 cm. Other no: Front of drawing 42.

The Steeple & Church of Irtlingbury to the North East

146. IRTHLINGBOROUGH

Title on drawing: *The Steeple & Church of Irtlingbury to the North East*

Artist: Unsigned, Peter Tillemans

Date: Probably 1719. Visits in the area are recorded in Bridges' MS Notes early in September 1719, while the only dated note on Irthlingborough is on 25 September 1721.

Bridges' text:

> The church now standing, dedicated to S. *Peter*, consists of a body, north and south ile, chancel and cross ile from north to south, leaded and embatled. At the west end, at some distance from the church and joined to it by the ruins of the colleges, is an embatled tower, on which is an octagonal turret.

The church at Irthlingborough remains much as shown here today, save that the "ruins of the colleges" were restored in the 19th century and incorporated into the building. Irthlingborough was one of a number of collegiate churches – that is it supported its own college of clergy who conducted services and performed other duties, such as running a school or almshouse. The tower already shows a decided lean, and eventually was rebuilt faithfully by the architect J.L. Pearson between 1888 and 1893.

The drawing has been overdrawn with squares prior to being engraved, and the engraving was used in the published text (Vol.II, p.337) where it is similarly shown with a title as on the drawing, but no signature or date.

Notes: BL. No.144. 32x21 cm. Other no: On reverse is written Numb.29.

North West View of Kettering taken from the Common Field calld the Linx Sepr 1721

147. KETTERING

Title on drawing: *North West View of Kettering taken from the Common Field calld the Linx Sepr 1721*

Artist: Unsigned, Peter Tillemans

Bridges' text:

> *Kettering* field hath different names; the *Warren*-ground, from a warren that was formerly there; the *Links*, covered with furze and brakes; and *Broom*-hills, which are not distinct lands but common. At the bottom runs the ditch-brook dividing these parts from the common field, which is in yard-lands, and is ploughed in hides.

A charming view showing the town dominated by the tall spire of the church. A number of substantial houses are indicated, but the view does not allow easy identification of individual properties. One building of significance can be seen in the valley, just below and slightly left of the church, where appears a roof with a tall chimney adjoining: is this Thomas Eayre's bell foundry? The position would be about right, with the track of Mill Lane over to the right.

Notes: BL. No.145. 44x19 cm. Other no: On front of drawing 53.

148. KETTERING

Title on drawing: *Kettering Church Northamptonshire*

Artist: Unsigned, Peter Tillemans

Date: Probably 1719. Bridges' MS Notes record visits in September and October 1719.

Bridges' text:

> The church. dedicated to S. *Peter* and S. *Paul*, consists of a body, north and south ile, and chancel, covered with lead. On an embattled turret, is raised an elegant spire.

This fine drawing shows the church from the east with its Decorated style east window in the chancel and the Perpendicular style north and south chapels. Behind rises firstly the parapet of the nave gable and behind the noble spire.

To the south of the church is the Manor House, which is thus noted by Bridges: "Mr *Sawyer*'s house in which are old stone window frames, was formerly the abbat's hall". The latter reference is to the holding of the manor by the abbey of Peterborough, prior to the Dissolution.

Notes: BL. No.146. 47x27 cm. Other no: On reverse is written Numb.64.

149. KETTERING

Title: None on drawing

Artist: Unsigned, Peter Tillemans

Date: Probably 1719 *(see previous drawing)*

This shows the north side of Kettering church, with its dominantly Perpendicular architecture. The mounding of the churchyard is indicated, but no gravestones are drawn.

Notes: BL. No.147. 34x31.5 cm.

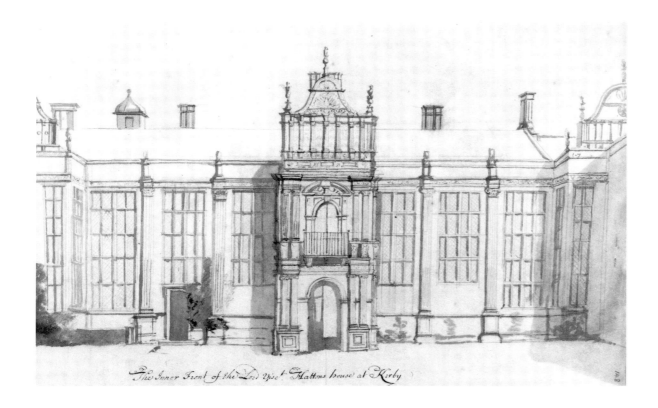

The Inner Front of the Lord Visct Hattons house at Kirby

150. KIRBY HALL

Title on drawing: *The Inner Front of the Lord Visc^t Hattons House at Kirby*

Artist: Unsigned, Peter Tillemans

Date: Probably 1719, although the only visit recorded in Bridges' MS Notes is 27 September 1722. However a visit to Gretton is recorded on 4 August 1719.

Bridges' text:

> *Kirby* is now only a single house, the seat of the lord viscount *Hatton*. This house, consisting of a square court, was built by the *Stafford* family, as appeareth from their crest, *a Boar's head out of a ducal coronet* and HUMFRE STAFFORD, on several parts of it. Here are three orders of pillars: above the second order is this legend IE SERAY . 1572 . LOYAL . and on the inner porch this date 1638. The gardens here are beautiful, stocked with a great variety of exotic plants, and adorned with a wilderness composed of almost the whole variety of English trees, and ranged in an elegant order.

A useful depiction of this house, now largely a ruin. What Tillemans has drawn is the south side of the courtyard with its roofs and windows intact. Today only the Hall, on the right of the porch, retains its roof, the range to the left, with kitchens below, is now roofless. Today looking at the windows to the left of the

porch we can clearly see a blocked row of lights where a floor cut across them, allowing a basement and two floors on that side of the house. Tillemans' drawing shows that when the roof was on and the windows glazed, this effect was invisible.

All the gables are complete with their heraldic finials, only partially surviving today. Behind the main range on the left of the porch a turret roof marks a staircase addition of the mid 17th century.

Bridges describes the porch with its orders of architecture, built in the early 1570s by Sir Humphrey Stafford. Stafford died in 1575 with the house not quite complete and it was purchased by Sir Christopher Hatton, whose descendants resided at Kirby through the 17th and 18th centuries. The 1638 date refers to a series of alterations which were made between then and 1640 and included, for example, the balcony doorway above the porch entrance.

The gardens described by Bridges lay to the west of the house, and here only small planting against the walls is obvious.

The house was rarely used after 1800 and was partly stripped of interior fitments and gradually fell into decay and ruin. It was taken into guardianship by the Ministry of Works in 1930 and is now administered by English Heritage.

Notes: BL. No.148. 40.5x29.5 cm. Other no: On reverse is written Num:97. An archaeological survey was undertaken of the parterre garden in the early 1990s and a conjectural restoration of the late 17th century garden was undertaken (1993/4).

Front of Sr Justinian Ishams house at Lamport to the Garden Sep 1721

151. LAMPORT

Title on drawing: *Front of Sr Justinian Ishams house at Lamport to the Garden Sep 1721*

Artist: Unsigned, Peter Tillemans

Bridges' text:

> Sir *Justinian Isham*, the present possessor of Lamport manor and all the lordship, hath here a very elegant seat; part of which is old, and part new built in his father's time, by *John Webb* son in law to *Inigo Jones.* He hath several drawings of mouldings, architraves, and freezes, made in the years 1654. and 1655. with some letters from Mr. *Webb* dated 1657. relating to the gate, and pilasters, and the execution of an intended depository. In the hall windows are several family coats of arms, brought some years ago from *Pightesley.*

A fascinating portrayal of the west front of Lamport as conceived by Sir Justinian Isham, 2nd Baronet, in the 1650s employing, as Bridges states, the architect John Webb. What Webb built was a reception pavilion, seen here, attached behind to the rather rambling Jacobean manor house. The doorway gave access into the main room, the High Room, filling the whole height of the right hand half of the block, as it still does. To the left below was a parlour and above a bedroom and behind an elaborate carved staircase. This pavilion

was used as the central portion of a new west front designed by Francis Smith of Warwick between 1738 and 1740, and at that juncture the formal garden was swept away and replaced by a circular carriage drive.

Tillemans has captured the rigid formality of the garden with its conical trees and tall hedges. The steps to right and left probably rose to embankments with terrace walks, similar to those surviving in other areas of the garden today.

The drawings alluded to in the printed text are still amongst the Isham family archives, and as well as elevations, still contain almost full-size details of mouldings and console brackets. These drawings are a rare survival of Webb's designs for a country house. The "intended depository" refers to a design by Webb for a circular domed mausoleum, never built. Had it been erected it would have been one of John Webb's major works, like the work at the Hall itself. The coats of arms in the windows mentioned are Isham heraldic panels of late 16th century date brought from the former Isham home, Pytchley, and are now in the windows of the staircase of Lamport Hall.

The Ishams purchased the Lamport estate in 1560 and remained there till 1976, when following the death of Sir Gyles Isham, 12th Baronet, the Lamport Hall Preservation Trust was established, and this now maintains and administers the property.

Notes: BL. No.149. 45x28 cm. Other no: On the front 52. The Isham archives are now deposited at the Northamptonshire Record Office. Webb was not, in fact, Jones' son-in-law, but a kinsman (see *Colvin*)

View of Langdyke Bush & Country Adjacent taken upon Helpston Heath near the Hedge 29 Aug. 1721

152. LANGDYKE

Title on drawing:

View of Langdyke Bush & Country adjacent taken upon Helpston Heath near the Hedge 29 Augᵗ 1721

Artist: Unsigned, Peter Tillemans

Bridges' text:

[In the introduction to the Hundred of Nassaburgh, Bridges narrates the history of the Hundred court:]

This court, curruptly called *Langley*-court, was formerly kept at *Langdyke*-bush: and within the memory of man hath been summoned there, and adjourned to the Lord *Exeter*'s house at *Helpston.*

Langdyke-bush stands about two furlongs to the left of the warren-house, or of the great road between *Stamford* and *Peterburgh*, upon a high ground, that overlooks the country to the north-west, near the corner of a hedge in the open field called *Helpston*-heath, with a white thorn tree on the other side.

The drawing fits precisely Bridges' description: left we have the plantation of the Bush, the roadway presumably in the shallow hollow centre, and the white thorn to the right. In the background among the trees is the tower and spirelet of Helpston and to the right of the thorn-tree the spire of Glinton.

Notes: BL. No.150. 44.5x27.5 cm. Other no: On the front of drawing 49.

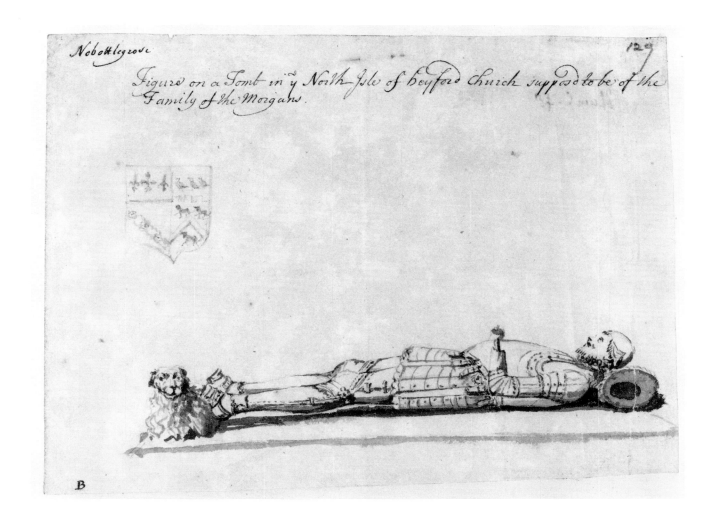

Nobottlegrove

129

Figure on a Tomb in y^e North Isle of Heyford Church suppos'd to be of the Family of the Morgans.

B

153. LITCHBOROUGH

Title on drawing: *Figure on a Tomb in y^e North Isle of Heyford Church supposed to be of the Family of the Morgans*

Artist: Unsigned, Peter Tillemans

Date: Probably 7 July 1719, when Tillemans dated his drawings of the Morgan monument at Heyford

Bridges' text:

[The inscription from the monument is quoted but no description}

The title on the drawing is incorrect, and, while there seem some discrepancies in the heraldry as drawn, compared with the true emblazon on the shield, it all accords with the monument for Sir John Needham (d.1618) at Litchborough. Tillemans visited Heyford on 7 July and drew Judge Morgan's monument and doubtless continued to Litchborough, but forgot the location when the title was added to the drawing.

The figure on its large tomb chest is carved of alabaster and is a fine piece of work. It was erected in 1633 by Sir John's widow, so an unusually late use of alabaster. The inscription tells us that "The Knight above named was Gentleman Pensioner unto the late Queen Elizabeth of happie memorie, and afterwards unto our late soveraigne Lord King James, and was by them both well esteemed, and likewise by other notable Persons of the best ranke and qualitie".

Notes: BL. No.129. 14x18.6 cm. At the bottom of the drawing is a letter B.

View of yᵉ Tower at Longthorp taken 10. Aug. 1719

154. LONGTHORPE

Title on drawing: *View of yᵉ Tower at Longthorp taken 10 Aug 1719*

Artist: Unsigned, Peter Tillemans

Bridges' text:

> In the New manor is an old tower, demised, under a lease from the Dean and Chapter, by the name of *West*-hall.

This is, of course, the well known Longthorpe Tower, famous for its remarkably complete 14th century wall paintings, in the care of English Heritage. This view from the north shows the structure of the *c.*1300 tower with its corner buttresses. Alongside is the gable of the Chamber/Hall range with a tall traceried window, and then behind a range with a wide tiled roof and a blocked arched opening at its further end, which was the doorway into the Hall. Mullioned windows in the tower suggest 17th century alterations. Only fragments of the hall range survive today.

Notes: BL. No.153. 32x20.5 cm. Other no: On reverse is written Num:71.

View of Sr Francis St Johns Dwelling House & Outhouses at Longthorpe July 1721

155. LONGTHORPE. Thorpe Hall

Title on drawing: *View of Sr Francis St Johns Dwelling House & Outhouses at Longthorpe July 1721*

Artist: Unsigned, Peter Tillemans

Date: Bridges' MS Notes record a visit on 28 July 1721.

Bridges' text:

> *LONG-THORP*, in earlier records written simply *Thorp*, is an hamlet of fifteen families. It is divided into two manors, distinguished by the names of the Old and New manor. The Old manor, under a lease from the Dean and Chapter, is held by Sir *Francis St. John*, created baronet in 1716, grandson to *Oliver St. John*, the attorney general, in the reign of *Charles* I, who hath here a good seat, the place of residence; but the manor house is let by him to an undertenant.

This is one of the most remarkable houses in the country, having been built between 1653 and 1656 to the designs of Peter Mills, an architect whose work is both highly distinguished and little known. It represents a typical fashionable house of its time with important rooms on the first floor, a hipped roof with flat viewing platform accessible from a staircase within the cupola. Visible shadowy projections on the right-hand side of the house are those of two bay windows. (This is useful verification of the existence of the bays as part of the original house; they have sometimes been attributed to the 19th century.)

Behind the house are outbuildings and stables, and surrounding the plot are high walls and impressive gatepiers. The view confirms that the windows originally had cross-mullion and transom windows.

The house, after years of use as a hospital and then following a period of neglect, was restored in 1989 as a Sue Ryder Home. Unfortunately one of its best interiors was sold by a previous owner and now forms part of Leeds Castle in Kent. The encircling walls with their rich piers still survive.

Notes: BL. No.154. 43.5x24.5 cm. For Peter Mills see *Colvin,* and Tim Mowl and Brian Earnshaw: *Architecture Without Kings* (1995).

156 (a)   157 (b)   158 (c)   159 (d)

LONGTHORPE. Thorpe Hall

Title on drawing: *Four Draughts of 4 Statues markt a b c d in Sr Francis St Johns Garden at Thorp near Peterborough*

Artist: Unsigned, Peter Tillemans

Date: Probably, like the previous drawing, 28 July 1719.

These drawings represent the sort of 'classical' statue which decorated many gardens at the end of the 17th century. They are often inspired by statuary seen abroad, say, in Rome or at Versailles. The figures here represent (156) a young huntsman holding a spear in his right hand and a horn in his left; (157) a draped female figure; (158) another male figure which again seems to be holding some implement; (159) another draped female figure, again holding some object.

No statuary exists today at Thorpe.

Notes: BL. Nos.244,245,246,247, and 248. Leaf 244 has the title only. (Size of drawings, 31x19.5 cm). Other no: On leaf 244 is written N.129.

South View of the Treshams House at Liveden taken in the Close 4 Aug.t 1721

160. LYVEDEN

Title on drawing: *South View of the Treshams House at Liveden taken in the Close 4 Aug.t 1721*

Artist: Unsigned, Peter Tillemans

Bridges' text:

> The new building is of free-stone, in the form of a Cross, with a projection of windows at each end, of four angles and five squares. It consists of three stories, of which the lower is half under ground: the middle seemeth to have been intended for a kitchen, as is probable from the chimney and ovens in one of the projections. The entrance by the door still remaining, was from the North. Above the first storey without, is stone-work in the form of escutcheons, and upon the second storey, in stone compartments, are representations of the nails, scourge, crown of thorns, *Judas*'s bag, with the ladder, hammer, and other instruments of our Saviour's crucifixion, with the abbreviations IHS and XPS . . . The mouldings and carvings are well preserved, and the cement as strong and hard as the stones themselves.

A delightful drawing of this intriguing building. Like the Triangular Lodge at Rushton (Plate 240) the building also has religious symbolism, both in its decoration, as mentioned by Bridges, and in its plan, a cross. It was begun in the 1590s but was unfinished when Sir Thomas Tresham died in 1605, and has remained an open shell ever since.

Bridges was clearly taken by the workmanship and it is even more a testament to the skill of the masons that it still stands today. The coursing of the stonework is superb and the carved decorations are as clear almost as when they were carved.

The New Bield was originally erected as a large garden pavilion, placed at the corner of a rising series of terraces with mounts and pools. The Lyveden garden layout is a rare survival of an almost untouched Elizabethan layout and deserves full restoration.

The view of the south side of the building shows the basement entrance between embankments. To the left a large mound indicates the garden and one of the spiral mounts. The cottage in the background still stands as the home of the custodian of the monument, which is now in the care of the National Trust.

Notes: BL. No.151. 44x23.5 cm. The building is described in Bridges' MSS with the date 5 August 1721. The garden layout is described with a plan in RCHM Vol. 1 p.8. A considerable clearance of the mounts and water garden has been effected within the last few years by the monument's custodian, Ted Faulkner.

161. LYVEDEN

Title on drawing: *This North West prospect of LIVDEN house by J. BRIDGES Esq^rs order was taken by G. NUNNS*

Date: Uncertain. A note in Bridges' MSS refers to the inscriptions being recorded in September 1718, which might be the date of the drawing.

A rather heavy handed drawing which pays special attention to the Latin inscriptions which run around the parapet.

George Nunns was a Northamptonshire surveyor and a number of estate plans drawn by him are known.

There is, for example, one of 1716 at Deene. He, or Eayre, may also have produced a measured plan of the building since on the reverse of the drawing is written "Mem. Plan Wanting at Mr Eayres^s Now in Ruins."

Notes: BL. No.152. 33x22.5 cm. Nunns is referred to in Joan Wake and Deborah Champion Webster eds., *The letters of Daniel Eaton*, Northamptonshire Record Society, 1971, p.130, letter 154, which shows he was still alive in 1729.

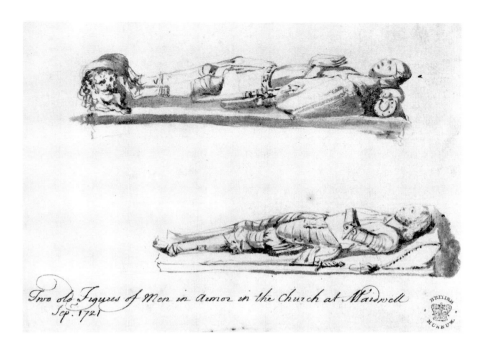

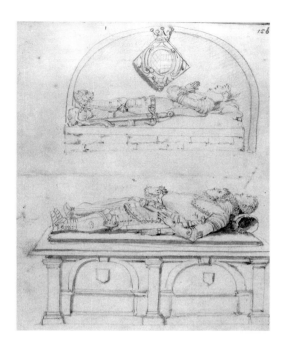

162. MAIDWELL

Title on drawing: *Two old Figures of Men in Armor in the Church at Maidwell Sepr 1721*

Artist: Unsigned, Peter Tillemans

Date: A visit is recorded in Bridges' MS Notes on 1 September 1721.

Bridges' text:

> In the chancel, near the south wall, are two old battered figures of men in armour.

These figures no longer exist at Maidwell, the only monument being a damaged tomb for Edward, Baron Dundalk and his wife Katharine, erected in 1634. Of the two figures in Tillemans drawing, the top one would seem to be that of a knight in armour wearing a cyclas over his mail suit and with a shield and sword on his left side, probably *c*.1400. The lower figure seems to be early 17th century, but it does not relate to the figure on the Dundalk tomb.

Bridges' MS Notes contain the statement under an entry labelled Maidwell:

> 2 old battered figures of Men in armour in ye Chancell drawn by T. & a Stone ridged with a Cross upon it.

Perhaps the earlier figures were of wood and have since decayed, or they may have been swept aside in the over zealous Victorian restoration.

Notes: BL. No.155. 16.3x21.2 cm. Other no: At the left hand corner is written a letter A. Neither of these two figures in Hartshorne's *Recumbent Effigies* (1876).

163. MARHOLM

Title on drawing: *In Marham Church 1. The Earl of Southampton adjoining to the Wall on ye S. side of the Church. 2. A Monument of Wm Fitzwilliam Esqr & his Wife Winifred on the S. side of the Chancel July 1721*

Artist: Unsigned, Peter Tillemans

Date: Bridges' MS Notes record visits on 28 and 31 July 1721.

Bridges' text:

> [Only the second of these is noted by its inscription]

The top drawing is of a tomb of a knight in armour carved from clunch and uncoloured, which today rests on an elaborate tomb in the medieval style which did not exist prior to the restoration of the church in 1868. Prior to that date it rested within an arched recess as shown here, with the coat of arms above for Sir William Fitzwilliam, later Earl of Southampton temp. Henry VIII, whom it was thought erroneously to represent. The effigy clearly dates from *c*.1400 and is usually identified as John de Wittlebury, whose family possessed the manor of Milton at that time.

The lower drawing is the tomb of Sir William Fitzwilliam (d.1599) and his wife Anne (d.1603). Sir William was Constable of Fotheringhay Castle during the time of Mary Queen of Scots' imprisonment. The effigies are once more of clunch but richly coloured and have been beautifully restored in recent years.

Notes: BL. No.156. 29x22 cm

164. MARHOLM

Title on drawing: [Partly torn away] . . . *for Wm Earl Fitz . . . am and Ann his Wife, 1720*

Artist: Uncertain, but very probably James Fisher, sculptor, of Camberwell

Date: 1720 [in the title].

Bridges' text:

> In the same chancel is a magnificent marble monument, with statues of Lord and Lady *Fitz-William* in their proper habits, as large as the life; and standing, one on each side, the figures of Piety and Grief. It is supported by four blue-veined marble columns of the Corinthian order, with capitals and friezes, and a pediment above. At the top is a large shield of white marble, with the family arms, supporters, and an Earl's coronet, with an urn; and on the two outside pillars are weeping cherubs.

This is a superb drawing and quite unlike Tillemans' style. The rather fanciful way in which the figures and decorations are drawn suggests that it is the original design for the tomb of William, 1st Earl Fitzwilliam and his wife, which the sculptor James Fisher of Camberwell contracted to make in 1718 for £900.

As it exists today only the central portion with the main figures survives. It is clear, however, not only from Bridges' text description but also from a description by Britton and Brayley in 1810 and also from a reference by Rev. Sweeting published in 1868 that it was originally much larger. The church was restored in the late 1860s and probably the lateral sections were removed then.

Notes: BL. No.157. 60x41 cm. For Fisher see *Gunnis*. The contract is among the Fitzwilliam papers, Northamptonshire Record Office. Sweeting's description runs: "West of this [the 1534 monument] is a monstrous erection, so large as to block up one light of each of the windows on the north side" (Rev. W.D. Sweeting: *Parish Churches in and around Peterborough* (London, 1868)).

165. MARHOLM

Title on reverse of drawing: *Ld. FitzW^m. at Marham*

Artist: Unsigned, but possibly A. Motte

Date: Uncertain.

This is a composite drawing made up by copying in reduced form the two previous drawings (Plates 163 and 164). It is very likely a drawing made preliminary to an engraved plate, hence the attribution to Motte.

Notes: BL. No.158. 27.5x22 cm.

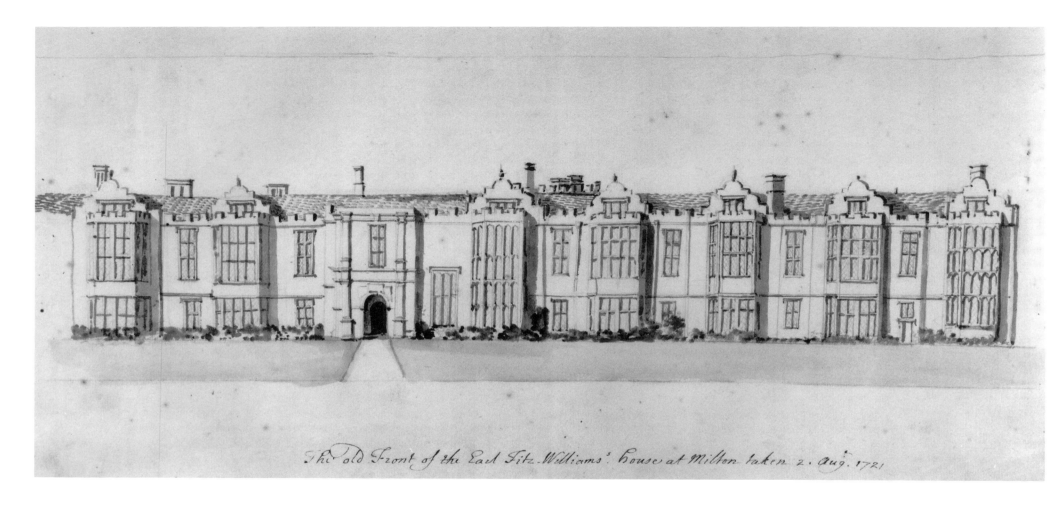

The old Front of the Earl Fitz. Williams' house at Milton taken 2. Aug.ᵗ 1721

166. MARHOLM. Milton

Title on drawing: *The old Front of the Earl Fitz. Williams' House at Milton taken 2 Aug.ᵗ 1721*

Artist: Unsigned, Peter Tillemans

Bridges' text:

> At *Milton*, in *Castre* parish, is the seat of the Earl *Fitzwilliam*. In the hall and parlour windows are many coats of arms, several of which were brought from *Fotheringhay* Castle.

Tillemans has drawn the north front of the house. The title says "The Old Front" presumably since a range to the right of what we see, erected in 1690, may have appeared almost like a new house, although it is no more than a new stable court.

We are looking at the Tudor Hall range with the porch leading into the Hall itself, ending with the first bay window to the right. The second bay from the porch, together with the windows on either side, marks the Parlour, then come further chambers and finally the facade ends in another bay, lighting the chapel. Behind and just visible and appearing as series of chimneys and battlements, is a range which contained a staircase. The curved gables are very like those at Apethorpe (Plate 3). It will be noticed that the main rooms are on the first floor.

In 1773 the architect Sir William Chambers was called in to make additions to Milton, and the gables disappeared, being replaced by a series of dormers within a hipped roof.

Notes: BL. No.159. 45x28 cm.

View of Nassington Church and Spire taken 3 Aug: 1721

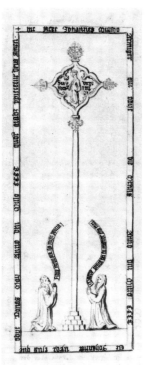

167. NEWTON BY GEDDINGTON *(left)*

Title on drawing: *A Brass Plate of John Mulsho in the Church at Newton*

Artist: Unsigned, Peter Tillemans

Date: Uncertain, but probably 10 July 1719 since the drawings of Geddington were executed on that day.

Bridges' text:

> . . . on an antique marble, is in brass a cross flory mounted on four steps: at the bottom, on the right side, is a man in a gown kneelling, as in prayer . . . on the other side is a woman, in like posture . . . At top, in the centre of the cross, stands St. Faith, with a glory about her head, and in her right hand a gridiron.
>
> [Bridges inserts the inscriptions where there are gaps above]

This is one of the more unusual brasses in the county and is now to be found in Geddington church, whither it was removed when Newton church was declared redundant and converted into a Field Centre. Cross brasses are not common, and to find one still with its figure of a saint is most unusual. The diminutive kneeling figures of the deceased add great charm to the composition.

Notes: BL. No.161. 31x18.5 cm.

168. NASSINGTON *(above)*

Title on drawing: *View of Nassington Church and Spire taken 3 Aug.¹ 1721*

Artist: Unsigned, Peter Tillemans

Bridges' text:

> *NASSINGTON*, a village of about eighty families, in an open field lordship, seated on a descent towards the river, hath the *Nyne* on the east, on the south *Fotheringhay, Rockingham* forest on the west, and *Yarwell* on the north.

A general view of the village looking from the south across the strip cultivation of the open fields. It shows the tall nature of the structure, with its solid west tower – all due to the Saxon origins of the building. The spire looks perfectly credible medieval, but it is recorded to have been rebuilt in 1640.

To the left of the church are the gables and roofs of the Manor House, still largely surviving and containing much evidence of medieval work.

Notes: BL. No.160. 45x28.5 cm. Other no: On front – 36.

Spelhoe

A View of Northampton from Queen's

ls on the London Road

169. NORTHAMPTON

Title on drawing: *A View of Northampton from Queen's Cross on the London Road*

Artist: Unsigned, Peter Tillemans

Date: Probably July 1721 when Bridges' MS Notes record the West prospect of the town being drawn by Tillemans (see Plate 172).

Bridges' text:

> *(There is a long description of the Eleanor Cross in Bridges' text under Hardingstone]*

A fine long view which with its animation and details has much to offer. From left to right, the view takes in the complete breadth of the town. On the extreme left is the post-mill which stood on the rising ground just west of the London road. Then comes the Eleanor Cross, perched in isolation on its steps, topped by the Maltese cross finial, which as Bridges' text tells, was added in 1713 and remained there till the 1840 restoration. Two viewers on horseback are discussing the monument while below, journeying towards the town, is a coach with outriders.

The buildings of the town are well shown. Just above the coach is the tower of St. Peter's church, with, a little to its right, in the distance the spire of Kingsthorpe church. Then coming back into the town, the fine spire of Holy Sepulchre, and in the centre the complex of buildings around All Saints' church: the church itself, the Sessions House and the large town centre houses. Slightly to the right again another large house, probably marking St. Giles' Square or the top of Derngate. Above this, on the northern edge of the town can be seen the gables of a large mansion which belonged to the Fleetwood family (see Plate 170). Moving right again, and on the edge of the town, the gardens and orchards which lay to the south-east of the town, so that St. Giles' church looks more like a separate village rather than a town church. Among the trees in the valley, just an indication of the park of Delapre.

Moving right again, out in the fields, is a windmill on a site now covered by the General Hospital, and far right, on the skyline the well wooded parkland of Abington. In the valley below, at the corner of the drawing, a footpath or track marking the ancient route from Hardingstone to Northampton.

Notes: BL. No.163. 73.5x24.5 cm. Other no: on reverse is written Numb.70 aa.

170. NORTHAMPTON

Title on drawing: *South West Prospect of the Town of Northampton taken in a By Road to Banbury upon the Rising of the Hill between Coton-End Feild & Hardingstone Feild 22 July 1721*
1. All S^s 2. St Sepulchres 3. St Giles 4. St Peters 5. The Castle & the Meeting House. 6. Mr Fleetwoods 7. The Sessions House 8. The Wells among the Trees

Artist: Unsigned, Peter Tillemans

Date: The date is confirmed in Bridges' MS Notes "W view of Northton by T. taken in ye Banbury byroad upon ye rising of ye Hill betw. Cotton end field & Hardingstone feild. July 22 1721".

This is an important drawing since it identifies positively the various buildings and locations. It is taken from the rising ground off the present Rothersthorpe Avenue, in the area of Briar Hill.

The road runs down hill to what was then known as Cotton End, and then on, leaving behind the open fields, to the town. On the left the "Meeting House" better known as Castle Hill, and then below it, although not distinguishable, despite the caption, St Peter's church. Holy Sepulchre stands proudly above its surrounding houses and to the right the many gabled front of "Mr Fleetwoods". This was a large house

almost on the scale of a manor house, which began its life as a religious building, housing the White Friars. At the Dissolution much of the friary was demolished, but what remained was incorporated into a large house erected by Sir William Samwell of Upton. Shortly after the Restoration in 1660 the property was acquired by the Fleetwood family who continued to live there till the end of the 18th century, and for whom there are several memorials in Holy Sepulchre church. The size of the house can be appreciated from the drawing, and it was almost certainly here that Duke Cosimo de Medici stayed when he visited Northampton in 1662, and it was to this house that the 2nd Earl of Northampton came, as Recorder for the town, on the day following the disastrous Fire in September 1675, to take command of affairs. It is not clear exactly when the house was demolished, but its disappearance is much to be regretted.

In the centre of the view is the tower of All Saints, and to its right the Sessions House and a number of other large town houses. To the right again the tower of St Giles' church, and further right the windmill noted on the previous view (Plate 169). Just beyond the mill are the trees sheltering "The Wells", that is Vigo Wells, where it had been hoped in 1702 that their chalybeate waters might be sufficient for the establishment of a spa, but the enterprise failed. The site lies to the east of Becket's Park, below the grounds of the Hospital. The name commemorates a battle at Vigo in north-west Spain in 1702, where the combined English and Dutch fleets won a victory against the Spanish and French.

Notes: BL. No.164. 43.5x20.5 cm. Other no: On the front of the drawing 22.

A View of the Country about Northampton taken from the Road between Northampton & Kingsthorpe Sep.ʳ 1721

a. Kingsthorpe Town & Steeple. b. Upton amongst the Trees. c. Duston. d. Dallington. e. Holdenby & Brington at a Distance. f. The River Nen

171. NORTHAMPTON

Title on drawing: *A View of the Country about Northampton taken from the Road between Northampton &*
Kingsthorpe Sepʳ 1721
a. Kingsthorpe Town & Steeple b. Upton amongst the Trees c. Duston d. Dallington e. Holdenby &
Brington at a Distance f. The River Nen

Artist: Unsigned, Peter Tillemans

Date: No precise date is possible, but Bridges' MS Notes record visits to Boughton and Billing at the beginning of September in 1721.

This is another splendid view, highly picturesque and evocative. Here is the true spirit of early Georgian England as we would wish to visualise it. It is taken from the Leicester road, somewhere in the region of Primrose Hill, near the present Roman Catholic Cathedral, looking down into Kingsthorpe Hollow.

In the foreground are horsemen and hounds out exercising taking the road which falls into a deeply wooded valley. Beyond, on the right, is Kingsthorpe with its prominent spire, then to the left, on the skyline, the band of trees denoting Holdenby and Brington "at a Distance". On the left, the trees on the skyline, shelter the tower of Duston church, and below in the valley is Dallington. Lower still in the valley is the northern tributary of the River Nene, its banks lined with pollarded willows.

While most of the letters in the caption denoting the places mentioned above are distinguishable, that marking Upton is not.

Notes: BL. No.166. 46x22.5 cm.

172. NORTHAMPTON

Title on drawing: *The Western View of the Town of Northampton taken above Kingsthorpe July 1721*

Artist: Unsigned, Peter Tillemans

Date: Likely to have been drawn on 22 July (see Plate 170).

Perhaps more striking than the buildings in this view is the effect of the field cultivation patterns, and the open aspect of the town. One feels that the churches, especially Holy Sepulchre and All Saints, are just a little exaggerated in scale.

The caption says "above Kingsthorpe", and the location seems to be somewhere in the region of Kingsthorpe Grove School, or even beyond, on what is now the St David's Estate.

To the left is St Giles' church with Hardingstone (?) on the horizon. Centre is the tower of All Saints, with to its left in the trees the Fleetwood mansion. Then beyond a number of large houses which probably marks Sheep Street, and further beyond Holy Sepulchre more houses in the area of what had been the lands of St Andrew's Priory, that is the Grafton Square area today. The windmill stood to the west of what is now Barrack Road and, in the valley, is the area of Kingsthorpe Hollow where there is still some evidence of stone buildings.

The view also shows well the geography of the surrounding countryside, with most notably, on the right, the rising land around Duston, a feature which, since it is now entirely built over, it is easy to forget.

Notes: BL. No.165. 42 x 24.5 cm. Other no: On front of drawing – 23.

173. NORTHAMPTON. All Saints Church

Title on drawing: *All Hallows Northton*

Artist: Unsigned, Peter Tillemans

Date: Probably 1719. Bridges' MS Notes record a visit on 22 July 1719.

Bridges' text:

> The church dedicated to All-Saints, situate about the middle of the town, was begun to be rebuilt after the fire of 1675. in the reign of King Charles II. and completed in the reign of Queen Anne. It consists of a body, north and south ile, and chancel leaded. In the midst is a cupola covered also with lead, and supported within by four pillars of the Ionic order. At the west end is a square tower in which are six bells. On the top of the tower is a small turrit.

This superb drawing shows the church standing proudly within the open piazza created after the 1675 Fire. The churchyard is surrounded by a wall with western and southern gateways. From the west a short avenue of trees gives onto the forecourt of the church, with just a single step up to the portico. The church is faithfully recorded and the only difference today is the smaller clock on the tower and the loss of the sundial above the gable on the south side of the nave. In Bridges' MS Notes is a reference to the statue of King Charles II on the portico being dated 1692 and that it was done "by the most Indifferent hand": an unfortunate reference to the Northampton sculptor John Hunt, who had been apprenticed to Grinling Gibbons. The statue stands there, of course, to record the gift of timber from the Royal Forests for the rebuilding of the town after the Fire.

The churchyard to the east is bounded by more trees. The rather sharp corner of the churchyard closest to the viewer is probably artistic license, since at that corner stood the Conduit and Tillemans may have omitted it to show the architecture of the church better. It is also known that work was being done on the water supply and management of the conduits and perhaps there were "road works" which Tillemans has chosen to ignore!

To the right, on the edge of the drawing, is the Sessions House, with its corner protected by iron railings, and beyond, jutting out, the large house which is now the Judges' Lodgings.

In the background, to left and right, are the town houses of Mercers Row and Wood Hill, giving a good idea of the type of building which had been put up after the 1675 Fire. It is not surprising when one sees this view that Daniel Defoe described Northampton as "the best built town in all this part of England".

The drawing has been squared over in preparation for an engraved plate.

Notes: BL. No.168. 45x28.8 cm. Work on the water system of the town is referred to in C. Markham & J. Cox: *Records of the Borough of Northampton*, Vol. 2, 1898, (pp.258-9). Of the various editions of Defoe, the most attractive is: Daniel Defoe, *A tour through the whole island of Great Britain* (Abridged and edited by P.N. Furbank and W.R. Owens), Yale, 1991, where also (p.211) is the statement: "The great new church, the town-hall, the jayl, and all their public buildings, are the finest in any country town in England, being all new built".

174. NORTHAMPTON. All Saints Church

Title: *All Saints Church Northampton*

Artist: Probably A. Motte

Date: Uncertain.

An outline drawing based on the previous one (Plate 173). Almost certainly this is a drawing prepared during the engraving process. While the architecture is more carefully drawn, the more mechanical approach has robbed the view of its charm.

Notes: BL. No.169. 32.5x28.5 cm.

175. NORTHAMPTON. Castle

Title on drawing: *Northton Castle*

Title on reverse of drawing: *Prospect of Northampton Castle Taken 9 July 1719*

Artist: Unsigned, Peter Tillemans

Bridges' text:

> A little without the west gate stood the castle, upon high ground, overlooking the meadows, S. *James's* abbey, and the country about Duston . . . The Keep was large; and in *Leland's* time bulwarks of earth were raised before the gate . . . The site of it belongs to Sir *Arthur Haselrig,* whose grandfather purchased it of one *Read* soon after the Restoration. In 1662, pursuant to an order of the King and privvy Council, the walls and gates, and part of the castle of *Northampton* were domolished.

The sketch is drawn from a point to the east of the site, alongside the Castle Hill Chapel, whose building with its vestry, is to the left. In the centre, within the left-hand portion of the higher wall of the castle ruins are indicated portions of a tower that survived till the 19th century. Otherwise the site looks very open and regular, and was converted into an orchard a little later, being thus shown on the 1747 plan of the town by Noble and Butlin and where the area is labelled Castle Orchard and Cherry Garden. In the lower enclosure appears a well or spring.

Behind the castle remains, just visible are the houses of St James' End, and on the extreme right the wooded uplands of Duston.

Notes: BL. No167. 31.4x20.6 cm. Other nos: On the reverse is written Num.80 and at the left-hand corner on the front is N.

127

176. NORTHAMPTON. Church of the Holy Sepulchre

Title: No title on drawing

Artist: Unsigned, Peter Tillemans

Date: Probably 1719.

Bridges' text:

> The church dedicated to the honour of the *Holy Sepulchre*, is situate at the north end of the town, is of a circular form, and consists of a body, north and south ile leaded. In the middle is a cupola covered also with lead, and supported by eight pillars of the Tuscan order; each pillar standing at the distance of eight foot from one another, and forming an angle with the pillar next adjoining. At the east end is a chancel with north and south ile, to which you enter the church by an ascent of three steps. At the west end is a broad embattled tower, on which is raised a pyramid spire of eight sides.

A drawing which usefully records the state of the church as it was to remain until the restoration and extension by Sir G.G. Scott in the 1860s. The tower and spire remain as illustrated, but the Round and the rest of the building were quite considerably altered.

The Round preserves its broad flat Norman buttresses and just to the left of the porch one small Norman window, still there today. The other windows in the Round are tall with three lights in the Perpendicular style, and there is another smaller Perpendicular style window above the porch, with a square head. No windows are indicated in the superstructure of the Round, but its pyramidal roof is clear. The Round is entered from the porch, whose outer mouldings appear somewhat irregular, with the right-hand jamb being at variance to the left.

The south aisle has a tiled roof, flat parapet and three large windows in its wall. All are of the Perpendicular style, two under arched heads and one under a square head. The two arched windows are like those in the Round, and under one can be seen a doorway. There were considerable alterations to this aisle in the 18th century since an engraving of 1784 shows it with just two windows, one at either end of the aisle. The doorway is still there but with no window above. Furthermore, on the engraving there is no tracery shown in the windows and it is likely that this was removed and the windows given clear glass to accord with the Georgian refitting of the interior. When Scott restored the church he rebuilt the aisle in his favourite Geometrical Decorated style.

Notes: BL. No.170. 39.5x25 cm. Other no: on reverse is written Numb.11 aa. Copies of the 1784 engraving are in the collection of Northamptonshire Libraries.

177. NORTHAMPTON. Church of the Holy Sepulchre

Title on drawing: *Draught of the Cross of Stone set in the Wall of a Cottage on the W^s in St Sepulchres Church Yard*

Artist: Unsigned, Peter Tillemans

This sculpture is of uncertain origin and date, but it clearly represents the Crucifixion and is probably the top of a churchyard cross or finial of a gable.

Presently it stands on a window-sill inside the Church.

Notes: BL. No.172. 12x6.5 cm. Other no: On the front of drawing the letter D.

178. NORTHAMPTON. Church of the Holy Sepulchre *(right)*

Title on drawing: *2 of ye 8 Pillars in ye Church of St Pulchre*

Artist: Unsigned, Peter Tillemans

Date: Uncertain. In Bridges' MS Notes there is a set of measurements of the church, its pillars etc. dated 24 July 1718, and elsewhere a note: The Dimensions of wch Pillars & Arches were taken by – Marriot.

A simple drawing recording a portion of the Round with two of the Norman pillars supporting their later Gothic arches. The detailing of the capitals is carefully represented.

Notes: BL. No.171. 25x19 cm. Other nos: On reverse is written Numb. 12 and at the bottom left-hand corner is written E.

179. NORTHAMPTON. St Giles' Church

Title on reverse of drawing: *South Prospect of St Gyles Church in Northampton taken 9 July 1719*

Artist: Unsigned, Peter Tillemans

Bridges' text:

> At the East end of the town is the church dedicated to S. *Giles*, consisting of a Body, North and South ile, and chancel, with a cross ile from North to South, all leaded. In the middle between the church and chancel is a square embattled Tower, with a Pinnacle and Weathercock at each corner.

A small drawing but despite its simplicity of some interest. It shows the church in fact from the north, not the south as the caption states, and like that of Holy Sepulchre it shows the church before restoration and enlargement in Victorian times. The main differences today concern the length of the nave and aisles: two further bays were added to the west end in 1853. As Bridges' text states, all the roofs are lead and have parapets. The central tower is as rebuilt in 1616 following the collapse of its predecessor, and the windows of the clerestory probably date from then also. The eastern north chapel has a curious arrangement of windows, probably due to rebuilding in 1512, when money was left to the church for that purpose.

Beyond the church is a view of the Nene valley looking across the fields, emphasising the position of the church right on the edge of the built area of the town.

Notes: BL. No.174. 15.8x20.2 cm. Other no: On front is written F. On reverse is also a light pencil sketch of a church spire, indistinct, but perhaps Kettering,

180. NORTHAMPTON. St Thomas' Hospital

Title: None on drawing

Artist: Unsigned, Peter Tillemans

Date: Probably 1719.

Bridges' text:

> Southward of St. *John*'s is the hospital dedicated to the memory of S. *Thomas Beckett*, founded and endowed by the citizens of *Northampton* about 1450, for the poor of the said town.

Another fine record of a long lost building. It shows the late Perpendicular facade, with its distinctive ogee arched window, niches and quatrefoil frieze. The central window is unusual in that the central mullion rises right to the apex of the arch, and its ogee shaped head can be paralleled at Canons Ashby church and the Bedehouse at Higham Ferrers. The niches have intricate decoration and that of the top shelters a statue of the patron saint.

The building survived till 1874 when it was swept away to make way for an access road to the Cattlemarket from Bridge Street, and its disappearance is much to be regretted.

A rather clumsy engraving based on the drawing is included in a composite plate in Bridges' published text (Vol.1 p.447).

Notes: BL. No.173. 24x15 cm. Other no: On the front of the drawing is written M.

Spilbur

G

181. NORTHAMPTON. St Peter's Church

Title: None on drawing

Artist: Unsigned, Peter Tillemans

Date: Probably 1719, and in Bridges' MS Notes a visit on 16 September of that year is noted.

Bridges' text:

> At a little distance from the west bridge is the church dedicated to St. Peter, consisting of a body, north and south ile, and chancel leaded, the two iles extending as far as the chancel. At the west end is a low antique embattled tower, in which are four bells. The tower is adorned with rows of small arches, and neat tracery work that incircles the western door.

The drawing is another good record of the appearance of the church, almost as it remains today. The tower is faithfully recorded with its rows of arcading and ornament. While Bridges describes the ornamental arches on its west face as encircling a doorway, the drawing shows these in their present position, over the west window: it is considered that they did originally form the decoration of a doorway and it is perhaps some memory of this that Bridges is recording. It is known that the tower collapsed in the early 17th century and was rebuilt eastwards of its original position, and the loss of the west doorway and the debased Perpendicular style windows in the aisles, all date from then. The aisle windows appear to have been blocked in the lower sections. The lead roofs referred to by Bridges are hidden by low parapets, but the water spouts issuing from them are prominent.

Notes: BL. No. 175. 30x23 cm. Other no: On reverse is written Numb.53 aa.

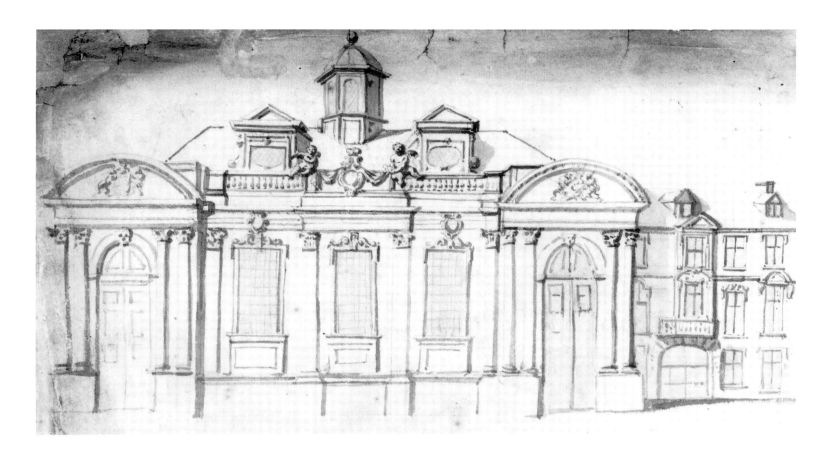

182. NORTHAMPTON. Sessions House

Title on drawing: *The Sessions House at Northton wᵗʰ yᵉ Prison adjoining*

Title on reverse of drawing: *Prospect of the Sessions House and Prison adjoining at Northampton taken 31 July 1719*

Artist: Unsigned, Peter Tillemans

Bridges' text:

> To the south-east of *All-Hallows* church is an handsome house built by Sir *William Haselwood*, and sold by him to the Justices of peace, who have applied it to the purposes of a county-gaol. Adjoining to it on the east is the Sessions-house, a very elegant structure and curiously ornamented.

This again is a most useful drawing showing these buildings as originally conceived. The Sessions House survives largely as shown here, save for the unfortunate removal of the cupola and dormers – how much they add to the appearance of the building.

The building to the right began its life as the town house of the Haselwood family from Maidwell and dates like the Sessions House from the late 1670s following rebuilding after the 1675 Fire. It is very typical of the style of many of the town's buildings of that date and shows the influence of the architect who directed the rebuilding of the town, Henry Bell of Kings Lynn. Indeed this facade is very similar in detail to the Duke's Head Inn at Lynn also by Bell, most notably for the scrolled pediments to the windows, almost a signature of the architect. Also clear is the original form of the windows with their cross-mullion and transom tracery and leaded casements.

This facade was completely rebuilt in 1845 and given more of a Palladian effect.

Notes: BL. No.176. 32x20 cm. Scrolled pediments like those on the Sessions House and the Gaol are found not only at Kings Lynn, but also in the courtyard of Kimbolton Castle (also attributed to Bell) and on the facade of the former Rectory at Ecton (*i.e.* Ecton House). A later use, *c.*1710, can be seen at Cottesbrooke Hall (Plate 43). For Henry Bell, see *Colvin*.

183. NORTHAMPTON. The Guildhall

Title: None on drawing

Artist: Unsigned, Peter Tillemans

Date: Probably 1719.

Bridges' text:

> Southward of the market-place is the old conduit, erected in 1478. and supplied with water brought to it in pipes from the spring called the conduit-head, in the field on the east of the town. Over this conduit was antiently an hall, in which several trades, who had constitutions or companies, were used to meet, for the regulation of offences committed to the injury of their business, and against their respective constitutions.

This is the building which preceded the building of the present Guildhall in 1864. It is one of the few buildings which survived the 1675 Fire, only its outside staircase having to be rebuilt.

The main room is clearly on the first floor and retains its medieval windows, entrance doorway and corner buttresses. Bridges quotes the date 1478, but the windows have the appearance of tracery at least a hundred years earlier than that, and perhaps it is the upper floor and battlement parapet which dates from then.

The ground floor was used as a prison prior to the acquisition of the Haselwood house (see Plate 182). It is not easy to be sure just what is represented at the right hand end of the ground floor lean-to, but probably a number of shops or booths of timber construction, and perhaps related to access to water supply, as alluded to by Bridges' text.

It seems extraordinary that this building survived till 1864 and then was demolished. It stood at the corner of Wood Hill and Abington Street: a tragic loss.

Notes: BL. No.177. 31.5x20 cm.

185. NORTHAMPTON. Queen Eleanor's Cross *(right)*

Title on drawing: No title, except the hundred name *Spelhoe*

Artist: Unsigned, Peter Tillemans

Bridges' text:

> See previous drawing (Plate 169).

This splendid drawing shows the details of the Cross admirably. It also records the restoration of the cross effected in 1713 when the Quarter Sessions voted "a Sume not exceeding £30" towards repairs. The top stage of the cross was probably rebuilt and at the summit a tall *cross pattée* was fixed, with sundials against each cardinal face. Further, lesser, repairs were carried out in 1762, but much of what we see here existed till 1840 when the architect Edward Blore undertook a restoration to recreate the medieval appearance. The *cross pattée* was removed, together with the sundials and other 18th century additions and the summit given its present broken column finial.

Notes: BL. No.178. 30x20 cm. Further discussion of the history of the cross occurs in Christopher Markham: *The Stone Crosses of the County of Northampton*, London, 1901, pp.8-14, and a more recent survey is contained in D. Parsons (ed.) *Eleanor of Castile 1290-1990. Essays to Commemorate the 700th Anniversary of her death : 28 November 1290*, Stamford, Paul Watkins, 1991.

184. NORTHAMPTON. All Saints Church. The Conduit *(above)*

Title on drawing: *Draught of the Conduit near All St Church in Northton Taken 9 July 1719*

Artist: Unsigned, Peter Tillemans

This is a useful record of this vanished structure. It stood just to the south-west of All Saints church, attached to a corner of the churchyard (see note to Plate 173). It takes the form of an octagonal tower with cusped arched divisions, carrying a double parapet with architectural decorations: a series of quatrefoils, some with shields within them. On top is a coronet of pinnacles. There is no indication of access to the spring which it covers.

The conduit was damaged in a storm in 1815, when its pinnacles were removed, and survived till 1831.

Notes: BL. No.179. 16x10 cm. Other no: On front is written B. A full discussion of the conduit is given in C. Markham & J. C. Cox, *Northampton Borough Records*, Vol.II, 1878. (pp.252-60), and there is further information in R.M. Serjeantson, *History of the Church of All Saints*, Northampton, 1910 (pp.302-3), where there are illustrations of the church with conduit in position in the late 18th century and its post-1815 appearance. The late Victor Hatley suggested that known work on the water supply from the conduit around 1719 may have resulted in partial demolition of the structure, perhaps explaining this rather sketchy representation.

186. NORTHAMPTON. Ancient seal

Title on drawing: *From an Impression in Wax drawn by A. Motte 1719*

Below the title is written *Dr Maine of Northton 1719 No.126*

Artist: Andrew Motte

The figure within the seal clearly alludes to St. Andrew and the seal is probably therefore related to the Priory of that dedication which stood on the north-west side of the old town. It is not easy to decipher the lettering around the seal, but it seems to read: s:ilici:de:ltat incat:norhm.

Notes: BL. No.182. 8x10.2 cm. Other no: On the front of the drawing is written a letter O.

187. NORTHAMPTON. Ancient seal

Title on drawing: *Mr Vertue drew this from an Impression of a Seale in ye hands of Tho. Rawlinson Esqr*

Artist: Presumably George Vertue

Date: Uncertain, but probably 1719.

The inscription round the seal reads: sigillum sancte crucis in umro Norhamtonie.

Notes: BL. No.181. 23x17 cm. Other no: On the front of the drawing is written P.

189. NORTHAMPTON. All Saints Church *(below right)*

Title: None on drawing

Artist: Thomas Eayre

Date: Uncertain.

This is a page of notes and sketches done to indicate the details of the portico of the church. It has a caption and below is written a further instruction by Eayre which indicates that these details had been drawn to assist the engraver in preparing a plate.

The caption is self explanatory:

> I have here More at Large Shown the form of ye Urns and of ye Banisters –
>
> No.1. the forme of all ye Urns 2. The Banisters above ye Columns and there is 10 in Each pt. 3. The Banisters on ye Topp of ye Tower – and 15 in Each Side ye Tower 4. The Vain or Weathercock
>
> I have omitted ye Shadows within ye Columns Mr Tillemans having already dun these If Mr Motte Keeps Strictly to Mr Tillemans drawing in all other Respects he may depend on its being good Tho Eayre

This note is valuable in verifying the larger drawing is by Tillemans and also giving an idea of the mechanics of turning one of his drawings into an engraved plate.

Notes: BL. No.180. 30x13.5 cm.

188. NORTHAMPTON. All Saints Church *(right)*

Title on drawing: *Port' Allhallows*

Artist: Unsigned, but probably A. Motte

Date: Uncertain.

Another careful outline drawing with detailed rendering of the balustrades, urns, Ionic capitals, etc. of the portico of the church. Probably put together using the notes made by Thomas Eayre (see Plate 189).

Notes: BL. No.180. 27.5x13.5 cm.

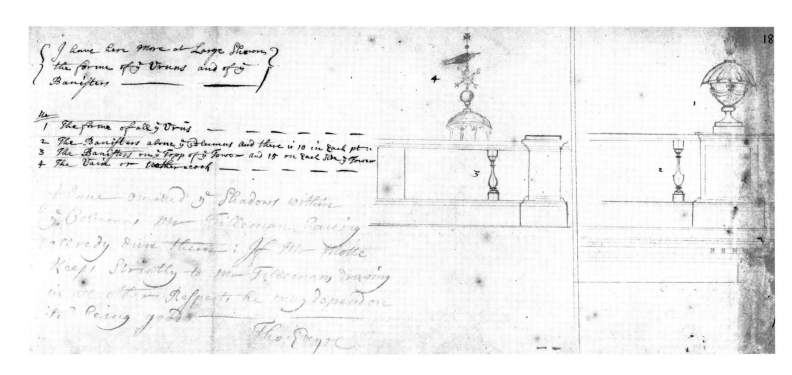

The Church at Norborough and Claypoles Chapel taken 31 July 1721

190. NORTHBOROUGH

Title on drawing: *The Church at Norborough and Claypoles Chapel taken 31 July 1721*

Artist: Unsigned, Peter Tillemans

Bridges' text:

> The church, dedicated to S. *Andrew*, consists of a body, north and south ile, and chancel covered with lead. The nave is raised, with windows on each side, above the iles. At the end of the south ile is a chapel, carried on beyond the ile, called *Cleypole*'s ile or chancel. The chancel of the church advances eastward beyond *Cleypole*'s ile, which is embattled, and hath a low round pyramidal tower at the east and west corner.

A good view of this church. It still has a somewhat bizarre appearance with the diminutive main building overshadowed by the ostentatious Claypole chapel. Perhaps the turrets had larger roofs than they do today – or is this just Tillemans' sense of exaggeration?

The main church is a good example of an early 13th century church, with its narrow buttresses, bellcote and Geometrical tracery in its aisle windows. The immense south chapel was originally built by the Delamere family *c.*1330-40 and is a splendid example of late Decorated architecture. The way it juxtaposes the church suggests that it might have been intended as a total rebuilding project, never completed. The window tracery is an uncommon form showing the florid Decorated beginning to turn towards Perpendicular, so as well as flowing shapes there are plenty of vertical lines. This is especially true of the south window of the chapel, barely visible in the drawing. The whole chapel is crested by battlements set on a stringcourse holding ballflower ornament. The turrets contain staircases which give access to the roof.

The Claypole family acquired Northborough manor in the 16th century, and later members of the family claim some historical note, since Oliver Cromwell's daughter married into the family, his widow living at the manor house.

The buildings on either side of the church are an interesting contrast. On the left is a simple thatched cottage with few windows, while on the right is a substantial stone house with leaded windows and a tiled roof ending in a gable topped by a finial. There is a walled garden with access into the churchyard. This is not the manor house, which stands some way to the west of the church, but probably the vicarage.

Notes: BL. No.162. 40x27.5 cm. Other no: On front of drawing – 33.

191. OAKLEY, LITTLE *(left)*

Title on drawing: *Wm Mountague Esqr^s Monument on the North side the Chancel of Little Ocley Church 4 Augt 1719*

Artist: Unsigned, Peter Tillemans

Bridges' text:

> A little lower, on the same wall, is a monument of the Composite Order, supported by two pillars gilt and painted. Under an arch is a man, habited in a cloke, in the attitude of prayer.

Here we have the monument of William Montagu d.1619. It is an elaborate and large mural monument, having been erected in 1620 by Montagu's nephew, Sir Edward of Boughton, later to become 1st Baron Montagu. There is considerable use of cherubs as ornamentation: there are two reclining on the pediment, two more within the spandrels of the niche arch, and another, holding a skull and hourglass, within the base pendant. The figure is somewhat over dominant and aptly deserves its description in *Pevsner:* "a big kneeler"!

Notes: BL. No.183. 31.5x19.5 cm. Other no: On the front is written A.

192. OAKLEY, LITTLE *(right)*

Title on drawing: *A Stone Monument in y^e Chancell of Little Okeley Church next to y^e Monum^t of W^m. Montagu Esq^e w^thout any Inscription*

Artist: Unsigned, Peter Tillemans

Date: Without much doubt the same as the previous drawing, that is 4 August 1719, a date which is confirmed in Bridges' MS Notes as a visit.

Bridges' text:

> Against the north wall of the chancel is a free-stone monument of the Doric order, projecting from the wall, and raised on three pedestals, each of which supports two fluted columns . . . *[Bridges then describes the heraldry]* . . . There does not appear to have been any inscription on this monument; which is supposed to be that of *William Markham* Esq. and *Elizabeth* his wife, who both died within two years of each other, and were buried in this church.

This is one of a series of memorials of similar design dating from the last decades of the 16th century, another example being in the north aisle of Fawsley church to various members of the Knightley family and probably dating from *c.*1573. All have a combination of carefully rendered architecture mixed with hybrid Renaissance decoration, using strapwork and grotesques. Distinctive on this monument are the pedestals of the columns and the curious pediment with scallop shell centre and strange clawed leg supports (almost indentical clawed supports occur at Fawsley). The workmanship also relates to two monuments at Fotheringhay (1573) (Plate 108) and to carved work at Deene Park (1571).

The manor of Oakley had come into the Cave family in Elizabethan times, when Elizabeth, daughter of Sir Edward Montagu of Boughton had married Sir Richard Cave. After his death in 1560 she married William Markham. It would be appropriate that the monument is to their memory, she having died in 1569 and he in 1571. It is not without significance to find another monument of the same type for one of the Caves (1568) at Stanford on Avon.

Notes: BL. No.184. 31.5x20 cm. Other nos: On reverse is written Num:94 and on the front the letter B.

Polebrook

View of the Town Church and Bridge of Oundle taken in Ascheton Field to the North

193. OUNDLE

Title on drawing: *View of the Town Church and Bridge of Oundle taken in Ascheton Field to the North*

Artist: Unsigned, Peter Tillemans

Date: Uncertain. Bridges' MS Notes record visits to Oundle on 7 October 1719 and 25 August 1721, and another view of the town is dated 4 August 1721. August 1721 seems the most likely, although the numbering sequence suggests 1719.

Bridges' text:

> *OUNDLE*, in domesday-book, and the earliest records, written *Undele*, on the east and south is bounded by the *Nyne* . . . Here are about three hundred and fifty families. The principal streets are *New-street*, all of stone houses covered with slate, *North*-end and *Chapel*-end . . . Over the stream, leading from *Oundle* to *Ashton*, is the north bridge, of which *Ashton* repairs one half, and *Oundle* the other.

This is another choice drawing by Tillemans, with his delight in activity. Central, like a cathedral, rises the spire of the church, and among the houses can be seen the roofs of several grand mansions. Looking almost like part of the church itself is, as Bridges' text notes: "the manor-house, in which Captain *Hunt* resides . . . called the Berystead", and to the left of the church the roof chimneys and dormers of Cobthorne (see next plate). Beyond this is a windmill and then in front the long causeway over the Nene, with its series of archways going back to the medieval period.

Over the causeway proceeds a coach with outrider, and in the field a shepherd leans upon his crook guarding his flock.

Notes: BL. No.185. 53.5x20 cm. Other nos: On the front, in pencil, is written 23, and on the reverse is written Numb.36.

View of Oundle to the South taken in the Meadows. 4 Aug 1721

194. OUNDLE

Title on drawing: *View of Oundle to the South taken in the Meadows 4 Aug 1721*

Artist: Unsigned, Peter Tillemans

Bridges' text:

. . . here are several other good houses, particularly Major *John Creed*'s, built some time before the Restoration by Major *Butler*, who brought the joists and beams from Liveden. It stands high, and descends with good gardens down to the river.

Another good prospect of the town. On the left is the Barnwell bridge, and on the edge of the town the series of garden plots stretching down towards the river. In the centre is the garden front of Cobthorne, one of Oundle's finest houses, noted in Bridges' text. The house was built in the 1650s and is an impressive example from that time, comparable to Thorpe Hall, near Peterborough (Plate 155). The drawing shows the typical cross-mullion and transom windows of the period and its impressive flight of chimneystacks. In its garden is an avenue of trees.

Beyond to the right, rising above the houses, is the spire of the church, and just beyond that more roofs, one topped by a cupola. The latter was formerly above the house on the corner of the Square and St. Osyth's Lane and would have given access to the flat roof of that house.

Notes: BL. No.186. 45x28.5 cm. The reference to Major Butler using the beams from Lyveden New Build is worth noting, although examination of the structure by the Royal Commission on Historical Monuments team in the early 1990s did not reveal any evidence of re-used timbers.

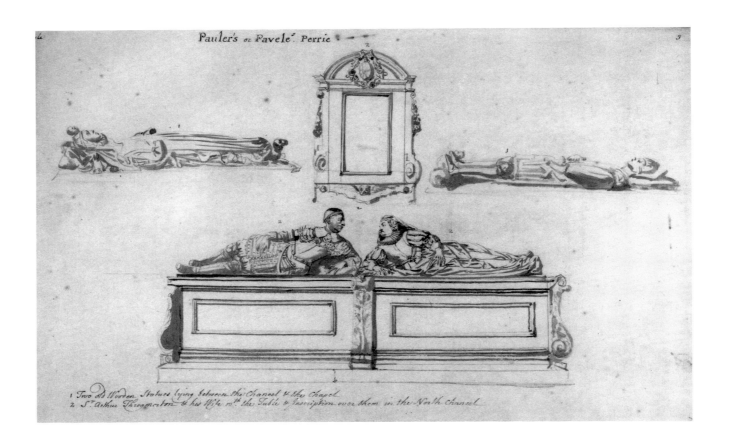

1 Two old Wooden Statues lying between the Chancel & the Chapel
2 Sʳ Arthur Throgmorton & his Wife wᵗʰ the Table & Inscription over them in the North Chancel

195. PAULERSPURY

Title on drawing: *Pauler's or Paveleˢ Perrie*

> *1. Two old Wooden Statues lying between the Chancel & the Chapel 2. Sʳ Arthur Throgmorton & his Wife wᵗʰ the Table & Inscription over them in the North Chancel*

Artist: Unsigned, Peter Tillemans

Date: Probably 1721, and Bridges' MS Notes record a visit in July 1721.

Bridges' text:

> The church, dedicated to S. *James*, consists of a body, north and south ile, chancel, and south-porch, leaded. At the west end is a broad embattled tower, in which are five bells . . . Under the upper arch between the chancel and burial place, upon an altar monument of free stone covered with wood, are the effigies of a man and a woman, with a child between them, carved in wood. On each side of the tomb were shields of arms, but these are now defaced, nor is there any inscription visible . . . At the west end of the burial-place is an elegant altar monument of white marble inlaid with black. Upon the tomb are represented the effigies of a man and his wife, looking at each other, the man in armour curiously cut out of freestone, and reposing his left arm on a pillow, and the Lady resting her right arm upon her veil . . ." [inscriptions also quoted].

The wooden effigies described by Bridges appear either side the plaque. Nearly all surviving examples date from the early 14th century and Northamptonshire has a goodly number in its churches. The knight is shown wearing a bascinet helmet, camail, cyclas and partial armour, while the lady has the usual flowing gown with a wimple headdress.

The larger tomb is that of Arthur Throckmorton and his wife, Mary, erected in 1626. It is an unusual design with the figures reclining and gazing at each other over their shoulders and is an excellent piece of carving. It is rare to find figures in freestone at this date, and while the use of stone might suggest a local hand, the quality suggests a London sculptor. The inscription plaque was originally on the wall above the tomb, but when the church was restored in Victorian times this was removed to a side wall and a window, which had been blocked to take the plaque, was reopened: a well-meaning act which unfortunately detracts from the effect of the tomb.

Notes: BL. No.187. 45x28.5 cm. Other no: On the front of drawing is written 3.

196. PETERBOROUGH

Title: No title on drawing

Artist: Signed by Thomas Eayre

Date: Uncertain. Thomas Eayre was measuring distances on 28 August 1721, so this date is a possibility.

A good example of Thomas Eayre's surveying, with his usual precise delineation of detail. The plan brings out well the way the city plan has developed around the Market Place and St. John's church, and the road down to the river. The Cathedral and its cloistral buildings are quite separate, with much evidence of orchards, and the hamlet to the east of the Cathedral shows the trend of the city to develop in that direction. The main stretch of the River Nene, then navigable easily to Peterborough, has a small tributary with narrow canals giving access closer to the city.

There is a sequence of numbers applied to the plan (Nos. 1 to 59) but there is no key to these nor was the plan engraved for the printed text. The caption alongside the bridge reads *The Place where St. Matthews or Bridge fare is kept*.

Notes: BL. No.188. 40x28.5 cm.

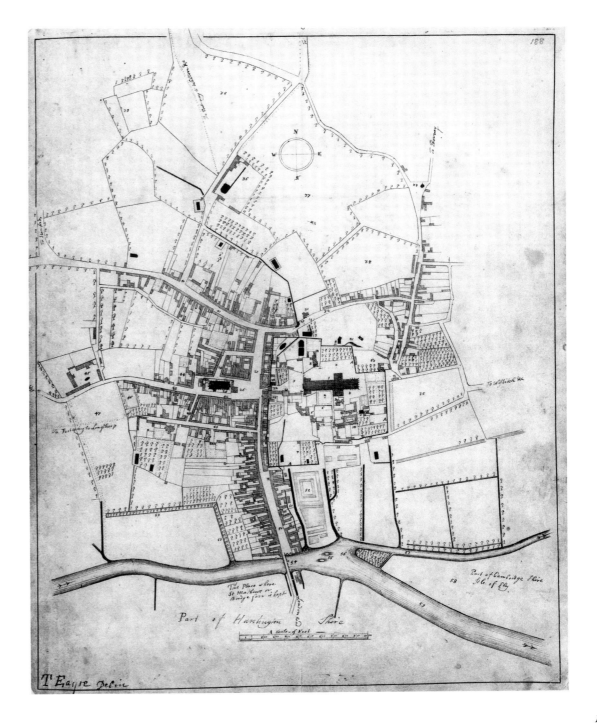

197. PETERBOROUGH

Title: No title on drawing

Artist: Unsigned, Peter Tillemans

Date: Probably 1719. In Bridges' MS Notes there are remarks on Peterborough dated August 1719 but also notes dated August 1721.

Bridges' text:

> The city of *Peterburgh* is situated on the northern bank of the Nyne . . . In *Peterburgh* are about four hundred houses, and thirty-two within the Minster precincts.
>
> *[There is a long extended description following, Bridges' Vol.II, pp.537-545]*

A highly decorative drawing showing the city from the south-east.

Far left is the bridge, a somewhat rickety looking timber structure, and in front of it boats and barges loaded with goods. In the centre of the town is the church of St. John with a thin narrow spire, or, as described in Bridges' text; "A pyramid shaft covered with lead". Close to the church a large building with dormers represents the Market House with to its right a tall standard denoting the Market Place and its cross. Finally the Cathedral, standing proudly above the cloistral buildings. From these, orchards and plantations run down to the river.

This prospect drawing was to form the origin of several others of varying detail.

Notes: BL. No.189. 80.5x26.5 cm. Other no: On the reverse is written Numb.58.

198. PETERBOROUGH

Title: No title on drawing

Artist: Unsigned, Peter Tillemans

Date: Probably 1719.

This seems to be a worked up drawing based on the previous view (Plate 197). It follows it in every respect but has additional human interest, typical of Tillemans' delight in activity in his prospects. There are strolling figures on the banks of the river, two rowing boats with passengers and an agricultural labourer returning from his toils with his rake over his shoulder.

Notes: BL. No.190. 42.5x13.5 cm.

199. PETERBOROUGH

Title: No title on drawing

Artist: Uncertain, but perhaps Andrew Motte

Date: Uncertain.

This is a smaller version of the prospect view (Plate 197) which is attributed to Tillemans. This version is little more than a mechanical transmission of the original and therefore could easily be Motte aiming towards an engraved plate.

Notes: BL. No.191. 29x7 cm.

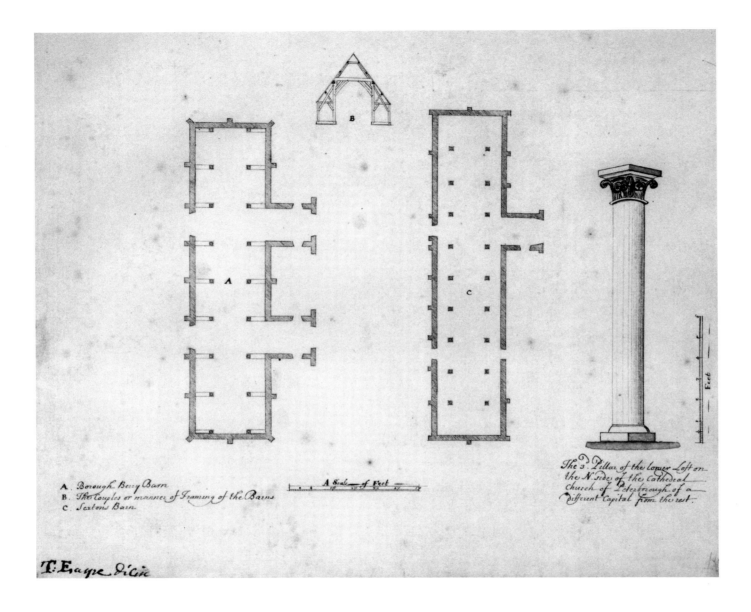

A. Borough Berry Barn
B. The Couples or manner of Framing of the Barns
C. Sexton Barn

A Scale of Feet

The 3. Pillar of the lower Loft on the N. side of the Cathedral Church of Peterborough of a different Capital from the rest.

T. Eayre dicin

200. PETERBOROUGH

Title on drawing: *A. Borough Berry Barn B. The Couples or manner of Framing of the Barns C. Sexton Barn. The 3ᵈ Pillar of the lower Left on the N. side of the Cathedral Church of Peterborough of a different Capital from the rest*

Artist: Signed by Thomas Eayre

Date: Uncertain, but there are notes on the Cathedral dated 1 August 1721.

Bridges' text:

> Farther on is *Burghberry* barn, standing on a moated ground of about four acres, where there is an horse pond, and a ditch for water passing through the middle.

> *[Bridges' text then gives dimensions]*

An interesting record of two large tithe barns which were situated on the western side of the city. They can be identified on Eayre's plan (Plate 196) where the Borough Bury Barn is on the north-west edge of the city (in numbered plot 36) and Sexton Barn is on the western edge of the city (in numbered plot 45).

Both of these barns existed till *c.*1900 but then were demolished – a great loss since they were excellent examples of their type, similar to those that still stand at Glastonbury, for example. Since both barns seem to have had similar roof structures, they were probably of the same date, some time during the 15th century.

The drawing again declares Eayre's keen archaeological observation.

Notes: BL. No.192. 48x30 cm.Both barns are described in Sir Henry Dryden, *Two Barns at Peterborough formerly belonging to the Abbey*, 1898. (Copy in the collection of Northamptonshire Libraries.)

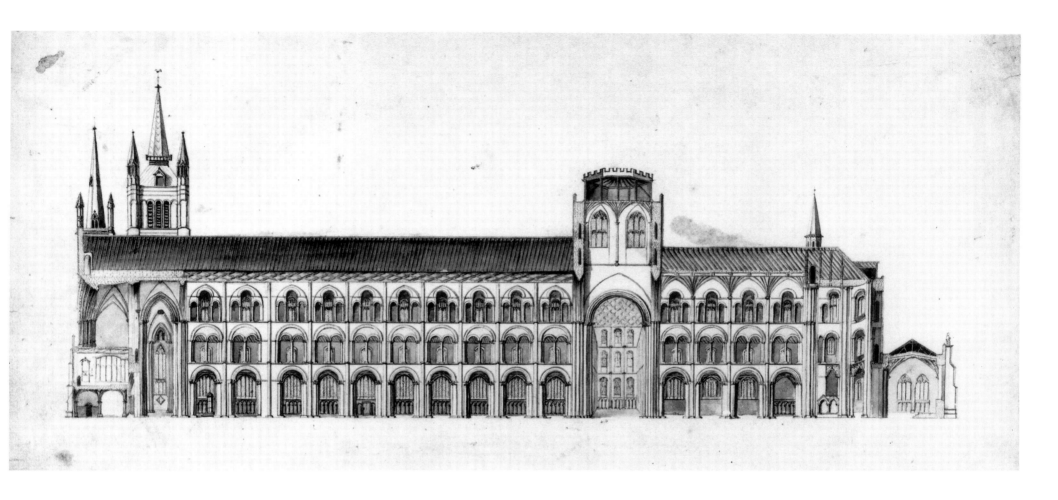

201. PETERBOROUGH

Title: No title on drawing
Artist: Thomas Eayre *(Signed)*
Date: Uncertain.

A finely drawn section of the Cathedral, taken from west to east across the sheet. It is a good example of Eayre working within strict architectural limits and, with his surveyor's hand, producing a drawing of distinction, and one that would have reproduced well as an engraving.

Notes: BL. No.193. 43.5x33.5 cm.

202. PETERBOROUGH

Title: None on drawing

Artist: Unsigned, but probably Thomas Eayre

Date: Uncertain.

A large view of the north side of the Cathedral. It is a little rough in execution and a little mechanical in draughtsmanship, hence the attribution to Eayre.

Notes: BL. No.194. 48x33.5 cm.

203. PETERBOROUGH

Title: None on drawing

Artist: Uncertain, but either by Eayre or Motte

Date: Uncertain.

This is a smaller and more finished version of the previous drawing (Plate 202), and has all the appearance of a pre-engraving drawing, so is likely to be by Motte rather than Eayre.

On the reverse is written:

> *Mem.I. The height of that part of the Roof of the Church that is marked a b to reach no higher than the dotted line. Mem.II. The Pyramid that is marked all round with dots to be finish'd no higher than the black line drawn across it. the rest being very faintly express'd with dots or points, to shew that there had been such a Pyramid formerly, tho not at present.*

This memorandum, which is in Eayre's hand, refers to the south-east turret of the larger north-west tower, where a spire is shown, but which no longer exists.

Notes: BL. No.195. 29x20.5 cm.

204. PETERBOROUGH

Title: No title on drawing

Artist: Unsigned, Peter Tillemans

Date: Uncertain, but probably 1721. A visit is recorded in Bridges' MS Notes during August 1721, and the following drawing (Plate 205) is dated 1 August.

A fine large drawing showing the eastern aspect of the Cathedral with the New Building and above it the choir apse and side chapels.

Notes: BL. No.196. 24.5x22 cm.
Other no: The drawing is labelled T.

205. PETERBOROUGH

Title on drawing: *The East end of Peterborough Minster taken 1 Augt. 1721*

Artist: Unsigned, Peter Tillemans

Another fine drawing showing the New Building with the apse and choir above. Well drawn Perpendicular tracery, decorative parapets and statuary finials all add to the effect.

Notes: BL. No.197. 27.8x29.8 cm. Other no: On the front of the drawing is written 34.

The East end of Peterborough Minster taken 1. Aug. 1721

206. PETERBOROUGH

Title: No title on drawing

Artist: Unsigned, Peter Tillemans

Date: While the other drawings seem to be August 1721, the numbers on this one suggest 1719, and there was a visit to Peterborough in August 1719 according to Bridges' MS Notes.

A splendid wash drawing showing all the detail of the West Front of the Cathedral, most carefully drawn. Little of the main facade has changed, but the towers are somewhat different. The taller of the north-west towers has a rather uncomfortable spire which had been added during the 17th century, while the side towers show signs of decay with broken pinnacles. All was made regular and correct when the Cathedral was restored by J.L. Pearson in the 1880s.

Notes: BL. No.198. 50.5x39 cm. Other no: On the reverse is written Num.66.

207. PETERBOROUGH

Title: None on drawing

Artist: Unsigned, Peter Tillemans

Date: Uncertain.

A superb drawing of the interior of the Cathedral choir. The architecture is as we know it today, but the fittings have all been changed.

On each side of the choir are banked two levels of stalls, these being a combination of some medieval traceried fronts and some plain panelled fronts. Behind are round arched canopied stalls with over and behind them medieval traceried screens. Painted designs are apparent and some of this work had survived from a refitting of the choir in the 1230s under Bishop Walter of Bury. It was a combination of Old and New Testament extracts with Royal symbols – leopards and crowned Ms. The medieval stalls were largely destroyed in 1643 and what can be seen here is the 17th century adaptation of what survived. In 1828 the stalls were removed but two still exist, resited in the North Transept. The 17th century three-decker pulpit can also be seen, and in the centre of the choir is the splendid eagle lectern given to the Cathedral *c.*1480 by Abbot Ramsey, and fortunately still extant.

Beyond is a classical reredos with on either side paintings, and the floor appears a simple stone paving.

Notes: BL. No.199. 54x42.5 cm.

208. PETERBOROUGH

Title: No title on drawing
Artist: Unsigned, Peter Tillemans
Date: Uncertain.

Another splendid drawing showing the Nave of the Cathedral from the west end. The building is open and free of seats and the familiar Norman architecture is serene.

The Choir is divided from the Nave by a Gothic pulpitum which is surmounted by an organ. Above can be seen the painted ceiling which remains one of the glories of the Cathedral.

Notes: BL. No.200. 56x44 cm.

209. PETERBOROUGH

Title: None on drawing

Artist: Probably Andrew Motte

Date: Uncertain.

This is a reduced version of the previous drawing (Plate 208) and probably represents a version prepared for engraving.

Notes: BL. No.201. 28.7x32.4 cm.

210. PETERBOROUGH

Title: No title on drawing
Artist: Unsigned, Peter Tillemans
Date: Uncertain.

Another good drawing showing the view along the North Choir aisle, looking from the New Building at the east end. The fan vault of the New Building, a triumph built for Abbot Kirkton *c.*1500, is clear, and beyond that the groined vault of the Norman aisle. There are stone benches along the wall under the windows. On the left is the mural monument for Bishop Cumberland (d.1718), one of the few known works by the sculptor Thomas Green of Camberwell.

Notes: BL. No.202. 36x28 cm. For Green of Camberwell see *Gunnis.*

211. PETERBOROUGH

Title: No title on drawing

Artist: Unsigned, Peter Tillemans

Date: Uncertain.

Another good drawing of the apse of the choir looking into the New Building. The ceiling of the apse is clear, a survival from the 14th century, with medallions containing Biblical figures and other patterns. Some of the Norman arches have Perpendicular tracery within them. Looking through to the New Building, we see it as it was fitted up in the late 17th century as the Cathedral Library. Beyond the central arch we see seated at a table a figure – one of Bridges' researchers, perhaps?

Notes: BL. No.203. 48.5x42.8 cm.

212. PETERBOROUGH

Title: None on drawing

Artist: Unsigned, but probably Andrew Motte

Date: Uncertain.

A reduced and simplified version of the last drawing (Plate 211), once again a preparation for an engraving.

Notes: BL. No.204. 29.2x24.5 cm.

213. PETERBOROUGH

Title: No title on drawing

Artist: Unsigned, but probably Andrew Motte

Date: Uncertain.

This is a composite drawing clearly done in preparation for an engraved plate. It incorporates a number of views which occur as separate drawings, but not all are so represented in the collection today.

At the top are four of the 13th century monuments (Plate 222); then there are five divisions with details of statuary, etc: then a row with three of the Minster gateways; then two views of the Infirmary (Plates 215 and 216); and finally a view of the Cloisters.

Notes: BL. No.205. 26.4x21 cm.

214. PETERBOROUGH

Title: No title on drawing

Artist: Unsigned, Peter Tillemans

Date: Uncertain.

This is another example of Tillemans' accurate recording of both architecture, decoration and heraldry. It shows the Deanery Gateway, built by Abbot Kirkton *c*.1500, with its large opening for vehicles and smaller archway for pedestrians. The large arch is closed by heavily panelled doors and in its spandrels can be seen the carvings of the arms of the See and Chapter of Peterborough: cross keys and cross crosslets, and cross swords and cross crosslets. This gateway now tends to be known as the Priory Gateway.

Notes: BL. No.206. 29x20 cm.

At the far end can be seen the remains of the entrance wall, and behind, further buildings. In the foreground is a water pump.

Notes: BL. No.208. 30x18 cm. Other no: On the reverse is written Numb.60.

215. PETERBOROUGH

Title on drawing: *Infirmary at Peterborough*

Artist: Unsigned, Peter Tillemans

Date: Probably 1719.

The Infirmary had been built *c.*1250 and was a large building with a nave and aisles. After the Dissolution houses were constructed within the aisles so that the arcades which formerly divided the building now form part of the facades of the houses. The tall 13th century arches are clear, while the house facades are an irregular series with an informal arrangement of mullioned windows of late 16th or early 17th century date.

216. PETERBOROUGH

Title on reverse of drawing: *Infirmary at Peterborough*

Artist: Unsigned, Peter Tillemans

Date: Probably 1719.

For commentary see previous drawing (Plate 215).

Notes: BL. No.207. 27.5x19 cm. Other nos: On the reverse is written Numb.64, and on the front is written a letter M.

217. PETERBOROUGH

Title: None on drawing

Artist: Uncertain

Date: Uncertain.

This is the first of a series of drawings of monuments and other items which existed at Peterborough Cathedral prior to the infliction of much damage to the building in 1643. The details are taken from a manuscript by the antiquary Sir William Dugdale (see Note). This drawing copies items of statuary, painted glass and monuments. At the top are three figures within Gothic niches representing the founders of the Abbey, Peda, Wulphere and Etheldreda, from the Hall of the Bishop's Palace; then two figures from windows of St Mary's Chapel (*i.e.* the Lady Chapel), with knights in armour, both with shields; then a slab with a brass indent also from the same chapel; and finally another slab with an inscription for Thomas de Uggford and a cross design, also in the Lady Chapel.

Notes: BL. No.209. 26.5x19.5 cm. The manuscript is quoted together with descriptions of the drawings in William Thomas Mellows, "Medieval monuments in Peterborough Cathedral", *Peterborough Natural History, Scientific and Archaeological Society*, 1937, and the captions here are based on this article.

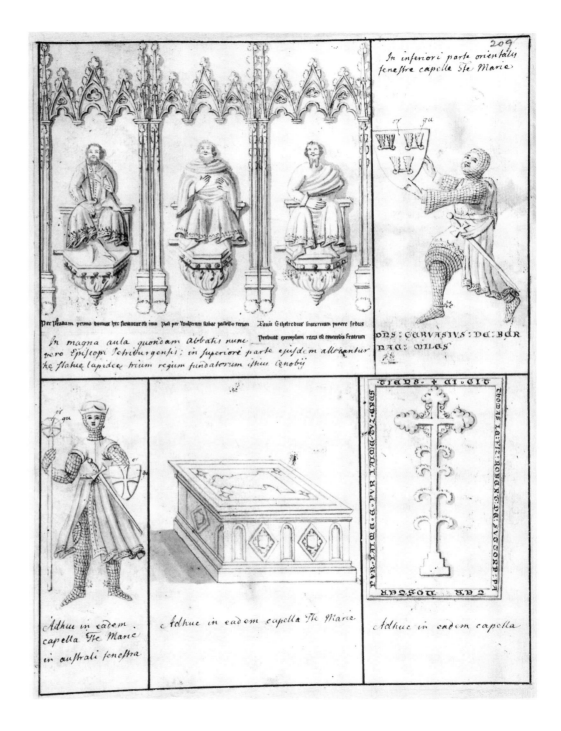

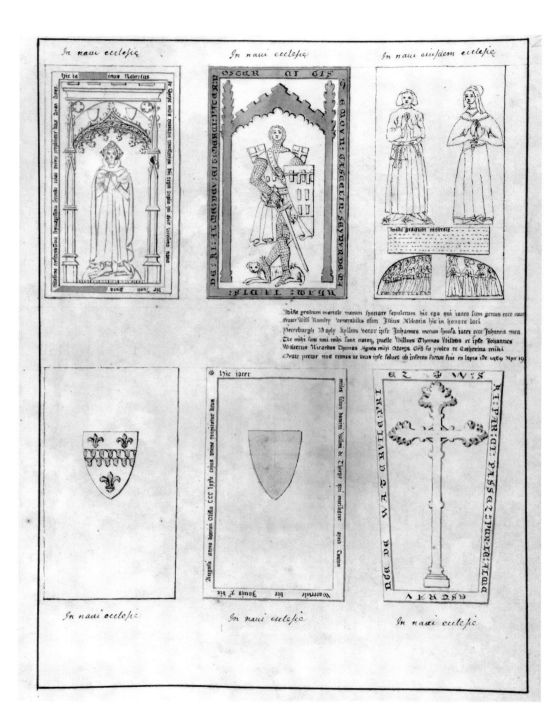

218. PETERBOROUGH

Title: None on drawing

Artist: Uncertain

Date: Uncertain.

Another drawing from the Dugdale manuscript (See previous drawing Plate 217). Mellows identified the figures as:

1. Sir Robert de Thorp, Chancellor to Edward III (d.1372)
2. Sir Edmund Gascelin, 2nd husband of Lady Isabella de Waterville of Marholm, temp. Edward II
3. A member of the family of Abbot William de Ramsey
4. No inscription
5. Sir William de Thorpe (d.1375)
6. Estaunea de Waterville

Several of these memorials were for owners of the Milton estate during the 14th century.

Notes: BL. No.210. 29x20 cm. For further information see Mellows *(op. cit.)*.

219. PETERBOROUGH

Title: No title on drawing

Artist: Uncertain

Date: Uncertain.

Another drawing from the Dugdale manuscript, recording three cross slabs and three figures of priors or abbots:

1. William Parys, Prior (d.1286)
2. John de Thingham, Prior
3. William Genge, Abbot (d.1408)
4. Godfrey de Croyland, Abbot (d.1321)
5. John Deeping, Abbot (d.1438)
6. Adam de Boothby (d.1338)

Notes: BL. No.211. 29x20 cm. See also Mellows *(op. cit.)*.

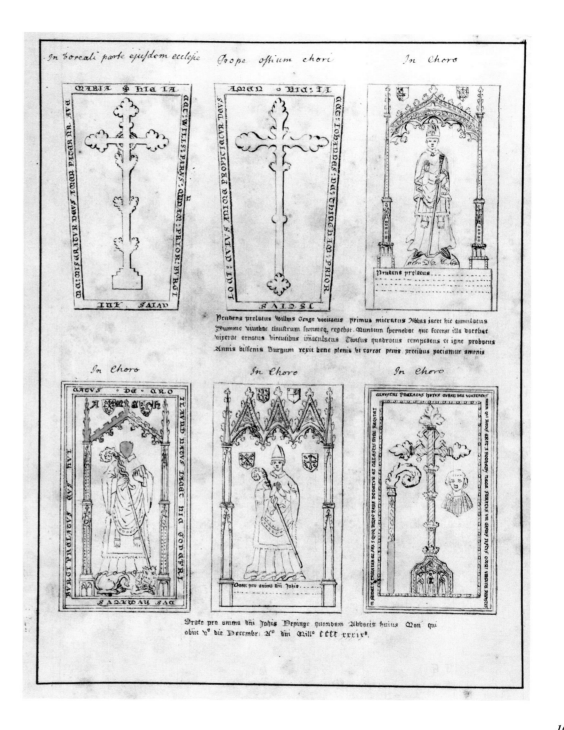

220. PETERBOROUGH

Title: None on drawing

Artist: Uncertain

Date: Uncertain.

A drawing of a slab with an intricatre canopy with lateral supporters containing niches and figures of saints. Underneath stands the figure of an abbot, his hands at prayer, supporting a crosier and around are four shields, three of which are missing. The extant shield shows a ram superimposed by the letter W, and this is sufficient to identify the memorial as that of Abbot William de Ramsey, d.1496, the donor of the lectern shown in the Choir (Plate 207).

Notes: BL. No.212. 28x19 cm. Other no: On the front is written 4 in pencil.

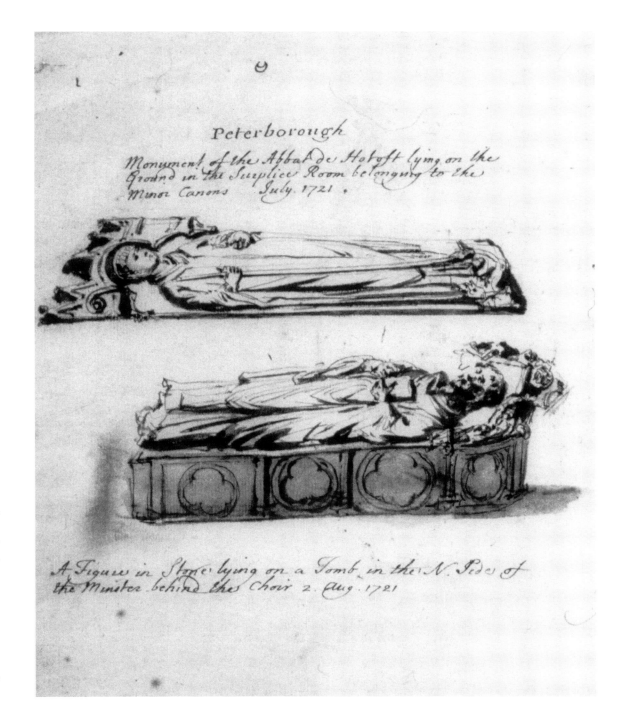

221. PETERBOROUGH

Title on drawing: *Peterborough Monument of the Abbot de Hotoft lying on the Ground in the Surplice Room belonging to the Minor Canons July 1721*

A Figure in Stone lying on a Tomb in the N Side of the Minster behind the Choir 2 Aug 1721

Date: These two dated drawings support the idea that the main sequence of drawings were executed in the summer of 1721, and indeed a visit is recorded in Bridges' MSS Notes on 1 August 1721.

Notes: BL. No.: No individual number, but on reverse of 14. 28x43.5 cm.

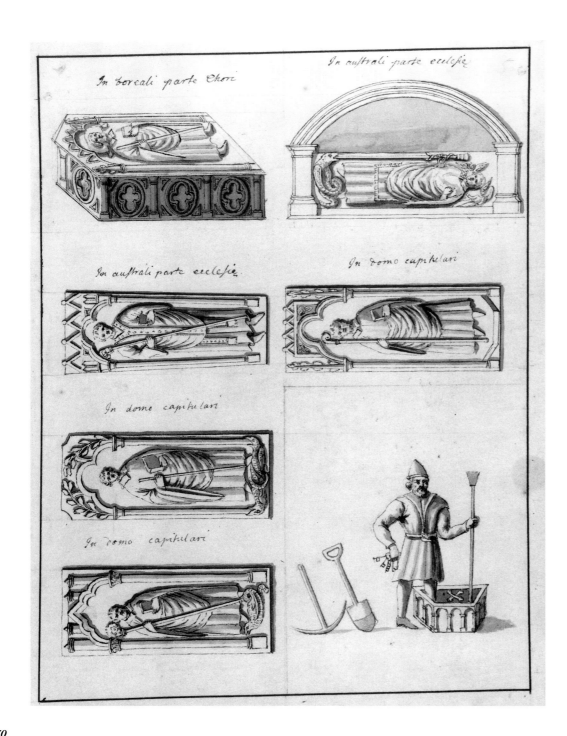

In boreali parte Chori

In australi parte ecclesie

In australi parte ecclesie

In domo capitulari

In domo capitulari

In domo capitulari

222. PETERBOROUGH

Title: None on drawing

Artist: Uncertain

Date: Uncertain.

Another composite drawing with six figures of abbots and a sketch of the painting known as "Old Scarlett".

The figures are, on the left-hand side, from the top:

 Abbot Benedict (d.1194)
 Uncertain
 Abbot Richard de London (d.1295)

 Albert Walter de St. Edmundsbury (d.1246)

On the right, from the top:

 Abbot John de Caleto (d.1262)
 Abbot Robert de Lyndsey (d.1222)
 Old Scarlett (d.1594)

Notes: BL. No.213. 29x20 cm.

223. PETERBOROUGH

Title: None on drawing

Artist: Uncertain

Date: Uncertain.

Another composite drawing with six divisions. W.T. Mellows identifies them as:

Top left:	Bishop John Chambers
Top right:	Tabard and funeral helm which recorded the burial of Mary Queen of Scots
Centre:	Tomb of Queen Katherine
Bottom:	Three brasses: William Smyth and Alice his wife, 1516; John de Harowden, Seneschal of Peterborough; unidentified.

Notes: BL. No.214. 29x20 cm. See Mellows *(op. cit)*.

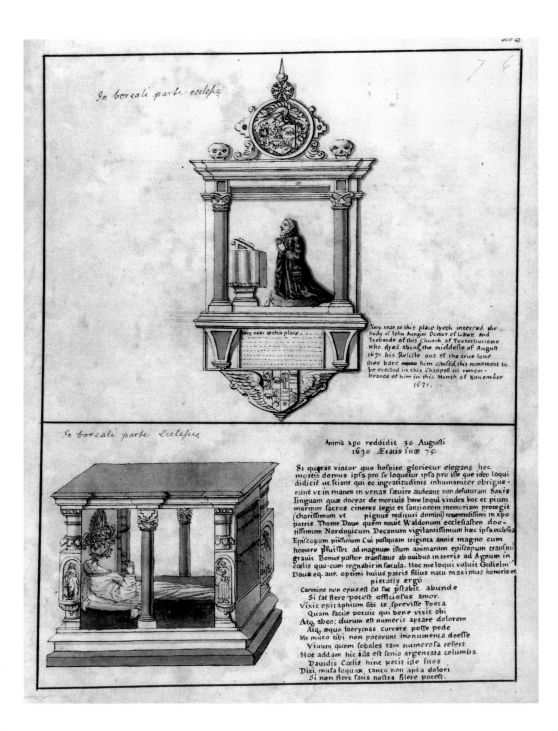

224. PETERBOROUGH

Title: None on drawing

Artist: Uncertain

Date: Uncertain.

Another drawing from the Dugdale MS. At the top is the monument of John Aungier, Doctor at Law, 1631, and below that of Bishop Dove (d.1630). Both display typical Jacobean decoration.

Notes: BL. No.215. 29x20 cm.

Peterborough Minster

216

Figure of ye Abbot Kirketon, as 'tis supposd, in ye Middle Window of ye Library

225. PETERBOROUGH

Title: *Peterborough Minster Figure of yᵉ Abbot Kirketon, as 'tis supposd, in yᵉ Middle Window of yᵉ Library*

Artist: Unsigned, but probably Peter Tillemans

Date: Uncertain.

A small sketch of this fragment of glass from the New Building. Abbot Robert Kirkton had held office from 1496 to 1528, and is remembered principally for the addition of the New Building at the east end of the Cathedral. Doubtless there was much more glass recording Kirkton's building work, and in the stonework there still exist many instances of his rebus and initials.

Notes: BL. No.216. 15x13 cm.

View of the Ruines of the Scite of Pipewell Monastery

226. PIPEWELL. Pipewell Abbey

Title on drawing: *View of the Ruines of the Scite of Pipewell Monastery*

Artist: Unsigned, Peter Tillemans

Date: Probably 1721, although the only visit recorded in Bridges' MS Notes is in August 1719.

Bridges' text:

> *Pipwell*, which took its name from a neighbouring spring, was antiently a small village, standing where the convent *West-Grange* was afterwards built, but on the foundations of the abbey fell to decay . . . Not far from the present woods are the vestiges of old buildings. On the south side, where the church is supposed to have stood, are ruins called the Hall-hollow. Within these few years, large

pillars, wrought and glazed pavement, with great quantities of painted glass, and a mutilated figure of the Virgin *Mary*, have been found near the ruins.

The woods of Pipewell, mentioned elsewhere in Bridges' text, are clearly seen as the background to the view, with the hamlet of Pipewell, consisting of mostly thatched cottages clustering along the roadway which border the monastery site in the valley below. The hillocks of the site of the Cistercian abbey are well depicted, together with the remnants of walling and a few buildings. One taller mound, to the right, appears to have been enclosed and planted with four trees.

The site was partially excavated in 1909 by Harold Brakspear but it is not easy to interpret his findings and some of Brakspear's conclusions are now suspect.

Notes: BL. No.217. 45x28.5 cm. Other no: On front is written 26. For discussion of the site see RCHM Vol.II pp.172-4.

227. RAINSBOROUGH CAMP

Title on drawing: *Rainsborow Camp*

Artist: Thomas Eayre

Date: Uncertain, although a visit is recorded in Bridges' MS Notes on 20 March 1721.

Bridges' text:

> To the south-west of *Newbottle* lies *Charleton*, an hamlet which in part belongs in part to the parish of *Newbottle*, and in part to *King's-Sutton*. On the south-west of it is the fortification called *Rainsborough*, which Mr. *Morton* conjectures was made by the *Danes*, to command that part of the country . . . The figure of the fortification is almost oval, and so the more likely to have been *Danish*. It is narrower to the east than to the west. It is now encompassed with only a single trench, and double bank. That on the inside of the trench is of the two highest. There are now four entrances into this encampment, two in the southern part, and two to the north. And a little below to the south-east is a much smaller piece of ground entrenched.

An excellent example of Eayre's archaeological surveying, with a section, view and plan.

This site is basically an Iron Age fort with some Roman occupation. Comparison of Eayre's plan with a more recently produced one prepared for the Royal Commission on Historical Monuments shows that Eayre has captured well the general shape of the earthwork. The hedge line is traceable today both as a field boundary and as a division in the pattern of the surviving field strips.

The Mr Morton referred to is John Morton, who had published in 1712 his *Natural History of Northamptonshire*, a work remarkable for its date dealing with natural history in its widest context.

The caption reads: *This Camp Within the Banks (besides allowance for the Ways) Contains 5a = Or = 10p or 2435 yards and Consequently was Sufficient to con=tain the like number of Men.*

Very distinctive is Eayre's treatment of trees and bushes.

Notes: BL. No.218. 46.5x28.5 cm. The monument is discussed in RCHM Vol.IV p.105.

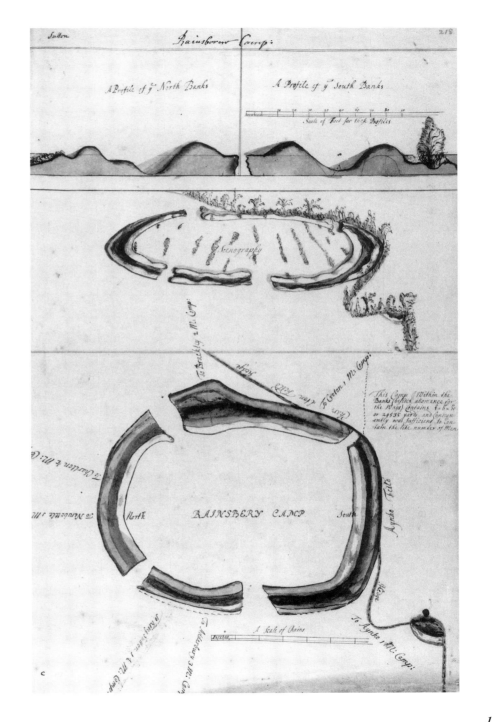

A Motte del

228. RAUNDS

Title on reverse of drawing: *The South View of the Church and Steeple of Raundes Taken Oct 3 1721*

Artist: Andrew Motte *(signed)*

Bridges' text:

> The church, dedicated to S. *Peter*, stands on high ground and consists of a spacious body, north and south ile, and a large chancel, all covered with lead.

This is a useful drawing since it gives us a chance to compare the draughtsmanship of Motte with that of Tillemans. Motte's approach is much simpler and broader than that of his colleague, although there is sufficient detail to enable the architectural styles of the building to be identified: Decorated style main building; Perpendicular south aisle; and the fine Early English west tower and spire.

Notes: BL. No.219. 27x19 cm. Other no: On the front is written a letter A.

229. RAUNDS

Title on reverse of drawing: *Ancient Painting upon the Screen in Raundes Church wth the Latin Passages in Scripture to which they refer in Eight Divisions*

Artist: Unsigned, Peter Tillemans

Date: Uncertain.

Bridges' text:

> The upper end of both iles is parted off by a screen. On that dividing the south ile, are painted eight different squares with inscriptions underneath, relating to the history of *Joseph*.

These panels were described in the *Gentleman's Magazine* in September 1791 (p.82), where each subject is identified. The Latin inscriptions were largely illegible at this date, but there is a reproduction of what survived on an engraved plate alongside the text.

The subjects are all taken from texts in the Book of Genesis, Chapters 37-45. The incidents are:

1. Joseph sleeping with the eleven sheaves of corn bowing to his sheaf of corn (Ch.37, v.5-9)

2. Joseph asking where his Brothers have gone and being told they have gone to Dothan (Ch.37, v.17)

3. Joseph is taken from the pit and sold to the Ishmaelites (Ch.37, v.28)

4. Joseph is in prison interpreting the dreams of Pharoah's servants (Ch.40, v.9)

5. Joseph is brought before Pharoah to interpret his dreams (Ch.41, v.24)

6. Joseph orders the people to fill the storehouses with corn (Ch.41 v.48)

7. Joseph's brothers are searched and the Pharaoh's cup is found in Benjamin's sack (Ch.44, v.12)

8. Joseph reveals his identity to his brothers (Ch.45, v.2)

Sadly these panels are no longer at Raunds. It is possible that they were severely damaged when the spire of the church was struck by lightning in July 1826 and collapsed.

Notes: BL. No.220 *(bottom)*, 221 *(top)*. Sizes 40x17.5 and 33x13.5 cm. I am grateful to the Rev. Leatherland for confirming that the panels are no longer in the church.

View of Rockingham Castle with a distant Prospect of three Towns in Rutland & Leicestershire Sepr. 1721
a. Two round Towers at the Entrance. b. The Church. c. part of the Town.

230. ROCKINGHAM

Title on drawing: *View of Rockingham Castle with a distant Prospect of three Towns in Rutland & Leicestershire Sepr 1721 a. Two round Towers at the Entrance. b. The Church. c. part of the Town.*

Artist: Unsigned, Peter Tillemans

Date: Bridges' MS Notes record a visit in July 1721, and another drawing is dated 11 July 1721 (See Plate 232).

Bridges' text:

> *ROCKINGHAM* is a village bordering on the *Welland*, famous for it forest and castle . . . The castle was built by *William* the Conqueror. In *Leland*'s time it was in great measure fallen to decay . . .

A view taken from the east, showing the hillside site of the castle overlooking the Welland valley. The uneven nature of the ground surrounding the castle is evident. While some of this reflects the fortifications of the castle, much derives from the existence of village houses and a roadway until early in the 17th century. The church, still isolated as here, stood close to the village street, the deep hollow of which is still obvious in the park today, leading from below the castle to the head of the present village street. Also in the foreground of the drawing is a large barn with a series of fences or walls uphill to its left: this no longer exists.

Above are the main buildings of the castle with the two towers of the late Norman period, and on either side ranges of Elizabethan buildings, shown in more detail on the next drawing (Plate 231). Above the range on the left is seen the top of the uneven wall of the medieval castle, and then behind the main house created by the Watsons following their acquisition of the property in 1553. There was much new building and rebuilding in the 1570s and '80s.

The villages in the valley are, from the right, Caldecott (spire), Great Easton (spire on skyline) and Bringhurst (tower alongside the edge of the castle). There is a windmill out in the fields towards Lyddington, and the well wooded nature of the valley is clear.

Notes: BL. No.224. 47x22.5 cm. Other no: On the front is written D. There is a duplicate of this drawing, signed by Tillemans, in the Overstone Collection, Reading University (Vol.p-z, fol.43A).

231. ROCKINGHAM

Title: None on drawing

Artist: Unsigned, Peter Tillemans

Date: Probably also 11 July 1721.

This important drawing shows in more detail the entrance side of the castle.

To the left is the large barn, and one can now see it has buttresses and a tiled roof. In the centre are the Norman towers, still with uneven tops. They were given battlements in the 1850s by the architect Salvin. The gatehouse has a long ridged roof over it. To the left of the gateway is a low range with a doorway and two mullioned windows and dormers, and rising above this, the main gable of the house, with to its right the turret of a bell tower. Just visible on the extreme left is the rising mound on which had stood the keep.

To the right of the gate towers is a similar low range of Elizabethan date, with rising above it the roof and chimneys of Walker's House, rebuilt in 1655.

A similar view to this was engraved for the published work by F. Chaplin and J. Robinson, together with another of the interior of the courtyard. They are, however, much simpler than this drawing and probably commissioned for the 1791 publication.

Notes: BL. No.225. 31.5x20 cm. Other no: On the front of the drawing is written B.

232. ROCKINGHAM

Title on reverse of drawing: *West Prospect of Rockingham Castle Taken 11 July.1719*

Artist: Unsigned, Peter Tillemans.

Another informative view, this time taken from the valley below the church. The church appears as it stood until Victorian times, when it was rebuilt in a much grander style. Here it appears as a rather mean little building showing, as does the castle itself, much evidence of building during the Elizabethan and Jacobean period, with mullion and transom windows. The castle appears behind its parapeted terrace, the main block just visible with its gables. To the left is Walker's House and to the right a lower range.

Notes: BL. No.226. 29.5x18.5 cm. Other no: On front of drawing is written A.3

233. ROCKINGHAM

Title on drawing: *View of two Mon^ts of two Ladys of the Rockingham Family in Rockingham Church 26 July 1721*

Artist: Unsigned, Peter Tillemans

Bridges' text:

> On the north side of the chancel is a neat marble monument, supported by two doric pilasters, with an urn at top . . . [there are then heraldic descriptions] . . . Under the arms are two cherubs heads, and below them the effigies, in full proportions, of a woman in a winding sheet, looking towards the heavens . . . Below the above is a handsome grey monument . . . [again heraldry is described] . . . Under the arms is a canopy supported by two pillars of the corinthian order. Below the canopy, on a pediestal in full proportion a female figure in a winding-sheet, looking upward, and pointing to a skull at her feet.

These descriptions are in the order of Bridges' text, while the drawings show the memorials in reverse order. That on the left is for the Hon. Margaret Watson (d.1713) and is a superb example of Baroque carving. The draperies are most sensitively accomplished and the figure stands in a pose derived from that of the Venus de Medici. The skull at her feet has a serpent entwined within it. Although unsigned, the monument is firmly attributed to William Palmer, an excellent sculptor whose name is almost unknown today. Today the monument stands in the south chapel of the church.

The other drawing portrays a monument of heavier design and less able sculpture, although still a good example of the Baroque manner. It is for Anne Lady Rockingham (d.1695) and still stands on the north side of the chancel. Also unsigned, this memorial is attributed to the sculptor John Nost and is comparable to that for Judge Levinz at Evenley (see Plate 105).

Notes: BL. No. On reverse of Drawing 15. 28x43.5 cm.

An old Oak called Fair Oak in Rockingham Forest in the
Bailiffwick of Cliffe

234. ROCKINGHAM FOREST

Title on drawing: *An old Oak called Fair Oak in Rockingham Forest in the Bailiffwick of Cliffe*

Artist: Unsigned, Peter Tillemans

Date: Probably 1719, and two visits to Kingscliffe are recorded in Bridges' MS Notes, on 11 and 12 August 1719 and on 7 October 1719.

A splendid drawing of an oak tree which may have had some special significance with regard to the Deer Park which had been attached to the Royal Hunting Lodge at Kingscliffe. The Lodge was already in existence by the mid 12th century, and the Deer Park is recorded in the mid 13th. Leland, *c.*1540, described it as "partly waullid with stone and partly palid", but what appears behind the oak is not part of the walling. What can be seen is a pencil sketch of Rockingham Castle with its Norman entrance towers and archway, and within the branch on the right is the line of the gable of the outbuilding (compare Plate 231). An intriguing example of Tillemans re-using paper.

Notes: BL. No.227. 40.5x28 cm.

235. ROTHWELL

Title on drawing: *S.E. View of yᵉ Town of Rothwell*

Artist: Unsigned, Peter Tillemans

Date: Probably 1719 and a visit is recorded in Bridges' MS Notes in August 1719. Another visit took place in September 1721.

Bridges' text:

The town, which stands on the south side of a rocky hill, contains two hundred ninety nine houses, and one thousand ninety one inhabitants . . . The town appears from several marks, to have been considerably larger than it is at present.

The drawing shows a distant view of the town with its regular pattern of hedged fields, probably old enclosures, while on the right is an indication of open fields. There is considerable indication of thatched roofs, especially on the left-hand side of the view.

The drawing has been overlaid with a lightly drawn squared layout indicating that it was prepared for engraving, and, indeed, this occurred when it formed part of a composite plate, illustrating Rothwell in the published text (Vol.II p.56).

Notes: BL, No.228. 40x26 cm. Other no: On the reverse is written Num:90.

236. ROTHWELL. Market House

Title: No title on drawing

Artist: Unsigned, Peter Tillemans

Date: Probably 1719 (See previous drawing, Plate 235).

Bridges' text:

> In *Rowell* is a remarkable market place, or sessions-house, a square stone-building, begun but left unfinished by Sir *Thomas Tresham*. Under the cornice on the outside, are carved the arms of many of the gentlemen of the county . . .

The drawing shows the north side of the building in the ruinous state in which it then stood. Its parapet has partially fallen, and the far side of the building can be seen through the unglazed windows. At various points small dark squares are drawn and some of these are almost certainly holes which housed the scaffolding which was put up when the building was erected. Normally these small holes are plugged with stone when the building is complete, but here they were either not plugged or the plugs have fallen out. Some of the arches are shown with pointed heads, but this is probably a mis-interpretation of perspective since the building is severely classical and anything other than a semicircular arch is inconceivable.

The Market House at Rothwell was built for Sir Thomas Tresham shortly after 1578 by the mason William Grumbold of Weldon as recorded in Bridges' text, as "a tribute to his sweet fatherland and County of Northampton but chiefly to this town his near neighbour. Nothing but the common weal did he seek; nothing but the perpetual honour of his friends". As Sir Gyles Isham has pointed out: "This indeed is the raison d'être of the building. The theme is friendship. The ninety coats of arms are other landed proprietors of Rothwell Hundred and many other Northamptonshire families". The heraldry is carefully delineated in the drawing. The amount of vegetation which clothes the cornices of the building would not today please an inspector from English Heritage!

The drawing was also engraved, complete with pointed arches, as part of the composite Rothwell plate (Bridges' text, Vol.II p.56).

Notes: BL. No.229. 31.5x22 cm. Other no: On reverse is written Num:33 cc. For a full discussion of the building see Sir Gyles Isham, "Sir Thomas Tresham and his buildings", *Reports & Papers of the Northamptonshire Antiquarian Society,* 1966.

Rushton

View of the Lord Cullens House and two Churches.

237. RUSHTON

Title on drawing: *Rushton View of the Lord Cullens House and two Churches*

Artist: Unsigned, Peter Tillemans

Date: The numbering system would indicate 1721, but the only recorded visits in Bridges' MSS are in 1719 and other drawings of Rushton are dated July 1719.

Bridges' text:

RUSHTON St. PETER'S consists only of four or five shepherds lodges, the parsonage, and lord Cullen's seat. It is pleasantly seated, declining southwards to the river Ise which runs here under a stone bridge of two arches . . . The manor is in Lord *Cullen*, to whose seat adjoins a garden and paddock equally elegant and pleasant.

This view, from the south, shows, left to right, the Hall, with just by it the church of St. Peter, then the village, and further right the Church of All Saints.

The Hall is the complex structure resulting from building by the Treshams in the late 16th and early 17th centuries, which was then greatly added to after Sir William Cockayne purchased it in 1619. There is enough detail to define on the left the tall chamber wing with its gabled projection; then comes the Hall with a large flat chimneystack and, just visible, a large mullion and transom window; finally another range projecting southwards with a complicated series of gables and levels. Behind the main block and between it and the church, is the courtyard, and the facade of the northern range is seen – a more regular Elizabethan wing with mullioned windows and dormers.

The whole of the southern side of the house was greatly embellished in 1848 so that today this facade is barely recognisable.

To the left of the house the garden layout is indicated with walled terraces and behind the house the planting of the wilderness. Almost central in the view is the road in a position somewhat to the west of where it runs today: it was realigned in 1799 when the St Peter's church by the Hall was also demolished and its monuments removed to All Saints (see Plate 239).

The Treshams acquired Rushton in 1438 and held it till 1619 when it was bought by Cockayne. That family lived there till 1828, being created Viscounts Cullen in 1642.

Notes: BL. No.231. 45x28.5 cm. Other no: On the front is written 25.

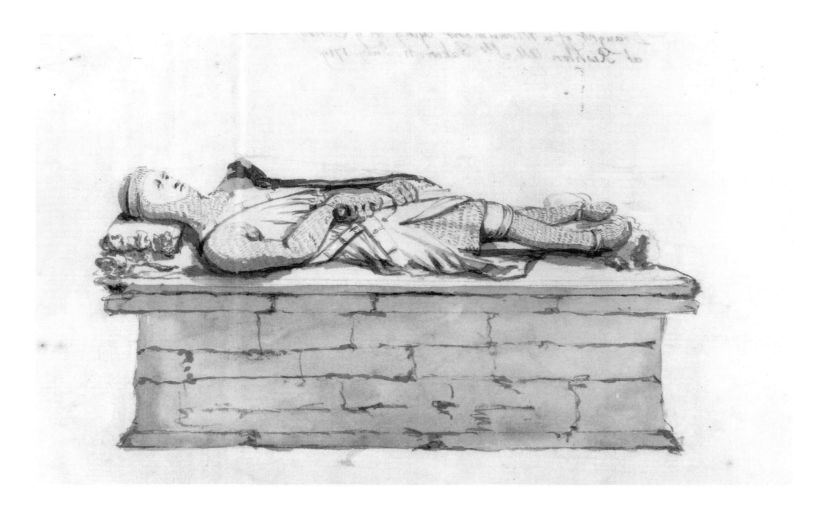

238. RUSHTON

Title on reverse of drawing: *Draught of a Monument lying in yͤ School House at Rishton All Sͭˢ Taken 11 July.1719*

Artist: Unsigned, Peter Tillemans

Bridges' text:

> On the north side of the chancel is a school-house, formerly a part of the church, where on a stone two foot high, seven foot long, and two foot four inches broad, is a marble figure, cross-legged and in armour. It is said traditionally to be the monument of *William de Goldingham.*

This effigy still exists and is a good example of late 13th century monumental sculpture in Purbeck marble.

The cross-legs, commonly believed to denote that the soldier went on the Crusades, have no such significance: they appear to be simply a means of giving strength so that the lower limbs could be successfully carved from the brittle Purbeck. Bridges' identification of the monument to William de Goldingham is usually accepted, since he died in 1296, and this date would fit the armour of the figure. He wears a suit of mail over which is a loose surcoat. The cushion at his head is unusual in that it has carved each side of it oak branches.

Notes: BL. No.222. 29.5x18 cm. Other no: On the front is written C.

Enough research has now been done to prove that there are effigies of knights with crossed legs who did not go to the Crusades, and equally effigies of knights without crossed legs who did!

239. RUSHTON

Title on reverse of drawing: *Draught of Sr Tho. Treshams Mon^t at Rishton St Peters lying on the North side of the Church Taken 11 July.1719*

Artist: Unsigned, Peter Tillemans

Bridges' text:

> Under the north pillar of the chancel, on a tomb of white marble, about a yard in height, is the marble effigies of Sir *Thomas Tresham* in a gown, with his hands erected.

As the title states, this monument was formerly in the church of St. Peter which until 1799 stood close to the Hall (see Plate 237). On the demolition of the church in that year, the monument was moved to All Saints. The effigy represents Sir Thomas Tresham (d.1559), an ardent Catholic who, through his support for Queen Mary I, was created Lord Prior of the Order of the Knights Hospitallers of St John of Jerusalem when that order was resurrected in 1557. He was only to hold office for a single year, since the order was abolished by Elizabeth when she ascended the throne in 1558. This is, in fact, the only effigy in England to show a member of the order in his robes. The front of the gown displays the Maltese Cross used by the Order, Malta having become their home after 1522.

The tombchest upon which the effigy rests is a good example of mid-16th century Renaissance decoration, with its distinctive shields and twisted columns. The whole is carved from alabaster and is one of a number of tombs which can be attributed to the Roilley family, tomb carvers based near Burton-on-Trent. The heraldry is especially splendid.

Notes: BL. No.223. 26.5x18. For the Roilley family of carvers see Edgecote (Plate 103).

240. RUSHTON. Triangular Lodge

Title: No title on drawing

Artist: Unsigned, Peter Tillemans

Date: Probably July 1719, since another drawing is dated 11 July and a visit is recorded in Bridges' MS Notes on 16 July.

Bridges' text:

While the Lodge is not specifically mentioned, the following quote on Sir Thomas Tresham is relevant:

This gentleman had a good taste in architecture, and began several buildings which he was not fortunate enough to finish.

This is a most attractive drawing of the Triangular Lodge, and faithfully records its architectural details, except there is no indication of the contrasting courses of white and brown stone. The view is taken from the south-east, with the entrance doorway almost totally hidden by a low building. These low buildings are reasonably substantial with tiled roofs and a good stone chimney.

Notes: BL. No.230. 28.5x20.5 cm. Other nos: On the front is written A and on the reverse Numb.44 cc. Also on the reverse is a pencil outline of the building, rather too large for the sheet and thereby excluding the central stack. The symbolism of the building is discussed in detail by Sir Gyles Isham, "Sir Thomas Tresham and his buildings" *(op. cit.).*

A View of the Scite of Sewardesley Priory now a Farm house call'd Shosly belonging to the Lord Lempster. 1 The Farm house 2. Vestigia or Foundations of the Chapel near a (3.) Barn built out of the Ruines

241. SEWARDSLEY

Title on drawing: *A View of the Scite of Sewardesley Priory now a Farm House calld Shosly belonging to the Lord Lempster 1. The Farm House 2. Vestiges of Foundations of the Chapel near a 3. Barn built out of the Ruines*

Artist: Unsigned, Peter Tillemans

Date: Probably 1721. An itinerary around this area took place between 17th and 20th July 1721, as noted in Bridges' MS Notes.

Bridges' text:

To the north-east of *Holcote*, at a small distance lies *Shordsley* or *Sewesley*, and more antiently *Sewardesley*, at present a farm-house of no considerable note, but formerly a nunnery of the *Cistertian* order, dedicated to the Virgin *Mary*. It was seated near a large wood, part of which is now called *Nun-wood* and *Chappel-coppice*. On the right hand side of the house, which in some parts of it consists of very old walls, and hath belonging to it a very old kitchen, are the remaining marks of ponds, which were fed by a water out of *Chapel-close*. The foundations of the chapel, not many years ago, were dug up to build a barn.

The farmhouse is in the centre of the view, and together with its outbuildings, has a thatched roof. Around the farmhouse are roughly fenced enclosures. The barn, mentioned in Bridges' text, is on the right-hand side and the remnants of foundations are on the low hillside close by.

There are only fragments of these buildings on the site today.

Notes: BL. No.232. 43.5x28 cm. Other no: On the front of the drawing is written 15. For a recent discussion of the site see RCHM Vol.IV pp.43-4.

242. SHUTLANGER

Title on drawing: *View of the Chapel at Shittlehanger now a Farm House*

Artist: Unsigned, Peter Tillemans

Date: Uncertain, but probably 1721.

Bridges' text:

To the west of *Stoke-Bruerne*, at the near distance of a mile, lies *Shittlehanger*, an hamlet of sixty houses, containing about two hundred and eighty inhabitants. It was formerly a place famous for shooting at butts, of which the marks are still remaining . . . Here is still in being an old chapel, fifty one feet in length, and now converted into a farm-house. The walls and window-cases are entire, as is also the porch with three arches of stone, which cross one another at the top. It is ten foot high, eleven foot long, and eight foot and a half in breadth. Behind the porch is a small stone-stair-case leading to a room over it, where possibly the bell hung, and on each side a buttress.

Although a simple drawing it well records the building which has for long been called "The Monastery", but which is in fact not a chapel remnant but the core of a 14th century hall house. As Bridges states, it preserves its original arched porch, some doorways and remains of windows. The drawing indicates considerable 17th century rebuilding, with mullioned windows, that to the left of the porch being of the cross mullion and transom type. The roof appears to be thatch. Remarkably there are still surviving today timbers of the medieval roof.

Notes: BL. No.233. 21.7x26.3 cm. The site is referred to in RCHM Vol.IV, p.131.

243. STAMFORD ST. MARTINS. Burghley House

Title on drawing: *La Bellissima Statua d Andromeda con il Monstro disotto, tutto dun medesimo pezzo de Marmo, nella villa Cecilliana chiamata Burleigh vicinia al Stamford*

Artist: Unsigned, Peter Tillemans

Date: Uncertain, but a visit is recorded in Bridges' MS Notes on 8 August 1719.

Bridges' text:

> *BURGHLEY,* or *Burleigh,* in the parish of *Stamford St. Martin,* is the noble seat of the earl of Exeter . . . The house has been much adorned . . . particularly by *John,* late *earl of Exeter,* and still more by *Brownlow,* the present possessor, who have enriched it with a variety of statues, pictures and carvings of the most elegant workmanship. Amongst the statues is that of *Andromeda,* made by Domenico Guidi, which cost the earl three hundred pounds at *Rome.*

A delicate drawing of this piece, showing Andromeda chained to the rock. The tail of the monster is behind her, while its head and jaws are at the base.

In the 1815 *Guide to Burghley House* this statue was then in the Great Hall, together with much other statuary. It is there catalogued as being by Peter Stephen Monnot. Monnot had been discovered by John, 5th Earl of Exeter while on his grand tour in Rome, and while there he commissioned a number of sculptures which were shipped back to England. This statue is no longer at Burghley, having been sold in 1954, and is now in America.

When the Earl died in 1700 he was buried in Stamford St Martin's church under a monument which had also been commissioned from Monnot, and which was set up at St. Martin's by the English sculptor William Palmer. It is a huge affair with lifesize effigies of the Earl and his Countess in classical garb, lying on a vast sarcophagus, attended by Wisdom and Art, also lifesize classical statues.

Notes: BL. No.234. 31x19.5 cm. For Monnot see John Drakard, *A Guide to Burghley House, Northamptonshire,* Stamford, 1815 (p.21) and *Gunnis.*

244. STEANE

Title on reverse of drawing: *Prospect of Steane House to the North Taken 2 July 1719*

Artist: Unsigned, Peter Tillemans

Bridges' text:

> *STENE*, formerly named *Stane* or *Stanes*, is bounded on the east and north by *Brackley* and *Hawes*, on the west by *Farningho*, and on the south by *Hinton*. There is but one house in the parish, except the Duke of *Kent*'s; though it is firmly believed in the neighbourhood, that there was once here a flourishing town, which was destroyed by the Danes.

This must be reckoned one of the greatest losses among Northamptonshire country house architecture. It is a really fascinating structure, with a mixture of architectural styles and features greatly intriguing. The manorial descent is complicated, but amongst its owners were Sir Reginald Bray, who possessed it between 1495 and 1503, and who is credited with an interest in architecture, having been concerned with the founding and building of Henry VII's Chapel at Westminster Abbey. It is recorded that Bray's heraldic device was in the windows of the Hall, so that parts of the building could well be from that date. By 1583 a Bray daughter had inherited the manor, and she married Sir Thomas Crewe of Crewe, Cheshire, and thus began a century of ownership by this family. During this time they were elevated to the peerage as Barons

Crewe of Steane. It was the great-grand-daughter of Sir Thomas who inherited in 1697, being the wife of Henry Duke of Kent. Thence the ownership passed to the Spencer family who demolished nearly the whole house between 1740 and 1750.

The central part of the building would appear to be a Great Hall, its large Gothic windows possibly dating from the Bray period, that is *c.*1500. The entrance is via a Jacobean arcade, probably dating from *c.*1620, when Sir Thomas Crewe built a chapel close by the house. Either side the Hall range are projecting gabled wings, both having mullion and transom windows of late 16th or early 17th century date. Then at either end project the facades of two curious Gothic wings. Both have at their corners, round towers with battlements, and in both there are windows with Gothic tracery. However, while that on the right appears a little irregular, with its odd tower profile and corner buttresses, and might well be medieval, that on the left is completely regular, with clear-cut angles and in its side wall mullioned windows under square labels. Possibly, therefore, this wing is an example of early 17th century Gothic, for which idea there is support in that the 1620 chapel, which still survives as a convincing example in the Gothic manner. The most interesting feature of the house is the top floor where there appears to be a Long Gallery. It would also seem to be early 17th century and has battlements and a cupola.

Today only small portions of the 17th century right-hand wing survive, incorporated in a house dating largely from the mid 19th century.

Notes: BL. No.235. 31x19.5 cm. Other no: On the reverse is written Num:84.

In Steane Chapel the Monument of Sr Thomas Crewe Kt Kings Serjt and Speaker of the House of Commons and of Temperance his Wife taken 11th July. 1721

245. STEANE

Title on drawing: *In Steane Chapel the Monument of Sr Thomas Crewe Kt Kings Serjt and Speaker of the House of Commons and of Temperance his Wife taken 11th July 1721*

Artist: Unsigned, Peter Tillemans

Bridges' text:

> . . . a fine altar monument composed of white, black, and grey marble, *(there follows a descriptions of the coats of arms)* . . . under an arch on an handsome tomb of black and white marble lies the statue of a person in the habit of a serjeant at law, reposing his head on his right hand, and holding a roll in his left; with his wife by him on a pillow, in the habit of the times.

This is one of a series of Crewe memorials at Steane. Sir Thomas died in 1633, but his wife had died in 1619. He has only a short inscription, but she has a long verse ending: *A true Temperance in deed and name, Now gone to Heaven from whence she came, Who with hir lot was well contented, Who lived desired and dyed lamented.* The authorship of the tomb is uncertain but there are similarities with the work of Nicholas Stone and the sculptor is likely to have been one of his pupils. It seems likely that it was erected after Lady Crewe's death, the inscription for her husband having been cut later.

Notes: BL. No.236. 28x22 cm.

View of the house at Stoke Park with the Woods & Stoke Bruern Church taken in the Road from Northton to Stony Stratford on the hill between Grafton & Stoke 10 Aug. 1721

246. STOKE BRUERNE. Stoke Park

Title on drawing: *View of the House at Stoke Park with the Wood and Stoke Bruerne Church taken in the Road from Northton to Stony Stratford on the Hill between Grafton & Stoke 10 Aug. 1721*

Artist: Unsigned, Peter Tillemans

Bridges' text:

On the south side of the parish of *Stoke-Bruern*, bounded by the river *Tove*, lies *Stoke-Park*, the seat of *Francis Arundel* Esq. The house was built by Sir *Francis Crane*, who brought the design from *Italy*, and in the execution of it received the assistance of *Inigo Jones*. It consists of a body and two wings, joined by corridors or galleries. The pillars, which support the galleries leading to the wings, are red, and of a different colour from the house.

As the caption says, the view is taken from the hill rising towards Grafton Regis, the road being drawn in with its bend in the valley below, more or less where the avenue leading southwards from the house ends. There is no avenue today, but the house is once again visible with a realignment of the main road between Grafton and Stoke.

We can see the full south spread of the house, with the central block, its tower and cupola, the colonnades and the two pavilions. There is a flat terrace in front of the house and some garden planting in front of each pavilion. Behind the house is a courtyard backed by a range of gabled outbuildings.

Sir Francis Crane was an important Court figure of the reign of Charles I. He is chiefly remembered as having established the Mortlake Tapestry factory in 1619. He acquired Stoke Park, which had been a Royal manor, in payment of a debt. After his death in 1636 it passed through a family line to his sister, who had married into the Arundel family. They held it till 1786 when it was inherited by an Arundel cousin, Levison Vernon, and the Vernons were there till 1928. In 1886 the main house was destroyed by fire, and never rebuilt. Instead a curious Jacobethan house was built onto the rear of the eastern pavilion. After the last War the house was unoccupied for many years and fell into disrepair. It was in danger of being demolished in the early 1950s, but fortunately was rescued by Robin Chancellor and Andrew Revai. The Victorian accretions were removed and the eastern pavilion adapted as a house. The western pavilion remains as a single space, with an interesting brick vaulted cellar.

The present garden layout incorporates a lily pond and fountain brought from Harefield Park, Middlesex, a property inherited by the Vernons.

On the skyline, to the right, is the village church of Stoke Bruerne.

Notes: BL. No.237. 40x27.5 cm. Other no: On the front is written 43. The statement about the colour of the stone refers to the different ironstones with which the house is built. The main structure was local pendle stone of a buff colour; the pilasters are a dark brown stone also local to Blisworth; while the colonnades are golden brown Duston stone. A similar colour combination was originally used by Inigo Jones for the Banqueting House in Whitehall, London.

Prospect of Mrs Arundels House at Stoke Park taken in ye Garden

247. STOKE BRUERNE. Stoke Park

Title on drawing: *Prospect of Mrs Arundels House at Stoke Park taken in yᵉ Garden* (Under the name of Arundel is Whitlocke crossed out)

Artist: Unsigned, Peter Tillemans

Date: Probably 1719, a visit being recorded in Bridges' MS Notes on 31 July of that year.

Bridges' text:

> This estate was given in consideration of money due to him Sir *Francis Crane* from the Crown, in the time of *Charles* I. The house was begun about the year 1630, and finished before 1636, during which interval he gave an entertainment here to the King and Queen.

This drawing shows in much more detail the arrangement of the facades of both the main house and the pavilions.

The attribution of the design of Stoke Park to Inigo Jones rests with Bridges (see extract quoted under previous drawing (Plate 246)). Crane's Court position would have enabled him to ask Jones for a design, and the statement that the design was brought from Italy may refer to the idea that its plan and design originated from buildings Jones had seen on his tour of northern Italy between 1613 and '14. This is the very first time that this form of the Palladian plan, with a central block and quadrant colonnades linking to pavilions, appeared in England. As well as the plan the design incorporates a version of Michelangelo's Capitoline Palace facade in Rome for the front of the pavilions. Today the pavilions, standing in isolation, look decidedly more Italian than English, so that Jones with his immediate knowledge of Italy is an obvious candidate as Stoke's architect.

The main house is a little puzzling: it seems rather less coherent than the pavilions, and a little old fashioned in comparison with them. Its end walls seem to have curved or Dutch gables, and the central entrance with its projecting tower is rather clumsy in its handling of detail. The main facade, however, does have some continuity with the tall Ionic pilasters and its range of cross-mullion and transom windows. Yet there are mullioned windows with leaded lights within the roof parapet and the chimneystacks look a little antique for 1630. All this supports the theory that the main house probably incorporated an earlier structure. Access to the upper levels of the pavilions seems to have been along the flat roofs of the colonnades. One pavilion was a library, the other a chapel.

Notes: BL. No.238. 40.5x27cm. Other nos: On the front is written rather large in pencil 46, and on the reverse is written Num:106.

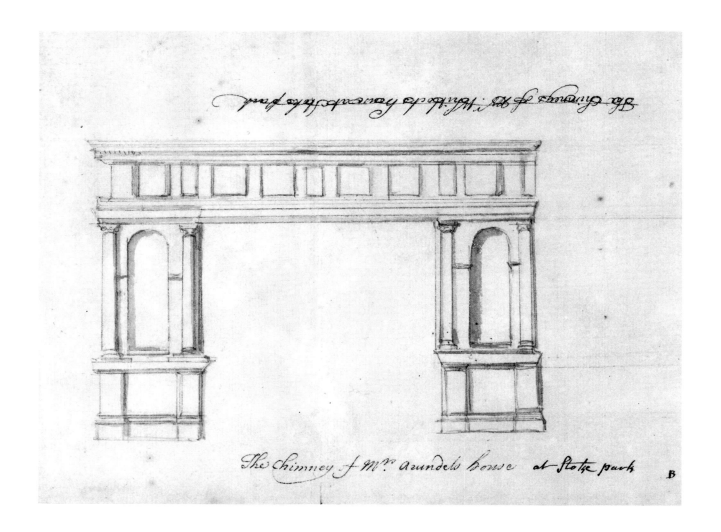

The Chimney of M^r arundels House at Stoke park B

248. STOKE BRUERNE. Stoke Park

Title on drawing: (At the top crossed out) *The Chimney of Mr Whitlocks House at Stoke Park.* (At the bottom) *The Chimney of Mrs Arundels House* (added in another hand) *at Stoke Park*

Artist: Unsigned, but probably Peter Tillemans

Date: Uncertain.

This sketch is of a large chimneypiece, possibly in the main room of the house, and while simple in execution, an examination indicates considerable sophistication. The top cornice, for instance, has a suggestion of a dentil frieze, and the pillars a suggestion of Ionic capitals. The spacing and the proportion of the rectangles in the frieze is also interesting.

The drawing has two titles, with both being in a sense correct! Isabella, widow of Francis Arundel took as her second husband Richard Whitlock, who was in residence when Bridges' text was compiled.

Notes: BL. No.239. 31x19.5 cm. Other no: To the right of the lower title is written B.

View of the Scite of Sulby Abby where there is now a Shepheards house with the Town of Welford at a Distance taken 12 Aug.ᵗ 1721

249. SULBY

Title on drawing: *View of the Scite of Sulby Abby where there is now a Shepherds House with the Town of Welford at a Distance taken 12 Augᵗ 1721*

Artist: Unsigned, Peter Tillemans

Bridges' text:

> The abbey stood in the ground called the Holm; the site of the house, with the grounds and pool, containing something more than sixty two acres. Upon the site of it is now a shepherd's house, and about it are risings and hollows, which seem to show the compass and extent of the walls. Coin-stones and other stones have been frequently dug out of the ruins.

The view is taken looking westwards across the site, with the location of the shepherd's house now covered by Abbey Farm. The site is not easy to interpret but the abbey church was to the right of the house.

Notes: BL. No.241. 43.5x24.5 cm. A considerable discussion of the site, together with a plan, is contained in RCHM Vol.III pp.183-4.

The old House of the first Russell that was Baron of Thornhaugh now a Farm House belonging to the Duke of Bedford July. 1721

250. THORNHAUGH

Title on drawing: *The old House of the first Russell that was Baron Thornhaugh now a Farm House belonging to the Duke of Bedford July. 1721*

Artist: Unsigned, Peter Tillemans

Bridges' text:

> Here is an old stone manor house, formerly the residence of the family of *St. Medard*, or *Semare*, who were lords of the manor. It stands about a quarter of a mile from the church, and is embattled all round, with a small embattled hexagonal tower. Part of a gate house, which is also embattled, is still standing. On the south side is a porch, inhabited by a tenant.

As Bridges' text goes on to relate, the estate eventually passed to the Russell family, cousins of the earls and later dukes of Bedford, who by the 18th century had become owners.

Unfortunately only small portions of this house now remain and hardly anything of the main block as shown exists. What is shown suggests a basically medieval structure, much regularised in the late 16th or early 17th centuries. One clearly medieval window remains on the first floor at the right-hand end of the building, and a number of buttresses also appear to be medieval. To the left is the top of a tower, presumably that described by Bridges. The wing to the left with its substantial chimney, could well have been the kitchen range, with lodgings over. There is quite an air of what the late Sir John Betjeman called "pleasing decay"!

Notes: BL. No.242. 44.5x28.5 cm. Other no: On the front is written 30.

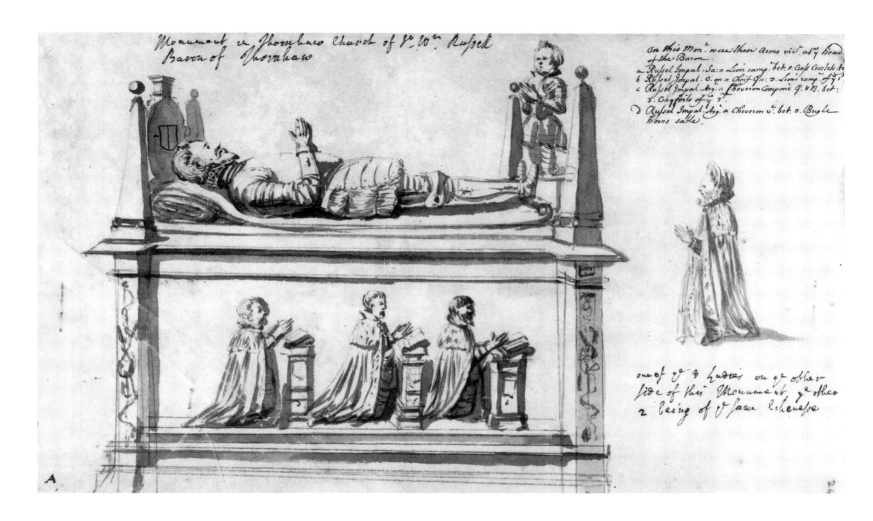

251. THORNHAUGH

Title on drawing: *Monument in Thornhaw Church of Sr Wm Russell Baron of Thornhaw*

Artist: Unsigned, Peter Tillemans

Date: Probably 1719.

Bridges' text:

On a stone monument in the south ile lies the figure of a man in armour, having his hands raised in the gesture of prayer; and a person, with a sword by his side, is kneeling at this feet. On one side, underneath, are three lords in their robes kneeling, with a table, desk, and book before each of them; and on the other side are three ladies in the same attitude. At the head of the principal figure are two pyramides, and two at his feet.

This fine freestanding tomb is in the south chapel of the church. It is an excellent example of the time, with its display of heraldry, obelisks and kneeling figures. Lord Russell, who died in 1613, had been Deputy Lieutenant of Ireland in 1580 and then displayed much courage in campaigns in Holland, being raised to the peerage on the accession of James I in 1603. The kneeling figure at his feet is that of the heir, Francis, who on the death of his cousin succeeded to the Bedford peerage. The small male figures on the tomb are those of Lord Russell's brothers, while the ladies are his daughters: all have their names painted above them. One of the ladies has a separate drawing on the sheet *One of ye 3 Ladies on ye other side of the Monument ye other 2 being of ye same likeness.*

Notes: BL. No.243. 29.5x18 cm. Other nos: On reverse is written Num:75, and on the front is written A.

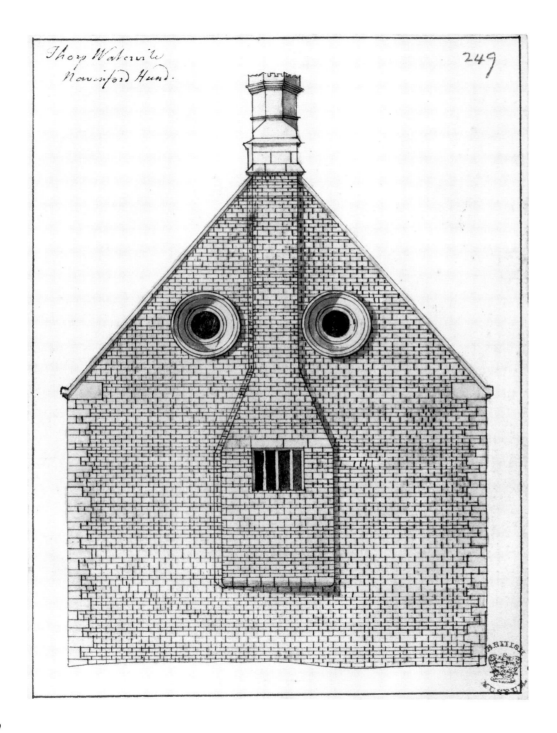

252. THORPE ACHURCH. Thorpe Waterville

Title on drawing: *Thorp Waterville Navisford Hund*

Artist: Uncertain, but perhaps George Nunns

Date: Uncertain. Thorp was visited on 10 October 1719 according to Bridges' MS Notes, but this drawing could well be later.

Bridges' text:

> In severall records, mention is made of a castle at *Thorp-Watervill*. It was probably built by *Azelin de Waterville*, soon after he was in possession of the lordship. But afterwards *Walter de Langeton* in the reign of *Edw.* I. erected here a large mansion-house, procuring for that purpose, without leave of the monks, and to their great detriment, a vast quantity of timber from the woods belonging to *Pipwell* abbey. It stood on a ground now a part of Lord *Exeter*'s estate, where is *Castle-hill*, and the vestiges of foundations are still visible. The Court for both manors is kept at the house of Mr. *Lee*. At the gold-end of this house without, are stairs which run on each side of the chimney, and within are passages under ground. In a barn of this gentleman's adjoining, and standing near the site of the castle, is very extraordinary timber-work, and at each end the appearance of a *chimney*.

The building of the castle here is usually attributed to Walter de Langton, Bishop of Lichfield, who held the manor from 1301 to 1307 and had licence to crenellate in 1301. It was put to siege in 1461 and is thought to have been largely destroyed at this time. What survives today as a large barn, is the building shown in the drawing, with its rather meticulous recording of its stonework. The gable end shows the chimneystack with its battlement top, set between two oeil-de-boeuf windows. Architectural evidence supports an early 14th century date. There is still good timberwork inside.

Notes: BL. No.249. 17.3x12.6 cm.

253. THRAPSTON

Title on drawing: *View of the Town of Thrapston and Iselip to the Eastward taken on the left hand of the Road from Titchmarsh*

Artist: Unsigned, Peter Tillemans

Date: The number sequence on the drawing suggests 1719, but a visit is recorded in Bridges' MS Notes in August 1720.

Bridges' text:

Here are one hundred and two houses, and four hundred fifty seven inhabitants. Foundations of buildings have been found in *Paradise*-close; and to the north of the church are two mounts, where a castle is supposed to have stood. Contiguous to it is the manor-house, where the court is now kept.

Another of Tilleman's attractive drawings, with the town of Thrapston to the left, and the village of Islip to the right. Thrapston is almost totally hidden by trees, but the church stands proud. The valley shows as well wooded with the hedgerows of fields, while in the foreground, with the line of the Thrapston-Titchmarsh road, is a series of open fields with indications of strip cultivation. The coach and its outrider allow one to interpret the roadway, and add a touch of period to the drawing.

Notes: BL. No.250. 29x19 cm. Other nos: On the reverse is written Num: 40. On the bottom left is written A.

View of the Church & Town of Towcester taken to ye South East on the Rising Ground enclosed next the Lord Lempsters house.

254. TOWCESTER

Title on drawing: *View of the Church & Town of Toucester taken to yᵉ South East on the Rising Ground enclosed next the Lord Lempsters house*

Artist: Unsigned, Peter Tillemans

Date: Probably 1719. There is a description in Bridges' MSS with the date 15 September 1719.

Bridges' text:

> In *Towcester* are about three hundred and fifty families. The town is chiefly situate on each side of the road, that goes from *London* to *Chester* . . . The church, dedicated to St. *Laurence*, consists of a body, north and south ile, and chancel, leaded. At the west end is an embattled tower, thirty yards high, in which are five bells.

(Bridges' text contains a much fuller account of which this is an extract)

This view is taken as the title indicates from rising ground within Easton Neston park. The church inevitably dominates the view, although today the growth of trees by the river all but obscures such an impression. It is not easy to identify individual houses, but the drawing suggests a number of fine properties with several gabled roofs with dormers and a series of chimneys. The cluster of houses on the right-hand side of the drawing is that which surrounds the Saracen's Head Inn and the Watling Street crossroads. Bridges makes mention in his description of "the *Berry-mount-hill* . . . which seems to have been raised against a northern enemy, lies on the north-east side of Towcester, and on the southern bank of the rivulet, that incloseth the town on the north". The mount, scarcely visible in the view, is represented by the planting immediately by the church. The curious mass against the clump of trees on the right side of the drawing is presumably a hay-stack. *(The mount is the subject of the next drawing.)*

Notes: BL. No.251. 43.5x18.5 cm. Other no: On reverse is written Num:51.

255. TOWCESTER

Title on drawing: *Berri Mount Hill or Berri Hill wth a view of Towcester Steeple*

Artist: Unsigned, Peter Tillemans

Date: Uncertain, but probably 1719.

Bridges' text:

> That this was indeed a *Roman* station, tho' not the *Tripontium* of *Antonius*, may fairly be gathered from the Roman coins, which have frequently been found here, and particularly up-on *Berry-mount-hill*. This mount, which seems to have been raised against a northern enemy, lies on the north-east side of *Towcester*, and on the southern bank of the rivulet, that incloseth the town on the north. It is surrounded with a mote, which is supplied with water from the brook. It is composed of earth and gravel, and is flat at the top. The diameter of it is about one hundred and two foot, and the height from the ground about twenty four.

In Bridges' MS Notes an entry dated 15 August 1719 adds that the mount was "planted wth cherry trees". The planting of the mound and its surroundings does in fact largely obscure the earthwork itself.

Berry Mount remains something of a mystery, but it is agreed that it is certainly not Roman. Its most likely date is of the late 11th or 12th century and it may be associated with the Royal estate which existed at that time. Its position suggests that it was erected to protect the road into the town, which in medieval times ran between the mound and the church, and remained there till the 18th century when Easton Neston park was landscaped.

Notes: BL. No.252. 28x28.3 cm. For a fuller discussion of Berry Mount see R.C.H.M. Vol.IV pp.158-9.

Wadenho

256. WADENHOE

Title on drawing: *Wadenho*

Artist: Unsigned, Peter Tillemans

Date: Probably 1719.

Bridges' text:

The church stands on rising ground, at a distance from the town, and nearer to the river . . . The church, dedicated to St. *Giles*, consists of a body, with two iles, covered with lead, and a tiled chancel. In a tower at the west end are three bells . . . The chancel, which is handsomely fitted up within, and the tower, were built at the charge of the present incumbent.

A careful drawing showing well the hillside position of the church, which is unusual being built into the slope, necessitating the elevation of the chancel upon a crypt. The cluster of village houses, with many stone chimneys, appears below the hill, with the river further to the right. Across the valley is the spire of Achurch. The note about the rebuilding of both tower and chancel is interesting since both still look largely medieval. The rebuilding was presumably carried out by Rev. Brooke Bridges, who was instituted in 1719, and perhaps Bridges the historian was instrumental in ensuring that the medieval character was retained. The difference between the lead coverd nave and tiled covered chancel is clear in the drawing.

Notes: BL. No.253. 46.5x21.5 cm. Other no: On the reverse is written Numb.39.

View of Walcot House taken sitting upon the Park Wall wᵗʰ Out-houses taken 29 Augᵗ 1721

257. WALCOT

Title on drawing: *View of Walcot House taken sitting upon the Park Wall wᵗʰ Out Houses taken 29 Augᵗ 1721*

Artist: Unsigned, Peter Tillemans

Bridges' text:

> In the hamlet of Walcot are only two houses; one an Inn, with stone doorcases, and windows of antiquity; the other, the seat of the Honourable *John Noel*, Esquire.

Within the account of the manorial history of Walcot, Bridges' text states that Sir Hugh Cholmley pulled down the old house and built the present one "an elegant and well finished structure".

Sir Hugh (1632-1689) is an interesting character. He was Governor of Tangier from 1663 to 1672 and made great improvements to the harbour there. In 1666 he married Anne Compton, daughter of the 2nd

Earl of Northampton, and was MP for Northampton in 1679. The Walcot estate was acquired in 1674 and the house presumably completed in 1678, the date on its rainwater heads. It is a fine, if somewhat plain, example of a double pile house, with a nine bay frontage, indicated in the shadow, with alternating segmental and triangular pediments above its ground floor windows. The roof has a wide projecting cornice and handsome pilasters, and its top is flat providing a prospect platform. Typical for its date, but seen rarely today, are the cross mullion and transom windows in the end wall.

Behind the house is a single storey L-shaped range with dormers and a tiled roof, with further outbuildings beyond. On the extreme left a large barn has a dovecote in its gable end and a small turret with a weather-vane. In front of the house, hidden by the wall, are gardens and an avenue of trees.

It is a fine and noble effect.

Notes: BL. No.254. 44x28 cm. Other no: On the front is written 51.

Sutton

255

Draught of the Brass
on Ludlows Stone in
the Chancel taken
3 July. 1719 at Wark
: worth

A

Draught of the Brass
on Sr John Chetwodes
Mon. on ye South side
of Warkworth church
taken. 3. July. 1719.

B

Draught of Amabilla
Stranges Brass plate
on ye South side of the
Church taken at
Warkworth 3. July. 1719

C

258. WARKWORTH

Title on drawing: *Draught of the Brass on Ludlows Stone in the Church taken 3 July. 1719 at Warkworth*

Draught of the Brass on Sʳ John Chetwodes Monᵗ on yᵉ South side of Warkworth Church taken 3 July. 1719

Draught of Amabilla Stranges Brass Plate on yᵉ South side of the Church taken at Warkworth 3 July. 1719

Artist: Unsigned, Peter Tillemans

Bridges' text:

The text of the inscriptions on the brasses is given.

The figures are, as the titles state, all from brasses at Warkworth. The bareheaded knight is William Ludsthorp, d.1408; the fully armoured figure is Sir John Chetwode d.1412; and the lady is Amabilla Strange d.1430. Amabilla was the first wife of Sir John Chetwode, and William Ludsthorp married Chetwode's daughter.

Notes: BL. No.255. 15x15.5 cm. The figures have written against them respectively A, B, and C.

259. WARKWORTH

Title on reverse of drawing: *Draught of 2 Mon^{ts} lying under the North Wall in ye N. Isle of Warkworth Church taken 3 July. 1719*

Artist: Unsigned, Peter Tillemans

Bridges' text:

> No mention, probably since there is no inscription.

The effigies can be identified as those of Sir John Lyons (d.1312) and his wife Margaret (still living in 1323). They are carved from freestone and are still within the recesses shown in the drawing. He wears a suit of mail over which is a long surcoat, and on his left side is a shield charged with the Lyons arms, together with a long sword. She is in a long gown with a wimple headdress. Both figures have their heads on cushions supported by angels.

Notes: BL. No.256. 14.4x19 cm. Other no: The drawing is labelled on the front D.

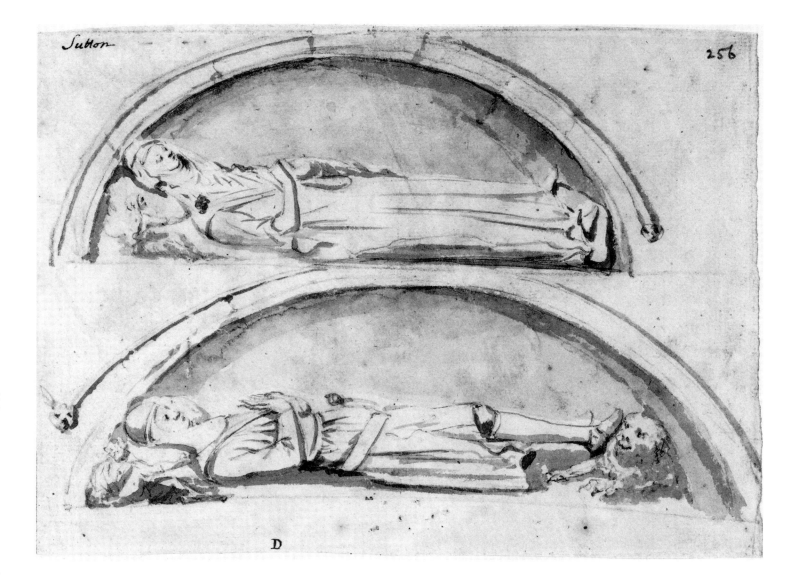

260. WARKWORTH

Title on reverse of drawing: *Draught of a Monument standing between the Body of the Church & N. Isle at Warkworth Taken on the S. side 3 July. 1719*

Artist: Unsigned, Peter Tillemans

Bridges' text:

Again not mentioned since there is no inscription.

This and the following drawing record both sides of the tomb of Sir John de Lyons, whose date of death is unknown, but who was still alive in 1346. The effigy is especially fine, with the heraldry of Lyons much in evidence, not only as the charge on the shield, but also with small lion heads as decoration to the armour and sword belt. The figure is important as a fine record of military dress and is a rare representation of the cyclas, a form of surcoat worn over an armour suit, which has a long back panel and short front apron.

Notes: BL. No.257. 15x14.5 cm. The effigies at Warkworth are fully described in Hartshorne: *Recumbent Effigies* (1876).

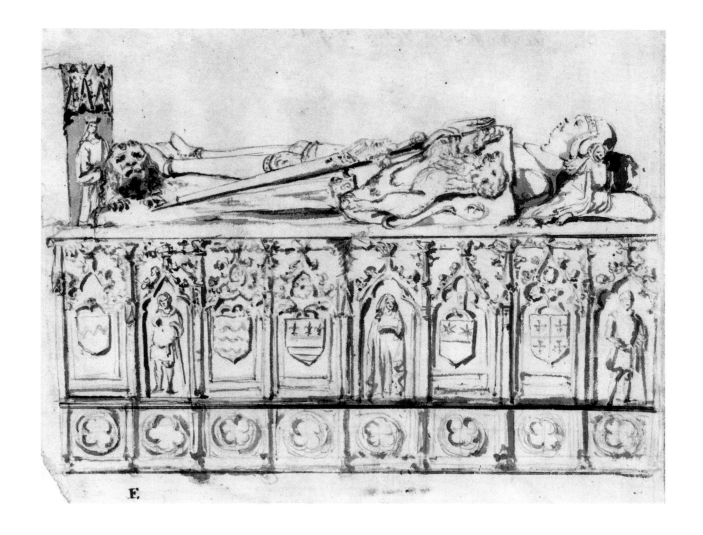

E.

261. WARKWORTH

Title on reverse of drawing: *Draught of a Monument standing between the Body of the Church & N. Isle at Warkworth Taken on the North side 3 July. 1719*

Artist: Unsigned, Peter Tillemans.

For commentary see previous plate (260).

Notes: BL. No.258. 18x16 cm. Other nos: On the front of the drawing is written E.

In ye Chancell S. Window

2 figures in ye E. Window of ye
N. Ile

262. WELDON

Title on drawing: *Weldon 2 figures in yᵉ E window of yᵉ N. Ile In yᵉ Chancel S. Window*

Artist: Unsigned, Peter Tillemans

Date: Uncertain, but a visit is recorded in Bridges' MSS in August 1719.

Bridges' text:

There is no mention of these fragments.

Notes: BL. No. 259. 19x15 cm.

263. WEEKLEY

Title on reverse of drawing: *Draught of two Mon^ts at the upper end of the North Isle of Geddington Church Taken 10 July 1719*

Artist: Unsigned, Peter Tillemans

Bridges' text:

> On an altar tomb in the north ile is the effigies of Lord Chief Justice *Mountague* . . . Against the north wall of the north ile, at the head of the above, on an altar monument supported by four Corinthian pillars are the figures of a man in armour, and, on his right hand, of a woman in the habit of the times.

The drawing is incorrectly inscribed, perhaps because the visit to Geddington was on the same day. There is no doubt that these are the Montagu monuments at Weekley, with the Montagu arms immediately obvious in the central panel on the altar tomb.

The larger monument is that of Sir Edward Montagu (d.1601) and his wife Elizabeth (d.1618). The tomb is typical of its date with its combination of architecture, heraldry and late Renaissance decoration, especially the obelisks and achievement in the pediment.

The simpler memorial is that of the father of the above, Sir Edward Montagu (d.1557), who following his rapid rise in the legal profession had amassed enough wealth to purchase the Boughton estate. He is shown in full judicial costume as befits his position as Chief Justice of the Court of Common Pleas. He was held in great esteem at Court and was one of the executors of the will of Henry VIII. The tomb chest is relatively simple but betrays in its use of twisted columns evidence of Renaissance design. A very similar design occurs on the tomb of his contemporary fellow judge, Sir Robert Brudenell at Deene (see Plate 46).

Notes: BL. No.105. 30.5x18.5 cm. At the bottom of the drawing is a letter 'B'. Attached to the drawing is a manuscript note: 'P.105 The two Monuments described on the back as being in / Geddington Ch. are actually in the neighbouring Ch. of Weekley – and always have been. 5 Oct 1905 J.A. Gotch, Weekley Rise, Kettering.'

Prospect of the Town of Wellingborough on the South West side taken on the Right hand of the Road from London between the Bridge

264. WELLINGBOROUGH

Title on drawing: *Prospect of the Town of Wellingborough on the South West side taken on the Right Hand of the Road from London between the Bridge & the Town.*

Artist: Unsigned, Peter Tillemans

Date: Probably 1719 and visits are recorded in Bridges' MS Notes in August and September 1719.

Bridges' text:

> *WELLINGBOROUGH* . . . is a large populous town, reclining on the side of an hill, at the distance of almost a mile to the north from the Nyne . . . It is chiefly situated on a red-stone-rock, of which the houses are generally built. In *Wellingborough* are above seven hundred families.

An attractive drawing, even if not especially informative. The town is seen below in the valley with the church dominant. There appears to be a house of some size just south east of the church, but otherwise no buildings stand out amongst the houses. Most of the houses at the edge of the town are thatched.

In the foreground just an indication of the track of the road, and in the background two windmills. (On the 1791 map of the county there is a windmill marked just to the north east of the town, to the south of Finedon road.)

Notes: BL. No.260. 51.5x21 cm. Other no: On the reverse is written Numb.28.

the Town

265. WELLINGBOROUGH

Title on drawing: *West View of Wellingborough Steeple Sepr. 1721*

Artist: Unsigned, Peter Tillemans

Bridges' text:

> The church, dedicated to *All-Saints*, consists of a body, north, and south ile, and chancel leaded . . . Over the west door is an oval window wrought with triangular stonework.

This good drawing faithfully records the detail of the late 13th century tower and spire. Above the richly moulded doorway is a rose window which today appears as a combination of intersecting arches radiating from a circle. The spire is typical of this part of the county with its broach form and corner pinnacles (*cf.* Denford and Wollaston). Either side are the aisles with their Perpendicular style windows. The second stage arched window is no longer visible, its space having been filled to accommodate a clock.

Notes: BL. No. 263 (together with Wilby church). 44.5x25 cm. Other no: On the front is written 53.

Ham[for]dsh[ire]

West View of Wellingborough Steeple Sep.r 1721

View of the Place cald the Benches at Perry park Corner in Whittlebury Forest taken 10 Augt. 1721

266. WHITTLEBURY FOREST

Title on drawing: *View of the Place cald the Benches at Perry Park Corner in Whittlebury Forest taken 10 Augt. 1721*

Artist: Unsigned, Peter Tillemans

Bridges' text:

> At this time there were two parks in *Pirie*, which were called by the names of the Old and New Parke . . . in the eleventh of *Henry* IV. this Sir *John de St. John* obtained a licence from the Crown to throw them both into one, and to add to them two hundred acres of field and wood, which lay contiguous to them. At the corner of this park, at a place called the *Benches* in *Whittlewood-Forest*, was formerly held the *Swainmote* Court for the said forest, and afterwards generally adjourned to *Whittlebury*.

There is little to say about this drawing, save that it shows a track through the forest with a fenced enclosure which has, on the right, a curious gate-like structure.

The Swainmote or swanimote court was a petty court set up specially to administer forest laws.

Notes: BL. No.261. 44.5x25 cm. Other no: On front is written 44. The Swanimote courts are discussed in Philip A.J. Pettit, *The Royal Forests of Northamptonshire,* Northamptonshire Record Society, 1968 (pp.24-26 especially).

South View of Wilby Church & Steeple Sep.r 1721

267. WILBY

Title on drawing: *South View of Wilby Church & Steeple Sep.r 1721*

Artist: Unsigned, Peter Tillemans

Bridges' text:

> The church, dedicated to the Blessed Virgin, consists of a body, north and south ile, and chancel leaded. At the west end is a tower, with a pinnacle at each corner, on which is raised an octagonal turret with a low spire. In the tower are three bells, and each corner a buttress.

The tower and spire are a remarkable feature of this church and one of the most decorative examples of its type, made all the more effective by being built in golden mid-Northamptonshire sandstone. The splendid spired lantern with its corner pinnacles is as an impressive example as the county can boast. The south aisle remains largely as shown, except that the clerestory had extra windows added in the 19th century. The chancel was totally rebuilt in 1853 with a high pitched roof.

Notes: BL. No.263 (with Wellingborough church). 44.5x25 cm. Other no: On the front of the drawing is written 53.

Woodcraft House now a Farm House belonging to Earl FitzWilliams. taken. 31. July. 1721

268. WOODCROFT

Title on drawing: *Woodcraft House now a Farm House belonging to Earl Fitzwilliams taken 31 July. 1721*

Artist: Unsigned, Peter Tillemans

Bridges' text:

> In the parish of *Etton* is *WOODCROFT*-house, an old manor place, and, from the remains of antiquity, apparently in former times a place of strength. It is surrounded with a large water, except on the western side, where the drawbridge is supposed to have been. The doors, and long passage through the gateway, with two large arches and seats of stone, and stone windows and staircases within the house, and a round bastion towards the north end, are of remarkable and anceint workmanship. Over the porch or gateway is a chamber, formerly the chapel: in the wall is a bason for holy water, a long stone seat, and a large window, now in part filled up, and made into a smaller. The walls are about four feet thick.

The length of the description in Bridges' text indicates the interest which this building aroused.

Woodcroft is the remains of a castle of late 13th century date. It is thought originally to have been of rectangular plan with a tower at each corner, but only one tower now survives. Of its 13th century walls only portions remain, having been incorporated into a house in Tudor times, when the Fitzwilliam family acquired it. There are still signs of the chapel inside the house above the gateway.

Otherwise the drawing captures the domestic quality of the building with planting visible within the courtyard and pigeons fluttering around the tower.

Notes: BL. No.265. 44x19 cm. Other no: On the front of the drawing is written 32.

Prospect of the Earl of Exeters House at Wirthorp to the West. 6 Aug.ᵗ 1719

269. WOTHORPE

Title on drawing: *Prospect of the Earl of Exeters House at Wirthorp to the West 6 Augᵗ 1719*

Artist: Unsigned, Peter Tillemans

Bridges' text:

> WOTHORP, in Domesday book written *Wridtorp*, in other records *Wridthorp*, and *Wyrethorp*, is a seat of the earl of *Exeter*'s, in the parish of St. *Martin*, *Stamford-Baron*. This seat, which hath a small park adjoining to it, is reported by *Camden*, to have been built by *Thomas Cecil*, the first earl of this family, who tells us also, that the founder pleasantly said, He built it only to retire to out of the dust, while his great house at *Burleigh* was sweeping. After the restoration, the duke of *Buckingham* resided here, with his family, for some years.

This extraordinary house, built in the early years of the 17th century, survives as a picturesque ruin. Much of the central block has collapsed, but the corner towers, roofless, still stand. In style it is a most curious piece of work, somewhat reminiscent of buildings associated with Robert Smythson, and with particular similarities with parts of Bolsover Castle. Its architecture is a good deal more Mannerist than one would expect for the early 17th century. There is evidence of a garden layout around the building.

The view shows the house set amongst trees. The central block projects on each facade with towers topped by lead turrets at the angles. The facade facing the viewer has three floors, each of three bays, two windows on the ground and first floors, and a single window in each gable. To the right, on the slope of the valley is a cottage, and behind the silhouette of a large house and the tower of Easton-on-the Hill church. Further right the Welland valley is indicated.

Notes: BL. No.264. 31x16.5 cm. There are excellent drawings of the house in its heyday by William Legg in the Library at Burghley. Legg was the architect of the west lodge to Burghley in 1800 and designed a number of buildings in and around Stamford (see *Colvin*).

Index to Text

All references are to page numbers